Uncommon Sense

By
Richard A. Posner
Gary S. Becker

16
EasyRead Large

Copyright Page from the Original Book

The University of Chicago Press, Chicago 60637
The University of Chicago Press, Ltd., London

Printed in the United States of America

18 17 16 15 14 13 12 11 10 09 1 2 3 4 5

ISBN-13: 978-0-226-04101-8 (cloth)
ISBN-10: 0-226-04101-8 (cloth)

Library of Congress Cataloging-in-Publication Data

Becker, Gary Stanley, 1930–
Uncommon sense : economic insights, from marriage to terrorism / Gary S. Becker and Richard A. Posner.
p. cm.
Includes index.
ISBN-13: 978-0-226-04101-8 (alk. paper)
ISBN-10: 0-226-04101-8 (alk. paper)
1. Economics—Miscellanea. 2. Law and economics. 3. Posner, Richard A.—Blogs. 4. Becker, Gary Stanley, 1930– —Blogs. I. Posner, Richard A. II. Title.
HB71.B435 2009
330—dc22
2009009198

∞ The paper used in this publication meets the minimum requirements of the American National Standard for Information Sciences—Permanence of Paper for Printed Library Materials, ANSI Z39.48-1992.

Set in 16 pt. Verdana

TABLE OF CONTENTS

GARY S. BECKER is University Professor in the Department of Economics, the Department of Sociology, and the Graduate School of Business at the University of Chicago.

RICHARD A. POSNER is a judge of the U.S. Court of Appeals for the Seventh Circuit and senior lecturer in law at the University of Chicago.

INTRODUCTION TO THE BECKER-POSNER BLOG

Blogging is a major new social, political, and economic phenomenon enabled by the Internet, a transformative technology of vast social importance (think of what it is doing to the conventional news media, such as newspapers!). The Internet has revolutionized access to information, and sometimes misinformation as well. Information on the Internet comes from many sources. It is a fresh and striking exemplification of Friedrich Hayek's thesis that the knowledge essential to society (he emphasized the economic activity of a society, but the point is general) is widely distributed among people and that the social challenge is to create mechanisms for pooling that knowledge. The mechanism that was the focus of Hayek's work, as of economists generally, is the price system (an explicit market). Price impounds the information of buyers and sellers concerning values and supply; the market is thus a method of aggregating information. The Internet illustrates the possibility of alternative mechanisms of such aggregation. The newest is the Internet-based "blogosphere." The Internet enables the instantaneous pooling (and hence correction, refinement, and amplification) of the ideas and opinions, facts and images, reportage and scholarship, generated by bloggers. The blogosphere differs from a system with explicit prices and monetary compensation because information in this sphere is usually made available without expectation of any monetary compensation or other financial rewards, although some bloggers have managed to attract advertising revenues and others (present company included) have made book deals. The blogosphere never the-less forms a "market," though one without explicit prices to users (the major cost, for both the bloggers and the blog readers, is time), in which tens of millions of participants interact in the provision of information. There are many examples of other markets, such as fraternal organizations, or men and women looking to find marriage partners, that do not involve explicit financial compensation either. But the blogosphere is new and would have been impossible without the electronic revolution that enabled the creation of the Internet. Apart from advertising revenue (our blog, however, does not carry advertising), compensation for posts in the blogosphere is also unusual since it involves such forms of compensation as the pleasures from writing—as in Wikipedia—or the pleasure from expressing opinions, or the pleasure from seeing one's name on the Internet.

The first Web log, or blog, was started in the United States about a decade ago, and the number has increased very rapidly. No one knows the exact number of blogs, especially since each day brings many new blogs throughout the world. The vast majority are personal diaries that are read only by family members and close friends. A relatively small (though large in absolute terms) number are addressed to larger audiences. Call these "network" blogs. Some primarily provide links to various online sources of news and opinion (including other blogs); others offer frequent, often daily, commentary on political and other (such as cultural) subjects. These are "opinion" blogs.

In December 2004, we started the "Becker-Posner Blog," http://becker-posner-blog.com /, an opinion blog that would have an unconventional format. We would post only once a week, and on a topic with considerable general interest. The posting would consist of a brief lead essay by one of us on a topical issue, followed by a still briefer comment by the other. This discussion format would enable us to use the Internet as a platform for serious but fresh, pointed, and lively analyses of major issues. Because we do not blog on a daily basis, do not (with infrequent exceptions) link to other online sites, and our pieces are in the nature of brief essays rather than informal, conversation-style jottings, we are outside the mainstream blog culture as it has evolved; but there is no reason why the mainstream should be considered so narrow.

One of us (Becker) is a Nobel-prize-winning economist who in addition to scholarly publications on a wide range of economic issues including education, discrimination, labor, the family, crime, addiction, and immigration, for many years wrote a monthly column for *Business Week.* Posner also has done some writing for the press and once had a very brief stint writing a column for the *Atlantic Monthly.* We thought the blog would have three advantages over a magazine column. First, it would elicit more comments, because it is easier to post a comment than to write a letter to the editors, and also because the space that newspapers and magazines are willing to devote to readers' letters is so limited that only a small number of letters is published, which discourages readers from writing letters. Second, the blog would attract more readers than a magazine column, as a consequence of more frequent (weekly rather than monthly) writing, the blog versus magazine format, and the unbundling of a column from a magazine. (Someone wanting to read Becker, for example, would no longer have to subscribe to *Business Week* to be able to read it.)

Posner is a federal appellate judge and also a writer of books and articles in a variety of fields, including antitrust, intellectual property, and other fields in which economics is applied to law, but also topical fields such as impeachment, contested elections, and national security issues. The rules of judicial ethics forbid Posner to comment publicly on pending or impending litigation or to participate in politics, as by endorsing candidates; hence the avoidance in the blog of certain topics that might seem a natural focus of our interest.

This book collects the postings in the first two and a quarter years of our blog (the latest piece reprinted in the book was posted on March 4, 2007)—more than 125 essays and comments. The range covered is vast—from global warming to New York City's ban on trans fats; from foreign aid to doping athletes; from the privatization of toll roads to the French propensity for riots; from Internet gambling to China's effort to buy an American oil company; from the governance of Harvard University to gay marriage; from orphan drugs to drunk driving; from fighting AIDS in Africa to the cost of the war in Iraq. What unites this promiscuous-appearing array of blog entries is that they are all about contemporary issues of economic policy, when "economics" is broadly understood (see below). Informal, topical, practical, and policy oriented, our postings do not address abstract economic issues, employ the technical apparatus of economics, or always rest on a rich foundation of empirical knowledge. Nor is the analysis exclusively economic in the usual meaning of this word; we have felt free to range widely in our consideration of policy-relevant factors.

The postings appear here without substantive changes, but with corrections of typographical errors and minor changes in punctuation and style. The postings are grouped by subject matter—sex and population, property rights, universities, incentives, jobs and employment, disasters and environment, crime and punishment and terrorism, and the world.

Many of the postings fit into more than one category; we place each in the category that best describes it. The arrangement within each group is mainly chronological, but when two or more postings deal with the same topic they have been grouped together. At the end of each part of the book, we have added "afterthoughts" reflecting (in part in response to comments) rethinking we have done of our postings, some of which are at this writing (December 2008) four years old. We thank Justin Ellis, Anthony Henke, Alison Sider, and Michael Thorpe for research assistance with the afterthoughts and help in correcting errors and omissions in the original postings. Gary Becker would also like to thank his wife, Guity N. Becker, for extremely valuable comments on drafts of his discussions.

One of the attractions of the blog format, compared with writing op-eds or columns for newspapers or magazines, is, as mentioned, that blog postings elicit more reader response. And indeed our postings have elicited many comments, often very thoughtful, and on occasion we have responded in the blog. Limitations of space preclude our publishing the comments or our responses in this book, but they remain available online; the blog contains an easy-to-use search feature that will call up any of our postings and with it the readers' posted comments plus any reply by us. Both of us have full-time jobs that limit the amount of time that we can devote to a weekly blog, and so the reader should not expect academic depth and thoroughness. We hope that we compensate with freshness and liveliness.

Because our blog does not discuss economic principles in the abstract, and yet most of our readers are not professional economists, we have thought it useful to set forth in this introduction some of the principles that guide us in analyzing public policy issues in our blog postings.

The foremost principle is that of rational choice. Not in the sense of a fully or explicitly reasoned process of deliberation—or even of a conscious weighing of alternatives—but in the sense simply of choosing means that are appropriate (given limitations of information) to the chooser's ends, whatever they may be. The assumption that people are rational choosers is a fruitful and powerful guide to understanding human behavior. It is not an unerring guide, however. Cognitive psychologists have challenged forcefully certain aspects of rational behavior in recent years. That challenge is reflected in our postings.

The ends that guide the means used in rational choice need not be selfish ones; altruistic behavior is common, especially but not only within the family. But like the assumption of rationality, the assumption of a rather narrow self-interest has considerable explanatory value. Most people are rather selfish in many areas of their activity, and it is perilous to ignore this when considering the design of public policy.

The model of human beings as self-interested choosers underscores the role of incentives in human behavior, and hence in policy. Indeed, while economics used to be thought of as the study of explicit markets in which goods are bought and sold along with aggregate economic phenomena such as inflation and unemployment, a newer definition regards it much more broadly as the study of how individuals and organizations respond to changes in their incentives, with rational choice assumed to be the principal guide to those responses. Incentives change when either benefits or costs change, as when the price of a good goes up and consequently the incentive to buy it goes down; and thus, for example, recent increases in the world price of oil due to a greater demand for oil have increased the incentive of oil producers to expand their output at the same time that the price increases have reduced consumption; the higher price is a benefit to the supplier but a cost to the consumer, so the reactions of the two are opposite. Similarly, incentives to consume foods containing trans fats have weakened in recent years after greater information became available on the harmful effects of trans fats on health.

The incentives of individuals and companies are often strongly affected by changes in public policies and in the physical and social environment, and our blog considers many of these effects, such as how taxes on capital affect investments, how individuals responded to the destruction wrought by Hurricane Katrina, how London's automobile-commuting tax has affected the amount of automobile commuting to central London, and how carbon taxes would affect commercial interest in building nuclear power plants.

Essentially all issues of public policy revolve around how the responses of different individuals and organizations to changes in incentives determine the aggregate responses of groups. For example, an increased tax on capital may affect different holders of capital differently, but economists study how the amounts of capital in an economy, industry, or other economic categories are affected rather than the effect on particular individuals. In order to understand these group responses, it is necessary to develop an analysis of how markets operate, be they formal markets, such as a stock exchange, or informal markets, such as the marriage market. Market responses can look quite different from the responses of the representative or typical individual or organization. This is why economists have devoted so much of their efforts to the analysis of markets along with that of individual behavior, and it helps to explain why economists' interests are often different from those of psychologists. Psychologists also study individual behavior, but they have less interest in aggregate responses to incentives and constraints, though social psychology does focus on group responses to stimuli.

In tracing the effects of costs and benefits, one must be careful not to confuse costs with purely pecuniary expenditures. A mere transfer of money from one person to another is not a cost from an overall social (as distinct from a private) standpoint because it merely rearranges society's wealth, although it may engender costs in the form of effort and other resources expended in attempting to effectuate the transfer of money from someone else to oneself. The time spent searching for a good to buy is clearly a cost, because that time would have a value in an alternative use; but it is not a monetized cost. The "full price" of a consumer good to an economist is the sum of the sales price, the search cost (mainly time), and the time spent consuming the good. We try constantly in the blog to identify and assess the full cost or price of various activities.

The effects of various actions on benefits and costs to an individual or organization depend critically on the extent to which they are incurred by the choosing subject rather than by others. If you give to charity, you obtain a benefit—otherwise you wouldn't give. But the benefit to each potential giver is likely to be much less than the full benefit to recipients; otherwise there would be much more charity than there is. Similarly, a factory that pollutes may impair the health and work environment of its employees, and this may require it to pay more in wages or health benefits. To that extent, the cost to the workers may be a cost to the factory. But most of the costs of pollution are borne by persons remote from the factory—persons with whom the factory has no actual or potential contractual relationship, because the costs of contracting ("transaction costs," in the terminology of economics) are prohibitive. These "external" costs are likely to have little or no effect on the decisions of normally self-interested factory mangers and owners on how much to spend on pollution control. Global warming, to which human-caused emissions of carbon dioxide into the atmosphere appear to contribute in an important way, is the current poster child of external benefits and costs. The costs incurred by an electrical plant to reduce its emissions of carbon dioxide would confer benefits primarily on others; equivalently, the costs imposed by such emissions are imposed primarily on others, not on the emitter itself.

Costs must be distinguished from "rents," another economic concept that recurs throughout the blog. A rent (not to be confused with rental) is a return that exceeds merely a reimbursement for a cost incurred. The classic example is fertile farmland. If demand for some agricultural good exceeds the capacity of the most fertile farmland to supply it, poorer land—land that is more costly to work—will be brought into production. The market price will have to cover the cost of that production, and so in a competitive market the price will be equal to the cost of producing the last unit of output that is demanded. That cost and hence the market price will exceed the cost of production of the most fertile farmland, and the owners of that farmland will therefore obtain a price in excess of their cost—a rent.

Another example of rent is the high incomes obtained by popular entertainers—these entertainers do not have perfect substitutes (just as poor farmland is not a perfect substitute for good farmland) and so they are able to command a price for their services that exceeds their costs of providing them. This, incidentally, illustrates the important point (already hinted at in the discussion of consumer search costs) that "cost" to an economist is "opportunity cost." The entertainer obtains rents because his or her alternative employment is less remunerative: the pop singer's next best employment might be as a waitress at a fraction of her earnings as a singer. Those earnings, which are what she gives up by being a singer, are the cost of her singing career (apart from expenses involved in a singing career, such as the cost of training, agent fees, and wardrobe expense). The difference between what she receives as a singer and the much smaller income that she would receive as a waitress is her economic rent.

"Rent seeking" is related to rents but it is a distinct form of behavior. It involves the seeking of wealth mainly through its transfer from others, such as from governmental subsidies and other favors, or sometimes through speculation on financial markets. Rent seeking is a natural human impulse, but it can also generate social waste. The prospect of such gains will induce expenditures on trying to obtain them that would be socially wasted if they do not also create value but merely enable the rent seeker to transfer wealth from others to itself. An example is a "patent race." A patent is a potential source of rents because the income generated by a patent may exceed the cost of inventing and producing the patented product, since the patent prevents competition that would eliminate a return to the patentee in excess of the cost of production. A race to be the first to patent an invention may confer social value by accelerating the creation of the invention, but if the acceleration is very slight, the additional social value may be much less than the costs incurred by the firms that competed to be first.

Institutional governance plays a big role in the analysis of economic policies. The main institutional types are the market, government, and nonprofit organizations such as most U.S. universities and (other) charitable foundations. The market (trade) has the important feature that social welfare is usually promoted by selfish behavior. The basic reason is that two selfish people will not trade unless they expect the trade to make both of them better off; hence the trade increases welfare, unless there are important negative effects elsewhere in the economy, as there may be for example where the manufacture of the traded product creates pollution. The market has another important feature, stressed by Friedrich Hayek, to whom we've already referred: it aggregates information (though, as the current financial crisis shows, not always efficiently), because information about supply and demand is compendiously impounded in prices. This feature may be absent within organizations, and the absence gives rise to "agency costs": the costs that arise from the effort of a principal (such as a corporation) to constrain his agents to serve the principal's interests rather than the agents' own interests. Agency costs are particularly acute in nonmarket organizations, such as government agencies and nonprofit organizations, as distinct from business firms, because in the case of those nonmarket entities there may be only weak market signals of agents' disloyal or incompetent performance, or there may be constraints in acting on these signals.

Presented abstractly as we have done in this introduction, economic principles may seem remote from practical issues. We hope the application of those principles in the blog entries that follow will dispel that impression.

I

SEX AND POPULATION

1

THE SEXUAL REVOLUTION

April 10, 2005

THE SEXUAL REVOLUTION—POSNER

The death of Pope John Paul II on April 2, 2005, is a reminder of the profound changes in sexual mores over the past half century in the United States and many other countries, of the pope's strong defense of conventional Roman Catholic sexual morality (including opposition to abortion, contraception, married priests, and all nonmarital sexual activity, including homosexual sex and even masturbation), and of the growing gulf between that morality and the actual sexual behavior of Roman Catholics in the United States (which is, on average, similar to that of other segments of the community), including the recent sex scandals involving the priesthood.

Let us consider first why sexual morality has changed so much over the past half century. If one takes an economic approach to the question, then since the benefits of sex in the sense of the pleasure or relief of tension that it yields have deep biological roots, it is probably to the cost side that we should look for an answer. The costs of engaging in sexual activity have fallen dramatically over the last half century (AIDS notwithstanding), for many reasons. One was the discovery that penicillin is a safe, certain, and inexpensive cure for syphilis. Another was improvements in contraceptive technology that have greatly reduced the likelihood of an unwanted birth (with minimal interference with sexual pleasure). It is true that the number of unwanted births has risen, but this is because other factors influence that number besides contraceptive technology. And to the extent that improved contraceptive technology induces more sexual activity by making sex safer, the number of unwanted births will not fall by the full percentage reduction in the probability of such a birth; the reduced probability per sexual act is somewhat offset by an increase in the number of acts. Legalizing abortion has further reduced the risk of an unwanted birth, although legalization can be viewed as a response to, rather than a cause of, a change in sexual mores or more plausibly as both.

Of fundamental importance is the changing role of women in society. The rise of the service economy, with its abundance of physically light jobs, together with the advent of highly efficient household labor-saving devices, has greatly increased women's job opportunities outside the home. That increase has in turn increased women's financial independence and thus reduced the gains to them from marriage. It has also increased the opportunity costs of childbearing: the higher a woman's income, the more she gives up if she leaves the labor force, whether temporarily or permanently, to have children. So this is another factor raising the cost of marriage to women.

The consequence of all these things has been to reduce the marriage rate and delay the average age of marriage, and also to reduce the cost of divorce to women (and to men, by reducing the benefits of marriage to men who want to have children and stay-at-home wives). With less and later marriage and more divorce, women spend less of their sexually active years married and so their demand for nonmarital sex—sex made in any event less risky by improved contraception and the availability of abortion—soars.

The increased demand for divorce was a factor in the successful movement for easy divorce, and easy divorce makes it impossible to channel sex into marriage. In communities (and there are still some) in which premarital sex is strongly disapproved, young people marry to have sex, but marriages so motivated are likely to end in divorce, producing more unmarried people and so more demand for nonmarital sex.

Another factor that influences behavior in the same direction, though one that predates the developments that I have just been discussing, is the long-term decline in child mortality, as a result of which it is no longer necessary for women to be almost continuously pregnant in order to have a reasonable number of children survive to adulthood. In addition, with the decline of the farm population and the rise of social security, children's value as farm labor and old-age insurance diminishes, and as a result the demand for children falls.

With more and more sex taking place outside of marriage, homosexual activity comes to seem less anomalous than in a society in which almost all sexual activity is (or at least is believed to be) confined to marriage. That is, once the link between marriage and sex is weakened, and sex comes to be thought of as worthwhile in itself rather than just as a means of procreation, nonprocreative sex—of which homosexual sex is a conspicuous example—begins to lose its opprobrium.

It may seem paradoxical to suggest that marriage and homosexuality are somehow linked; but they are. In societies like that of ancient Greece, in which men are expected to marry in order to procreate but are not expected to establish an intimate emotional connection with their wife (for example, in ancient Greece husband and wife did not eat together, and the wife rarely was even permitted outside the house), it is not difficult for homosexual men to marry. But when companionate marriage becomes the norm—when men are still expected to marry, but marriage connotes much more than occasional intercourse—homosexual men become anomalous; the institution of companionate, as distinct from patriarchal, marriage tends to extrude them from a fundamental social institution. Companionate marriage is still the marriage norm, but fewer people are married, so unmarried men are less conspicuous.

The major Western religions, especially Christianity, and within Christianity especially Roman Catholicism, are increasingly defined by their opposition to the modern loosening of sexual mores. This is not because these religions have become increasingly prudish (though Catholicism takes a harder line against abortion than it did until the nineteenth century, and though a concern with sexual conduct plays a notably small role in the New Testament), but because their teachings on sex have become ever more removed from the behavior of their votaries. Pope John Paul II seemed unusually conservative in matters of sex not because he was making Catholic sex doctrine more severe, but because he was refusing to yield to strong pressures to relax it. He was swimming against the tide. Even though the United States is in the midst of a very striking religious revival, religion's grip on behavior has weakened. Hence the contrast between vastly increased tolerance for homosexual behavior and powerful opposition, much though not all of it religiously based, to gay marriage. Hence, too, the great difficulty the Catholic Church is having in attracting young men into the priesthood, especially young heterosexual men—an all-male occupation holds obvious attractions for homosexual men, especially if the behavioral constraints of religious doctrine are weakening even for persons who desire a religious career.

To the extent that as a result of economic and technological change, sex ceases to be considered either dangerous or important, we can expect it to become a morally indifferent activity, as eating has mainly become (though not for orthodox Jews and Muslims). At this writing, that seems to be the trend in many societies, including our own. This is not historically unprecedented; many cultures have been far more casual about sex than our own—ancient Greece, for example.

I emphasize that this has been an essay in positive rather than normative moral theory. My concern is not with whether the changes in sexual mores that I have been discussing are right or wrong, but with trying to explain what has brought about the changes. I believe they can largely be explained in economic terms.

COMMENTS ON THE SEXUAL REVOLUTION—BECKER

Pope John Paul II was conservative on family matters, but was highly innovative on more important questions for the Catholic Church in the long run. These include his early, continued, and open hostility to communism when many intellectuals and some church leaders were supportive or accommodating, his steering of the clergy in Latin America and elsewhere out of active involvement in politics, his much more favorable attitude to capitalism than his predecessors, his rapprochement to the Jews and

Muslims, and his commitment to peace, even when he differed with America and other powerful nations.

This explain the worldwide outpouring of grief over the pope's death, including the vast majority of Catholics who were violating church doctrines on contraceptives and divorce. He will be long remembered for these enormous contributions, whatever happens to the sexual revolution.

I start this way in my comment on Posner partly to express the high regard I have for Pope John Paul II (I should make clear that I was elected to the Pontifical Academy of Sciences while he was pope). A reason more directly relevant to our topic this week is that the conflict between the actual behavior of most Catholics and the Church's doctrines on contraceptive use and other family matters is not unusual when dealing with culture and norms. Indeed, it dramatically illustrates the fact that powerful economic and social forces usually trump religious views and other social norms, until these views and norms adjust to the new forces. Birth rates, divorce, and premarital sex provide a powerful example of this well-known principle.

For many reasons, most mentioned by Posner, families in modern countries generally have few children, and instead invest a lot in the education, training, and health of each child. These reasons include the high value of human capital in technologically advanced economies; low rates of child mortality; the growth of female education, earnings, and labor force participation; and the decline of manufacturing and rise of the service economy. Among other things, these forces increased the financial independence of women that gave them a greater say in family matters, and made them much more willing to divorce than in the past.

As a result of these forces, the vast majority of families in the world have fewer than three children. There is no effective way to do this, while continuing normal sexual activity, without extensive reliance on effective contraception. So as economic development has spread throughout the world, family after family, regardless of their religious views, have greatly increased their contraceptive use in order to have fewer children. Birth rates in Spain, Italy, Poland, and other predominantly Catholic countries are among the lowest anywhere. Ireland is the most religious country in the Christian world by virtually all measures of religiosity, yet Irish families are using contraception extensively. Their birth rates have plummeted, even while they loved Pope John Paul II, and remain highly devout Catholics. Clearly, these families are separating their decisions about contraception from their degree of religiosity.

Low birth rates were made easier by better and more efficient contraceptives. The attractiveness and effectiveness of condoms continued to improve throughout the past eighty years. The pill, the most effective method of birth control, was developed only in the 1950s. Abortion became safer and legal in growing numbers of nations. The legalization of abortion illustrates that it is difficult to be certain about how much of the improvement in birth control methods were a response to pressure from families wanting few children and how much was due to technological innovations that proceeded largely independent of such demand.

Whatever the causation, better ways to prevent births became available not only to married couples, but also to their teenage children. The rapid growth in premarital teenage sexual activity not only in the United States, but also in many other nations, is the strongest manifestation of the "sexual revolution." Teenagers could now explore sex without much fear of pregnancy, a fear that was a major form of "birth control" in the past. Surveys on premarital sexual activity among American nineteen-year-old females indicate that the fraction that had engaged in premarital intercourse grew from about 25 percent in 1950 to around 80 percent currently. The number of sexual partners women had by age twenty also increased greatly.

Data further indicate that the larger numbers of teenagers engaging in premarital intercourse know more about and have easier access to effectives contraceptives than did sexually active teenagers in the past. About 60 percent of the women in 1960 who engaged for the first time in premarital intercourse used no contraception, while condoms were used 20 percent of the time. By the mid 1990s, about two-thirds used either condoms or the pill.

Yet even in recent years, a quarter of teenage women who engage in inter course for the first time use no contraception. This is a larger fraction of all teenagers than the total fraction of teenagers in 1950 who engaged in premarital intercourse. So the sharp growth in sexual activity among young persons was not simply due to better and better-known contraceptives, but also to a greater willingness to engage in sex prior to marriage. This is strong evidence that the sexual revolution led to a much more permissive and receptive attitude toward sex outside of marriage even without birth control, although abortion is now an option for many women.

Events such as economic growth and new technologies often induce changes in behavior despite prevailing norms that initially oppose this behavior. As this new behavior becomes more common and habitual, norms evolve to catch up to the behavior. This adjustment of norms to behavior rather than simply vice versa is widespread, including attitudes toward sex, divorce, women working, husbands helping out with child care, and children supporting elderly parents. Time will tell whether the attitudes of the Catholic Church on sexual matters will also evolve, but I believe that the Church will still be attractive to many Catholics even if their behavior violates Church teachings on questions like contraception.

So it is possible to understand the basis of the sexual revolution using an economic approach, but the approach must recognize that norms and habits are also important. These norms and habits usually adjust eventually to new forms of behavior, and the new norms greatly accelerate this behavior after they do adjust.

I disagree with Posner that sex will become, either morally or in other ways, just another consumer activity, like eating. Sexual intercourse is a very intimate relation between two people that grew as humans evolved during the past fifty thousand years when they apparently began to separate into families. This relation carries a lot of emotional attachment and baggage that will not vanish simply because contraceptives are effective and birth rates are low.

2

GAY MARRIAGE

July 17, 2005

THE LAW AND ECONOMICS OF GAY MARRIAGE—POSNER

The surprising decision of Spain, once the most Catholic country in Europe (except for Ireland), to recognize gay marriage—a decision that comes in the wake of a similar decision by Canada and, of course, by the Supreme Judicial Court of Massachusetts—presents an appropriate occasion on which to consider what light economic analysis might shed on the issue.

Economics focuses on the consequences of social action. One clear negative consequence is the outrage felt by opponents of gay marriage and of homosexual rights in general. Philosophers like John Stuart Mill would not consider that such outrage should figure in the social welfare calculus; Mill famously argued in *On Liberty* that an individual has no valid interest in the activities of other people that don't affect him except psychologically. (Mill had in mind the indignation felt by English people at Mormon polygamy occurring thousands of miles away in Utah.) But that is not a good economic argument because there is no difference from an economic standpoint between physical and emotional harm; either one lowers the utility of the harmed person.

The issue is more complicated to the extent that some of the outrage is based on fear that making homosexual relationships respectable by permitting homosexual marriage will encourage homosexuality. Most people don't want their children to become homosexuals, and this aversion is a factor in the utility calculus. However, they are probably mistaken in thinking that homosexuality is chosen; there is compelling evidence that sexual orientation is an innate (probably genetic) rather than acquired characteristic. It is not clear what weight, if any, society should give to opinions formed on the basis of scientific error.

Obviously there are benefits to homosexual couples from marriage—otherwise there would be no pressure to extend marriage rights to them. (Whether, given the alternative of civil unions, there are incremental benefits to marriage is a separate question that I discuss later.) Some of these benefits appear to impose no significant costs on others and thus are clear social gains: an example is that a married person does not have to have a will in order to bequeath his property at death to his spouse. Unless "outrage" costs are high, such benefits would, in an economic analysis, warrant recognizing gay marriage.

However, other benefits to married couples impose costs on third parties; an example is social security spousal and survivor benefits, to the extent they are not (and usually they are not) fully financed by the social security taxes paid by the person bestowing or obtaining the benefits. But such redistributive effects are equally imposed by heterosexual marriage, so they don't make a strong argument against homosexual marriage, especially since homosexual marriages are unlikely to be a significant fraction of all marriages. Only 2 to 3 percent of the population is homosexual and, judging from experience thus far, lesbians, who are far outnumbered by male homosexuals, seem much more interested in homosexual marriage than men are. Although I am not able to verify this figure, I believe that about two-thirds of gay marriages are lesbian, even though only about a third of homosexuals are lesbian. If this pattern persists, the total number of gay marriages will probably be very small relative to the number of heterosexual marriages.

The more fundamental economic question is why marriage is a legal status. One can imagine an approach whereby marriage would be a purely religious or ceremonial status having no legal consequences at all, so that couples, married or not, who wanted their relationship legally defined would make contracts on whatever terms they preferred. There could be five-year marriages, "open" marriages, marriages that could be dissolved at will (like employment at will), marriages that couldn't be dissolved at all, and so forth, and alimony and property settlement would be freely negotiable as well. The analogy would be to partnership law, which allows the partners to define the terms of their relationship, including the terms of dissolution. As with all contracts, the law would impose limits to protect third-party interests, notably those of children.

If outrage costs are set to one side, a purely contractual approach to (or replacement for) marriage makes sense from an economic standpoint because it would permit people to define their legal relationships in accordance with their particular preferences and needs. For those who did not want to bother to negotiate a "marriage" contract, the law could provide a default, one-size-fits-all solution—the conventional marital status embodied in state marriage statutes. That would reduce transaction costs for those people content with the standard "form contract." The law would, however, have to decide what contractual relationships qualified for social security and other public benefits to which spouses are entitled under current law.

The contract approach to marriage may seem radical, but that is because of a lack of historical perspective. Marriage has changed enormously over the course of history. In many cultures, it has signified the purchase of a woman by a man's family. In other cultures, instead of a bride price, there is a dowry (an approximation to the purchase price for a husband, paid by the wife's family.). Arranged marriages, often of children, have been common. Divorce at will by the man only has been common; likewise, of course, polygamous marriage (including in the Old

Testament). Trial marriages, defeasible if the wife fails to become pregnant, were a Scandinavian institution. Shia law recognizes temporary marriages. "Companionate" marriage, in which husband and wife are expected to be best friends, is a modern institution. In short, marriage has changed greatly in history, and it would be foolish to think that the current marriage conventions will remain fixed for all time. With the rise of no-fault divorce, the enforcement of prenuptial agreements, and the decline of alimony, marriage is evolving in the direction of contract. That evolution has contributed to the movement for gay marriage. For, as marriage becomes more like a contract, it becomes harder to see why homosexuals—who as I say are free to form other contracts—should be excluded from its benefits.

Under a contractual approach, gay marriage as an issue would disappear, because the state would not be being asked to "recognize" gay marriage and by doing so offend people who are distressed by homosexuality. No one thinks that homosexuals should be forbidden to make contracts, and marriage would be just a contract so far as any legal consequences were concerned. It would be left to individual religious sects to decide whether to permit church marriages of homosexuals.

The most remarkable aspect of the current controversy is that it is mainly about a word—"marriage." The reason is that although most Americans still oppose civil unions (among American states, only Vermont and Connecticut authorize civil unions, though New Jersey authorizes a related arrangement called domestic partnership; a number of foreign nations now authorize civil unions, some under the name "registered partnership"), I imagine that if the homosexual-rights lobby dropped marriage from its agenda and put all its effort into lobbying for civil unions, many states would soon recognize them, and eventually the federal government would follow suit and grant parties to such unions the legal status of spouses for purposes of social security and other federal laws; when that happened, there would be no practical difference between civil unions and marriage. Why so much passion is expended over the word "marriage" baffles me. After all, even today, and even more so if civil unions were officially recognized, homosexual couples can call themselves "married" if they want to. And this brings to the fore the disadvantage of treating marriage as a legal status. Were it just a contract, government would have no role in deciding what word the parties could use to describe the relationship created by it.

Although personally I would not be upset if Illinois (where I live) or any other state decided to recognize homosexual marriage, I disagree with contentions that the Constitution should be interpreted to require state recognition of homosexual marriage on the ground that it is a violation of equal protection of the laws to discriminate against homosexuals by denying them that right. Given civil unions, and contractual substitutes for marriage even short of civil unions, the discrimination involved in denying the right of homosexual marriage seems to me too slight (though I would not call it trivial) to warrant the courts bucking strong public opinion; and here it should be noted that although the margin in the polls by which homosexual marriage is opposed is not great, the opponents tend to feel more strongly than the supporters. Most supporters of homosexual marriage, apart from homosexuals themselves (not all of whom favor homosexual marriage, however), and some (not all) of their parents, support it out of a belief in tolerance rather than because of a strong personal stake, whereas many of the opponents are passionately opposed, some because they fear homosexual recruitment, contagion, etc., but more I think because they believe that official recognition of homosexual marriage would devalue their own, heterosexual marriages.

Of course it is often the duty of courts to buck public opinion; many constitutional rights are designed for the protection of minorities. But when, as in this case, there is no strong basis in the text or accepted meaning of the Constitution for the recognition of a new right, and that recognition would cause a powerful public backlash against the courts, the counsel of prudence is to withhold recognition. Doing so would have the additional advantage of allowing a period of social experimentation from which we might learn more about the consequences of homosexual marriage. One state, Massachusetts, already recognizes homosexual marriage, as do a small but growing number of foreign nations (Spain, Canada, Belgium, and the Netherlands). Perhaps without judicial intervention gay marriage will in the relatively near future sweep the world—and if not it may be for reasons that reveal unexpected wisdom in the passionate public opposition to the measure.

ON GAY MARRIAGE—BECKER

When I have discussed gay marriage with some conservatives, they strongly opposed using the word "marriage" for gays. Yet many of them accepted that gay partners should have the right to sign contracts that determine the inheritance of their property, provide various stipulations about living arrangement, the disposition of assets in case they break up, and many other conditions. Most of these persons might accept, I believe, that a gay partner can qualify for the social security benefits that spouses get, can be covered under employment medical plans of their partner, and so forth.

But to call these contracts "marriage" makes them see red. It is not that they believe (and I agree with them) that allowing the word marriage will significantly increase the extent of homosexuality. Whether homosexuality is due to genes or environment, allowing the term "gay marriage" to be used is likely to be a very small factor in determining the number of men and women who become gay.

The objections to gay marriage seem even stranger when one recognizes that gay couples have been allowed for a while to engage in much more significant behavior that has been associated throughout history with heterosexual couples. I am referring to the rights that gay couples already possess to adopt children, or to have one lesbian partner use sperm from a male to become pregnant, bring a fetus to term, and have a baby that the lesbian partners raise together, or the right of one gay male partner to impregnate a woman who bears a child that is raised by the two gay partners.

No one knows yet what is the effect on children of being raised by a gay couple. Yet it is a far more important departure from how children have been raised throughout history, with potentially much greater consequences, than using the word "marriage" to describe a gay union. I believe, although there is little evidence yet, that the effects on children raised by gay couples will usually be quite negative, in part because fathers and mothers have distinct but important roles, in part because their family structures will differ so greatly from that of their classmates and other peers. Another reason is that gay couples tend to have much less stable relations than heterosexual couples, although the data that demonstrate this is mainly from gay couples without children. To the extent the greater turnover extends to gay couples with children, which I believe it will, then greater turnover adds a further complication and difficulty for the children raised by gay couples.

So given this radical change when children are conceived and raised by gay couples, I find the furor stemming from the desire to use the term "marriage" to describe a union between two gays to be quaint and incomprehensible. But as Posner says there is commotion and anger about gay marriage, both pro and con, whether justified or not. Given the strength of these convictions, it is better to have the issue of gay marriage resolved by the legislative process of different states rather than by largely arbitrary judicial decisions that may support or oppose the use of the word "marriage" to describe unions of homosexuals.

Whatever the outcome of such legislation, gay couples should have the right to contracts that specify their desired asset allocation; conditions, if any, under which they can break up; visitation rights if they have children and break up; and any other aspects of their relation that they consider relevant. With the enforcement of these contracts, they would have practically all the rights that married heterosexual couples have, even when they cannot call their relation marriage.

Indeed, I have long argued (see, for example, my 1985 *Business Week* column reprinted in G. S. Becker and G. N. Becker, *The Economics of Life)* that heterosexual unions should be based on contract rather than judicial decisions or legislative actions.

Contracts are more flexible instruments than laws since they allow the terms of a marriage to fit the special needs of particular couples. The courts would become involved only in seeing that the contract is being enforced when one party believes it is not and in insuring that adequate provision is made for any children if a marriage dissolves.

If married heterosexual couples also had to base their relations mainly on contract, as I continue to advocate, gay couples may not feel strongly that they suffer from discrimination if they cannot be considered legally "married." I agree with Posner that the contractual approach is not likely to be adopted in the foreseeable future. However, it does suggest that gay couples might actually be in a better position than heterosexual couples if gay couples could use contracts to define their rights and obligations, while heterosexual couples were mainly subject to less flexible judicial and legislative law. In fact, courts frequently override the provisions of marital contracts among heterosexuals, which they may be less likely to do when dealing with contracts between gays.

3

POLYGAMY

October 22, 2006

IS THERE A CASE FOR LEGALIZING POLYGAMY?—BECKER

For a long time I have found the practice of polygamy intriguing, and have wondered why opposition to this form of marriage is so strong in the United States and most of the world—see my *A Treatise on the Family* (Harvard University Press, 1981, 1991). I have been reflecting on this subject again as a result of the arrest several months ago of a fundamentalist Mormon leader in Utah who was charged with practicing polygamy, among other things. The Mormon Church since the 1890s had suspended the practice of polygamy under pressure from the U.S. government. The act of having more than one spouse is now a felony in Utah, punishable by up to five years in prison, although authorities usually do not go after polygamists.

While the ferocious opposition to polygamy seemed strange even in the 1970s when I first wrote about this practice, it is much stranger now in light of developments during the past couple of decades. These developments include a successful movement to legalize contracts between gays that allow them to live as married couples, even though there is ongoing emotional debate about whether such couples can legally be considered "married." Gay couples can also adopt children. They can legally have their "own" children too through using male sperm to impregnate one partner of a lesbian couple, or through hiring women to become pregnant from the sperm of one member of a male homosexual relation. Men and women can be "serial" polygamists in the sense of marrying several times over their lifetimes after divorcing their prior spouses. Married women and men can have boyfriends and girlfriends without any legal difficulties, and have children with persons other than their spouses.

I have no problem at all with serial polygamy, with allowing gays to have contracts that are equivalent to being married, or to allowing gay couples to be called married. I have much more difficulty with children being raised by gay couples since that form of parenting is a venture into the unknown, but maybe that too is OK. My intent here is not to comment on these practices, but to ask why then does the strenuous opposition to polygamy continue?

Although polygamy encompasses both polygyny, where a man has several wives, and polyandry, where a woman has several husbands, polygyny has been far more common in human (and other) societies. This explains why I concentrate on polygyny, although my arguments apply also to polyandry.

The most frequently encountered argument against polygyny is the claim that it exploits women, and is a continuation of the traditional subjection of women to men. Women were indeed exploited in many monogamous and polygynist traditional societies, when they were frequently forced to marry men that they did not want to.

That hardly describes the situation these days in the United States, the rest of the developed world, and much of the developing world. Women choose their partners, and refuse to marry men who they do not want to marry, regardless of their parents' feelings or the ardor of suitors. In this world, a woman would not have to enter into a polygamist household if she would not want to. Would-be polygamist men would have to persuade second or third wives that it is worth it, because of their wealth, good looks, kindness, or in other ways. If she is willing to become an additional wife, why should laws prevent that?

What about a first wife who suddenly finds out that her husband is planning on taking additional wives? She could divorce him, share their property, and receive child support for any children they have in virtually all states without having to prove any "fault" on his part. Moreover, she could write a contract before marriage stipulating that he cannot take additional wives. The contract could provide for damages in the event of a divorce due to such a violation of the contract. Judges would surely take that into account in distributing property, custody rights over any children, and the size of child support.

Some oppose polygyny because they believe too many women would be "swept off their feet" by smooth-talking actual or potential polygamists. If that were a great concern, women could be required to be older before they could legally marry into polygamist households, or a "cooling off" period could be mandated before they could do that. Yet isn't it offensively patronizing to women to believe they cannot make their own decisions about whether to enter into marriages that contain other wives? We do not offer men any special protections against the "wiles" of women, so why do women need such protection? Indeed, I believe that in marital decisions women are more thoughtful and farsighted than men, partly because marriage has meant much more to women than to men.

The claim that polygyny is unfair to women is strange since polygyny increases the demand for women as spouses in the same way that polyandry would increase the demand for men. If men were to take multiple wives, that increases the overall competition for women compared to a situation where each man can have at most one wife. This argument against polygyny is like arguing that a way to increase the economic prospects of minorities is to place an upper bound on how many members of these groups a company can employ. Of course, actual laws that try to improve the economic circumstances of minorities often in effect take the opposite form by placing lower, not upper, bounds on their employment in different companies. That too is not sensible but I save that for another day.

Even though women as a group would gain from allowing polygyny, and men as a group would be hurt, not all members of each group would be affected in the same way. Men who do not have much to offer women would be more likely than under monogamy to remain unmarried, at least until they become older and wealthier, or more matured. Similarly, educated and otherwise attractive women who have a lot to offer might suffer if they have to face competition from several women who individually have less to offer, but collectively can offer as much or more. Perhaps opposition from such groups that would be hurt by polygamy is the political economy explanation of why that form of marriage has been outlawed in most of the world.

My argument for polygamy is one of principle to bring out certain fascinating issues. For, in fact, polygyny would be rare in modern societies even if fully allowed. Polygyny was popular in the past when men valued having many children. That is no longer the case, since few couples want more than three children, a number that usually can be easily attained with a single wife. So the main motivation for polygyny has vanished with the arrival of the knowledge economy where fathers as well as mothers now want a small number of educated children rather than many ill-educated offspring. Note that polygyny is rare even in those Muslim countries that allow it, such as Iran.

I conclude with two questions. Why the strong opposition to polygyny if it would be so rare? If modern women are at least as capable as men in deciding whom to marry, why does polygyny continue to be dubbed a "barbarous" practice?

SHOULD POLYGAMY BE LEGAL?—POSNER

Becker has posed an intriguing question: if a woman thinks she would be better off as a second or third (or nth) wife rather than as a first and only wife, or not married at all, why should government intervene and prohibit the arrangement? From an economic standpoint, a contract that makes no one worse off increases social welfare, since it must make both of the contracting parties better off; otherwise they would not both agree to the contract.

The question has achieved a certain topicality because of the movement to legalize homosexual marriage. One of the standard objections to such marriage is that if homosexual marriage is permitted, why not polygamous marriage? The basic argument for homosexual marriage is that it promotes the welfare of homosexual couples without hurting anybody else. That seems to be equally the case for polygamous marriage.

But is it? My view is that polygamy would impose substantial social costs in a modern Western-type society that probably would not be offset by the benefits to the parties to polygamous marriages. (For elaboration, see my book *Sex and Reason* [1992], particularly chapter 9.) Especially given the large disparities in wealth in the United States, legalizing polygamy would enable wealthy men to have multiple wives, even harems, which would reduce the supply of women to men of lower incomes and thus aggravate inequality. The resulting shortage of women would lead to queuing, and thus to a high age of marriage for men, which in turn would increase the demand for prostitution. Moreover, intense competition for women would lower the age of marriage for women, which would be likely to result in less investment by them in education (because household production is a substitute for market production) and therefore reduce women's market output.

Of course, forbidding the wealthy to buy a particular commodity is usually inferior to taxation as a method of reducing inequality. Yet we do forbid the buying of votes, which could be thought a parallel device to forbidding the "buying" of wives: one vote, one wife. We think that vote buying would have undesirable political consequences. So might polygamy. In societies in which polygamy is permitted without any limitation on the number of wives, wealthy households become clans, since all the children of a polygamous household are related through having the same father, no matter how many different mothers they have. These clans can become so powerful as to threaten the state's monopoly of political power; this is one of the historical reasons for the abolition of polygamy, though it would be unlikely to pose a serious danger to the stability of American government.

In polygamous households, the father invests less time in the upbringing of his children, because there are more of them. There is also less reciprocal affection between husband and wife, because they spend less time together. Household governancc under polygamy is bound to be more hierarchical than in monogamous marriage, because the household is larger and the ties of affection weaker; as a result, "agency costs" are higher and so the principal (the husband, as head of the household) has to devise and implement means of supervision that would be unnecessary in a monogamous household. (An additional factor is that women in a polygamous household have a greater incentive to commit adultery since they have less frequent sex with, and affection for, their husband, so the husband has to watch them more carefully to prevent their straying.) This managerial responsibility deflects the husband from more socially productive activities.

A woman who wanted a monogamous marriage could presumably negotiate a marital contract that would forbid the husband to take additional wives without her consent. However, she would have to buy this concession from the husband, which would make her worse off than if he were denied the right (in the absence of a contractual waiver of it) to take additional wives. Allowing polygamy would thus alter the distribution of wealth among women as well as among men.

Against all this it can be argued that polygamy would be uncommon in a society such as that of twenty-first-century United States. But the less common it is, the fewer the benefits to be anticipated from legalizing it. And I am not sure that it would be all that uncommon. Although few American couples want to have more than two or three children, a polygamous union is not a couple. If a couple has three children, the ratio of adults to children is 2 to 3. In a polygamous household consisting of a husband, two wives, and four children, the ratio of adults to children is higher: 3 to 4. So the per-parent burden is less, even though there are more children.

Because polygamy is illegal everywhere in the United States, few Americans think of it as an option. If it were made respectable by being legalized, who knows? There are four hundred American billionaires, and several million Americans with a net worth of at least $6 million. Nor, with most women working, is it obvious that a man would have to be wealthy in order to attract multiple wives, though presumably men who wanted to be polygamists would have to be able to offer some financial inducements, since most women would prefer to be a man's only wife. As more and more men attempted to become polygamists, the "price" they would have to pay for a wife would rise, so polygamy would be a distinctly minority institution. But it would not necessarily be trivial in size or harmless in its social consequences, which would be likely to exceed those of homosexual marriage. Polygamy is banned in most advanced societies and flourishes chiefly in backward ones, particularly in Africa. This is some evidence against legalizing it.

4

SEX SELECTION

February 12, 2007

IS SEX SELECTION OF BIRTHS UNDESIRABLE?—BECKER

In China in 2005, 118 boys were born for every 100 girls born. This ratio is far above the normal biological ratio of about 106 boys to 100 girls. The sexual disparity in China has resulted from a combination of low birth rates, a preference in China for boys when parents only have one or two children, and the spread of ultrasound techniques in that country that allow the sex of fetuses to be identified and then aborted if parents do not like the sex. Similar trends have emerged in India and South Korea as well.

More sophisticated and expensive methods permit parents to raise their chances of a male baby even before a woman becomes pregnant. Considered most reliable is a method that involves in vitro fertilization, drugs to stimulate the mother's ovaries, surgery, and other steps. The total cost can exceed $20,000, so this method clearly is only available to richer persons.

Are there good reasons to object to sex selection, either by abortion or more sophisticated methods? On February 1, 2007, the Committee on Ethics of the

American College of Obstetricians and Gynecologists (the ACOG) did issue an opinion objecting on the grounds that it is unethical for physicians to participate in sex selection by parents that was based not on potential for sex-linked genetic disorders, but solely on family balancing of personal preferences. This opinion about the ethics of sexual selection applied "regardless of the timing of the selection (i.e., preconception or post conception) or the stage of development of the embryo or fetus."

Such an opinion seems strange in light of the general support by physicians and the Supreme Court of abortions by parents "solely" to satisfy their personal preferences about timing or number of children. What is so different about sex-selected abortions that would lead the ACOG with its over fifty-one thousand members who provide health care to women to oppose abortions to satisfy parental desires for additional boys or girls while supporting the general right to abortion? The ACOG tries to provide an answer by claiming that sex selection through any method may "ultimately support sexist practices."

It is not clear what the ACOG means by sexist practices, but all the evidence on sexual preferences in the United States and other richer countries indicates an overwhelming desire for variety—boys and girls—rather than a strong preference for either sex. So sex-selected abortions in these countries is unlikely to have much of an effect on the overall sex ratio, although it would affect the distribution of boys and girls in different families.

I concentrate my remaining discussion on the implications of sex-selected abortions in countries where it raises the number of boys relative to girls. China, South Korea, and other countries have tried to implement control over sex selection by making it illegal to use ultrasound techniques to select the sex of children. However, these regulations are notoriously difficult to implement since doctors may say "congratulations" when an ultrasound test reveals a boy, and remain silent when the fetus is a girl.

Abortions of girl fetuses would reduce average family size if parents who prefer boys would end up with larger families than they would like because they cannot control the sex of their offspring. The effect on family size could go the other way, however, if the fear of having girls discourages parents from having additional children. These effects on family size could be important, but I ignore them in the following discussion and concentrate on the effects of a lower number of girl babies relative to boys compared to the biological natural girl to boy ratio of a little below 50 to 50.

One might expect parents who abort fetuses of sexes they do not want to treat their children better than they would otherwise since they now are satisfied with the sexes of their children. In such cases, sex-selected abortions against girls would improve rather than worsen the average treatment of girls since parents would be happier with the girls they have than if they had girls who were not really wanted. It is no surprise, for example, that orphanages in China predominantly have girls (and some handicapped boys), given the preference for boys in the traditional Chinese culture.

What about the overall effects in a society of skewing the sex ratio of births toward boys? The fewer girls who are born presumably would be better off since they would be better educated, and in other ways better treated by parents who want them. This would be reinforced if the effect of sex selected abortions is to lower the overall birth rate since it is well established that families with fewer children invest more in each one, girls as well as boys.

As children become adults in cohorts with a high ratio of boys, the advantage of girls and women increases since they are scarcer. It is claimed that young women in China are already at a premium as potential mates because strong sex selection has been going on ever since the one child policy was introduced in the early 1980s. Prior to the spread of ultrasound techniques, sex selection occurred through sending girls to orphanages, neglect, and in some case even engaging in female infanticide.

To be sure, if the value of girls as wives and girlfriends, and in other ways, rises because they are scarcer, then the value of boys as husbands and boyfriends tends to fall. However, it is not apparent why that should call for policies that prevent sex-selected techniques, unless the interests of men were motivating these policies. To use an analogy, a shift of demand in an economy toward services and away from manufacturing because of a shift in "preferences" toward services—as has occurred in the United States and other rich countries—benefits women relative to men since women are more likely to work in services than are men. Yet no one would claim that society should prevent such preferences because they help (indirectly) one sex over another.

The great statistician and biologist, R.A. Fisher, used a celebrated biological analysis to explain why the sex ratio remains close to 50 to 50 in nonhuman species. An economic analysis based on incentives gives results that are related to Fisher's result. An improvement in the position of women due to a decline in the number of girls relative to boys leads to some correction in the sex ratio as parental choices respond in the long run to the more favorable position of girls. If women are in greater demand as wives and in the economy when they are in scarcer supply, some parents will decide that having girls has advantages, possibly through receiving generous bride prices when daughters marry. This would shift "preferences" toward having girls. The long-run outcome would not necessarily be the biologically natural ratio of a little more boy births than girl births, but it should be closer to that ratio than the current ratios in some Asian countries.

SEX SELECTION—POSNER

I have little to add to Becker's convincing discussion. One small point worth noting, however, is a new technology for sex selection, described in an interesting article by Denise Grady in the February 6, 2007, *New York Times.* It is called "sperm sorting" and enables male or female sperm to be concentrated in semen, greatly shifting the odds in favor of producing a child of one sex rather than the other. The cost is only $4,000 to $6,000, which is much less than in vitro fertilization, since the "enriched" sperm can simply be inseminated in the woman rather than requiring in vitro fertilization. Sex selection by sperm sorting may actually be cheaper than ultrasound plus abortion, the conventional method; if so, and it comes to dominate, the ethics of sex selection will be separable from the ethics of abortion motivated by sex selection.

The key points that Becker makes, both of which I agree with, are, first, that sex selection by U.S. couples is unlikely to result in an unbalanced sex ratio, and, second, that in countries such as China and India in which there is a strong preference for male offspring, girls will be treated better if sex selection is permitted, since there will be fewer girls born to couples who did not want them. Of course, as there will fewer girls, period, the net effect on total female utility is unclear: fewer reduces total utility but happier increases it. Since the net effect is uncertain, feminist opponents of sex selection should consider whether, if unwanted girls are born, there are feasible techniques for improving their treatment so that if sex selection is forbidden (assuming that that is feasible—Becker suggests that it is not), there can be reasonable confidence that net female utility will increase rather than decrease.

I also agree with Becker that there is a tendency to self-selection, since as the percentage of girls and women declines, men's demand for them rises, and observing this couples will tend to shift their reproductive selection in favor of girls. Since there is no reason why this tendency must overcome a preference for boys, an unbalanced sex ratio could persist indefinitely. But this is unlikely in rapidly developing countries such as China and India. A strong preference for male children tends to be found in societies in which there is a great deal of subsistence agriculture, a weak social insurance system, and a reliance on private violence (as in a revenge culture) to protect personal and property rights; all these factors increase the demand for male children. As these conditions (the first two of which are important in China and India, and all three of which are important in Iraq, for example) change, the preference diminishes, as we observe in the wealthy societies of Europe and North America, where there is no longer a net preference for having male rather than female children.

Apparently sex selection is actually more common in urban areas than in rural areas of India. But presumably the reason is that access to ultrasound for detecting the sex of a fetus, and to abortion, is greater in cities, and this effect could dominate the greater preference for sex selection in rural areas. Urban Indians might prefer boys because of a lag in the adaptation of traditional values to urban conditions.

The transition to a 50 to 50 sex ratio, even if inevitable, is likely to take a long time. Suppose at time 1 there is a large excess of male births, followed at time 2 by a dawning recognition that girls are more valuable than had been realized at time 1. Probably time 1 and time 2 will be separated by twenty or thirty years (or more, if there is a "values lag," as I suggested earlier), and so there will be at least one entire adult generation in which the sex ratio is skewed in favor of males. Should countries that face this imbalance worry about it to the extent of taking measures against it? We have a natural experiment, which can help us to answer the question, in societies that permit polygamy. The effect of polygamy (technically polygyny—multiple wives—but polyandry is virtually unknown) is to raise the effective ratio of men to women, since a number of women are removed from the pool available to the nonpolygamous men. In a society in which there are 100 men and 100 women, but 10 of the women are married to one of the men, the male to female sex ratio, so far as the rest of the society is concerned, is 99 to 90. The result is to raise the average age of marriage for men and reduce it for women, reduce the percentage of married men and increase the percentage of married women, reduce promiscuity by increasing women's bargaining power, and possibly increase male emigration and female immigration. None of these effects seem likely to harm society seriously as a whole.

In contrast, research that I discuss in my book *Sex and Reason* (1992) finds that the low effective male to female sex ratio of the black population in the United States (due largely to abnormally high rates of imprisonment and homicide of young black males) promotes promiscuity because there is more competition among women for men, and reduces the marriage rate and family formation.

In sum, sex selection, at least in favor of males, appears not to have negative external effects. It presumably confers net private benefits (like other preference satisfaction), or otherwise it would not be practiced. (There are no external effects in societies, such as that of the United States, in which sex selection is unbiased.) The case for forbidding it is therefore unconvincing (at least when sex selection is not implemented by abortion, to which there are independent objections) unless it can be shown to create a net decrease in female welfare.

5

IMMIGRATION REFORM

February 21, 2005

SELL THE RIGHT TO IMMIGRATE—BECKER

Rich nations are facing enormous pressure to increase the number of immigrants because of their sharp limits on the number of legal immigrants accepted, and the huge numbers who try to cross borders illegally. This immigration pressure stems in major part from the very large gap between the earnings of workers at all skill levels in the United States, Western Europe, and Japan compared to the rest of the world. In addition, low birth rates in the developed world create excellent opportunities for young persons from poorer nations, and travel between nations has become much cheaper.

The United States, the leading destination for immigrants, uses quotas that give preference to family members of persons already here legally, to applicants with greater skills, to persons who applied earlier, and some other criteria. Since I am a free trader, readers might expect my preferred alternative to the present system to be nineteenth-century-style unlimited immigration. I would support that if we lived in the nineteenth-century world where government spending was tiny. But governments now spend huge amounts on medical care, retirement, education, and other benefits and entitlements. Experience demonstrates that in our political system, it is impossible to prevent immigrants, even those here illegally, to gain access to these benefits. I believe that with unlimited immigration, many would come mainly because they are attracted by these government benefits, and they would then be voting to influence future government spending and other public policies.

Given these realities of free immigration, the best alternative to the present quota system is an ancient way of allocating a scarce and popular good; namely, by charging a price that clears the market. That is why I believe countries should sell the right to immigrate, especially the United States that has so many persons waiting to immigrate. To illustrate how a price system would work, suppose the United States charges $50,000 for the right to immigrate, and agrees to accept all applicants willing to pay that price, subject to a few important qualifications. These qualifications would require that those accepted not have any serious diseases, terrorist backgrounds, or criminal records.

Immigrants who are willing to pay a sizeable entrance fee would automatically have various characteristics that countries seek in their entrants, without special programs, point systems, or lengthy hearings. They would be younger since young adults would gain more from migrating because they would receive higher earnings over a relatively long period. Skilled persons would generally be more willing to pay high entrance fees since they would increase their earnings more than unskilled immigrants would. More ambitious and hard-working individuals would also be more eager to pay since the United States provides better opportunities than most other countries for these types.

Persons more committed to staying in the United States would also be more likely to pay since individuals who expect to return home after a few years would not be willing to pay a significant fee. Committed immigrants invest more in learning English, and American mores and customs, and become better-informed and more active citizens. For obvious reasons, political refugees and those persecuted in their own countries would be willing to pay a sizeable fee to gain admission to a free nation. So a fee system would automatically avoid time-consuming hearings about whether they are really in physical danger if they were forced to return home.

The payback period for most immigrants of a $50,000 or higher entrance fee would generally be short—less than the usual payback period of a typical university education. For example, if skilled individuals could earn $10 an hour in a country like India or China, and $40 an hour in the United States, by moving they would gain $60,000 a year (before taxes and assuming two thousand hours of work per year).

The higher earnings from immigrating would cover a fee of $50,000 in about a year! It would take not much more than four years to earn this fee even for an unskilled person who earns $1 an hour in his native country, and could earn $8 an hour in the U.S.

These calculations might only indicate that $50,000 is too low an entrance price, and that an appropriate fee would be considerably higher. But with any significant fee, most potential immigrants would have great difficulty paying it from their own resources. An attractive way to overcome these difficulties would be to adopt a loan program to suit the needs of immigrants who have to finance entry.

One could follow the present policy toward student loans, and have the federal government guarantee loans to immigrants made by private banks. However, I objected to that program in a January 9, 2009, entry in this blog, and suggested instead removing the federal guarantees while retaining that education loans are not dischargeable through personal bankruptcy. The same approach would work for immigration loans since these are also investments in human capital. Of course, it would be difficult to collect from immigrants who return home, and that would lead to higher interest rates on these loans. But such forfeiture would be discouraged too if banks forced immigrants to make large enough down payments in order to get their loans.

Countries that charge a sizeable fee would have an incentive to raise the number of immigrants accepted because they would bring in tax revenue that cuts the tax burden on natives. For example, 1 million immigrants per year who each paid $50,000 would contribute government revenue of $50 billion per year. Moreover, immigrants who would enter under a fee system would generally make little use of welfare or unemployment benefits, would pay hefty taxes on their earnings, and would tend to be younger and healthier. So the overall direct economic benefits from larger numbers of immigrants would be much greater than under the present admission system. This would help quiet anti-immigration rhetoric as it induces countries to take more immigrants.

In addition, since anyone willing to pay the entry price could then legally immigrate, this approach should also cut down the number who enter illegally. Still, some persons will continue to try, especially if they want to avoid paying the fee, or only want to work for a short time in the United States. However, border and other immigration personnel would become more efficient in combating illegal entrants since they would have to deal with smaller numbers. It should become easier also to expel and even punish illegal entrants because they would get less sympathy from the American public than under the present system. After all, they usually could have entered legally, but tried to chisel out of paying.

In summary, charging a fee to immigrate would raise tax revenue, increase the number of immigrants accepted, and also raise the quality of those accepted.

It is a win-win situation for countries accepting immigrants, and for the vast majority of persons who would like to immigrate.

IMMIGRATION REFORM—POSNER

I approach the issue of immigration reform (theoretical reform—neither Becker nor I are considering the political obstacles to radical changes in immigration law) somewhat differently. I begin by asking: why restrict immigration at all? The only answer I consider fully compatible with a market-oriented approach to social issues is that the immigrant might reduce the net social welfare of the United States, if, for example, he was unemployable or on the verge of retirement, or was a criminal, or was likely to require highly expensive medical treatment, or if he would impose greater costs in congestion or pollution than he would confer benefits, with benefits measured (crudely) by his income before taxes and by any consumer surplus that he might create. I assume that the welfare of foreigners as such does not enter into the U.S. social welfare function; but immigrants who create net benefits in the sense just indicated contribute to the strength and prosperity of the nation.

The problem of the "undesirable" immigrant—the immigrant who wants to free ride on the services and amenities that the United States provides its citizens—could be solved by means of a two-stage process. In the first stage, the prospective immigrant would be screened for age, health, IQ, criminal record,

English language capability, etc.; the screening need not be elaborate. If the would-be immigrant "passed" in the sense that he seemed likely to add more to U.S. welfare than he would take out, he would be admitted without charge. If he flunked the screening test, an estimate would be made of the net cost (discounted to present value) that he would be likely to impose on the United States if he lived here and he would be charged that amount for permission to immigrate.

An alternative, less revolutionary, approach to screening out free-rider immigrants would be, first, to deny immigrants access to Medicaid and other welfare programs until they had lived in the United States for a significant period of time, and, second, to auction off a certain number of immigrant visas to the highest bidders. Immigrants willing to take their chances without access to welfare programs (not that all access could be denied—no one could be refused emergency medical treatment on a charity basis), and immigrants willing to bid high prices in an immigration auction, would be likely to be productive citizens, in the first case, and to cover any costs they would impose on the nation's health or other welfare systems, in the second case.

Either the more or the less revolutionary alternative would impose significant transition costs, but that would be true of any radical change in immigration policy. The obvious cost (though not really a cost, rather a redistribution of income) would be that by increasing the supply of labor, an immigration policy that made it easy for employable workers to enter the U.S. labor force would reduce wages in the labor markets that the immigrants entered. A closely related but subtler consequence is that the downward effect of large-scale immigration on wages (a short-run effect, in all likelihood) would complicate the process of determining the correct fee to prevent free riding: an immigrant who might be able to pay his way at the existing wage level might be unable to do so if the wage level fell as a result of massive immigration. Similarly, congestion and pollution externalities might increase at an increasing rate with massive immigration, requiring a further adjustment in the fee charged the "undesirables."

Either approach seems to me preferable to a flat fee for all would-be immigrants. A flat fee would not do away with the need to screen, since some would-be immigrants might impose net costs on the United States that were greater than the fee; that is why Becker's approach includes screening. The flat fee would exclude two types of immigrant that should, in a market-oriented approach, be admitted. One type would be "undesirables" willing and able to compensate the United States for the expected costs that they would impose—and so they would not be free riders after all; a very wealthy person on the verge of retirement would be an example of such an "undesirable." The second type would be highly promising would-be immigrants (for example, persons with a high IQ) who for some reason—perhaps because they reside in extremely poor countries—simply could not pay the down payment on the fee.

The fee would, it is true, increase government revenues, which may seem a plus. But it would do so at the usual cost of distorting the allocation of resources, in this case by excluding immigrants in the second class.

I note two complications. First, it may be desirable to adhere to the current policy of granting asylum to foreigners who are escaping persecution, even if they do not seem likely to be able to pay or to earn enough to cover the costs they'll impose on this country. My reason is not sentiment, but the fact that people who are persecuted tend to be either nonconformists or members of particularly successful minorities, and in either case they, or at least their children, are likely to be productive citizens even if their U.S. employment prospects are dim. Second, the United States in formulating immigration policy may have to worry about "brain drain," and, what may be more important, "leadership drain," from poor or unstable countries. For example, it would be highly unfortunate if all the Iraqis who have the ability and motivation to build a democratic, free-market society fled to the United States. Thus it may sometimes be in our national interest to exclude persons who would otherwise be highly desirable immigrants, in order to shore up forces or tendencies in their own countries that promote U.S. interests. However, I do not know how to mesh this concern with either my or Becker's proposals.

6

PUTIN'S POPULATION PLAN

June 4, 2006

GRAPPLING WITH RUSSIA'S DEMOGRAPHIC TIME BOMB—BECKER

Russia has the highest death rates among all countries with at least moderate levels of economic development. The present life expectancy for a typical male is about fifty-eight years, below what it was twenty years ago in Russia. For comparison, life expectancy for males is about seventy-five years in the United States, which itself is below that of Japan and a number of Western European nations.

Even more worrisome to many Russians are the very low birth rates during the past couple of decades. The total fertility rate—the number of children born to the average woman over her lifetime—is expected to be just 1.28 in 2006, or just a little more than one child per couple. Russian fertility is among the lowest in the world. Russia's low birth rates and high death rates make it one of the only half dozen countries (mainly in the former Soviet bloc) with declining populations. The Russian decline is currently about seven hundred thousand persons per year, but the rate of decline will accelerate as the number of women in childbearing ages continues to fall. A World Bank report projects that with unchanged birth and death rates, Russia's population would fall from its present level of about 140 million persons to under 100 million by the year 2050. If this happens, such a huge nation would then be largely empty of people.

Neo-Malthusians and others may believe that a lower population is a blessing because it reduces pollution, and raises labor productivity by lowering the number of workers per acre of land and per unit of capital equipment. However, low birth rates reduce the number of persons of working ages relative to retired persons, thereby making it more difficult to raise enough revenue from taxes on workers to pay for the retirement benefits and medical care of the aged.

Whatever may have been true when countries mainly depended on traditional agriculture, in the modern world a smaller population in a country like Russia that already has relatively few people per square mile also tends to lower productivity. Although international trade provides an outlet for specialized workers, a lower domestic population still discourages specialization and the division of labor because it reduces the extent of the domestic market. Lower population may also discourage investments in developing new products that get higher returns when there are more people to buy them.

So in my judgment President Putin is correct in his recent expression of concern not only about Russia's high death rate, but also especially about its low birth rate. He wants to encourage women to have more children, but he is deviating sharply from past leaders like Stalin who offered Medals of Glory to mothers who had many children. Putin has become sufficiently market oriented to encourage larger families by appealing to Russian pocketbooks. The high world price of oil and natural gas has provided Putin with abundant resources to play with, and he wants to use this energy bonanza to slow, and if possible reverse, the demographic decline of Russia.

Putin has proposed a ten-year program with very generous benefits for Russian women who have a second child—about 70 percent of Russian women of childbearing ages presently either have no children or only one child. Under his plan, women who do have a second child will get up to $110 more per month in child allowances, they would be able to take leave from work for up to eighteen months while receiving 40 percent of their salaries, and they would get larger subsidies for child care. But the most novel aspect of Putin's proposal is to give a cash bonus of over $9,000 to women who have a second child. This bonus is considerably larger than the annual earnings of a typical Russian worker, men or women, and it could be used for mortgage payments and for many other large outlays. Putin acknowledges that this program would require lots of money (perhaps 1 percent of Russian GDP), but he claims that it is necessary in order to "change the attitude of the whole society to the family and its values." Of course, Russia will not have the resources to implement the program if oil and gas prices fall sharply during the next few years, which is a real possibility.

Will Putin's financial approach work? I believe it will in the sense that the program is likely to induce many more Russian women to have a second child. To be sure, other countries have tried to increase birth rates through financial incentives, and these programs have had only mixed success. Guy Larouque and Bernard Salanie have made a very careful evaluation of the generous but extremely complex system of monthly child credits in France. Their estimates indicate that child subsidies to French women have raised France's total fertility rate by some 5 percent, or by about 0.1. Although France now has one of the highest fertility rates in Western Europe, their study suggests that this is only partly due to the elaborate French child subsidy system.

Putin's proposal is much more generous than the French program, although the Russian subsidies would only apply to women who have a second child. I believe that his plan would be quite effective, not only because it is generous, but also because the centerpiece is a cash bonus rather than a stream of monthly payments. The U.S. military has discovered that reenlistment rates are more affected by sizeable bonuses than by what would seem to be an equivalent series of payment in the form of higher annual compensation during the reenlistment period. Bonuses are more effective probably because younger people are usually short of ready cash for big purchases, such as apartments and homes, cars, and other consumer durables.

Such liquidity constraints are far more important in Russia than in the United States since the Russian financial sector is extremely primitive and undeveloped. The typical Russian family does not have credit cards, or access to commercial loans on homes or car purchases. So the value of a large cash payment for having a second child is likely to be very appealing, especially to less-educated women and other lower income families.

For this reason, I expect the Russian approach to child subsides to be more effective at raising birth rates than child subsidies have been elsewhere. Extrapolating the French results would give a very large effect of the proposed Russian system of subsidies and bonuses on Russian fertility (based on an e-mail from Bernard Salanie). Partly for reasons mentioned by Posner, the actual results are likely to be smaller, so I would guess that Russian fertility would increase by about 10–20 percent from current levels, or from the present total fertility rate of 1.28 to perhaps as high as 1.55. Since even this upper limit leaves Russian fertility far below the level (2.1) that would be sufficient to maintain its present population level, such a generous subsidy system is unlikely to revolutionize the way Russians view large families. Many of the factors that have led to small families, such as the high level of women's education, expensive housing, and high divorce rates, would not be greatly affected by these baby subsidies. Still, an increase of the fertility rate to 1.55 would greatly slow the rate of decline in the Russian population.

The Russian experiment will be carefully watched by many of the almost one hundred countries with total fertility rates that are below, many of them far below, replacement levels. If Russia succeeds in significantly raising its number of births, other countries that fear a long-run sharp decline of their population are likely to follow with their own programs to encourage women to have more babies.

PUTIN'S POPULATION PLAN—POSNER

I am going to go out on a very long limb and predict, contrary to Becker, that Putin's plan will fail. The major reason is that it lacks credibility. Having a child is a long-run investment, and Russians cannot be confident that the long-run features of the plan—the increased housing allowances and child-care subsidies—will be implemented throughout the childhood of the second children. Even the short-run features are uncertain. The generous upfront cash grant cannot be withdrawn from the bank until the child is three years old, which means three and three-quarter years after conception. And the paid-work-leave provision is supposed to last twenty-seven (eighteen plus nine) months after conception. I assume, without knowing, that the work-leave provision is to be funded by employers—and will there be any actual enforcement? If I were a Russian, I would be extremely skeptical that the plan will be fully funded and implemented, and this would make me reluctant to invest in a second child.

Moreover, a plan that costs 1 percent of GDP (that would be more than $100 billion in the United States, though it is only about $15 billion in Russia) must be financed, and depending on how it is financed, it may reduce the after-tax incomes of couples, thus offsetting, perhaps to a considerable degree, the benefits conferred by the plan. (Of course if the plan is a failure, it will not cost 1 percent of GDP, but that would just make it a cheap failure.)

Even if Becker's estimate of the effect of the Putin plan is correct—that it would raise the birthrate by 15 to 20 percent—that would still leave the birthrate far below the replacement level. So this expensive plan, even if successful (which is what would make it expensive), would merely reduce the rate of population decline. That rate is a function not only of the birthrate but also, as Becker points out, of the very poor health of the average Russian man. So if the main goal is to retard population decline, Russia might in lieu of the Putin plan allocate an additional 1 percent of its GDP to health care. Current health expenditures in Russia are only about 6 percent of GDP; a 17 percent increase (1/6) in health expenditures might have a dramatic effect on longevity. The broader point is that before Russia throws a huge amount of money (by Russian standards) at a problem, it should be careful to make sure that there are no better uses for the money.

Should Russia worry about population decline? Curiously, when population decline is heavily influenced by excess adult mortality, the decline has less effect on the dependency ratio (the ratio of nonworkers to workers) than when it results solely from a low birthrate. Japan has a very high dependency ratio because of that nation's combination of high longevity with a very low birthrate. Russia has low longevity and thus relatively few (male) retirees.

Apart from the effect on the dependency ratio, I don't think a country should worry much or maybe at all about a declining population. A declining population means less pollution and congestion and, as Becker also notes, a higher ratio of land to population—the Black Death in Europe in the Middle Ages contributed to a substantial increase in average wages as a result of the reduction in the population (by about a third—which is almost the reduction predicted for Russia by mid-century); and that wage increase, some economic historians believe, set the stage for Europe's subsequent economic takeoff. The effect in Russia would not be nearly so dramatic, however, because Russian population density is already low, although this is a little misleading because large parts of Russia are virtually uninhabitable.

Judging from the economic success of countries with very small populations, such as Switzerland, Singapore, and Denmark, the fact that a greater population increases the opportunities for specialization is not important to a nation's prosperity. The reason is free trade. A small country specializes in a few products and trades them for products in which other countries specialize. Put differently, given free trade, the relevant market is the whole world, and the size of the global market is not significantly affected by Russian demographic trends.

AFTERTHOUGHTS TO PART I

BECKER AFTERTHOUGHTS

I still strongly believe that selling the right to immigrate would be the best way to solve the immigration "problem." One advantage of selling that I did not mention is that many illegal immigrants in a country like the United States would be willing to buy their right to legal status. Converting from illegal to legal status eliminates the risk of deportation, and also opens up a wider range of job opportunities. It is especially hard for illegal immigrants to get skilled jobs. I would not claim that selling immigration rights would eliminate all illegal immigration—it would not—but for this and other reasons it is likely to greatly reduce the severity of the illegal immigration problem.

I discuss the generous subsidies that Putin proposed when president to encourage Russian women to have more children. Russian birth rates have stayed low, but apparently his proposal has never been fully implemented. Since my posting, an unpublished Ph.D. dissertation by Albert Kim ("Impact of Birth Studies on Fertility: Empirical Study of Allowance for Newborn Children: A Pronatal Policy," Department of Economics, University of Chicago, 2008) has studied other experiences with child subsidies, especially in Quebec, and finds only modest effects of such subsidies on the birth rate.

POSNER AFTERTHOUGHTS

I note here recent developments concerning two of my posts, one on Russia's population policy and the other on sex selection in China and India.

Russian officials claim that the population program instituted in 2006 has been a great success, which if true would be contrary to the view I expressed in my post on the program. The officials say that births grew by 8 percent in 2007 and the annual decline in population fell from 550,000 to 240,000 in this year. But according to the U.S. Census Bureau's Web site, the Russian fertility rate increased only infinitesimally, from 1.3693 in 2004 to 1.3837 in 2006, to 1.3981 in 2008 (the replacement rate—the rate necessary to prevent population from declining in the absence of immigration—is approximately 2.1), with the number of births per one thousand women increasing only from 10.78 in 2006 to 11.03 in 2008. According to the United Nations Population Fund (UNFPA), the number of women of active childbearing age is decreasing as a result of earlier fertility declines, and this will reduce the impact of fertility policies.

With regard to sex selection, which strongly favors males in developing countries, such as China and India, I suggested in my post that the sex ratio would gradually shift away from favoring males as these countries become more urban and less agricultural. According to India's Sample Registration System, in five of India's major states, the ratio of female to male births increased from roughly the year 2000 to 2005 in the two states with the lowest ratios (Punjab and Haryana) from .775/1 to .808/1 and from .803/1 to .837/1, respectively; it also increased in two of the other states and remained the same in the third. Yet over the same period, the ratio of male to female births in China (China reports the male/female ratio, India the female/male ratio) rose from 116.9/1 to 118.58/1. Interestingly, U.S. census statistics show less imbalance between male and female births in both China and India and no change between 2000 and 2005.

II

PROPERTY RIGHTS

7

KELO AND EMINENT DOMAIN

June 26, 2005

ON EMINENT DOMAIN—BECKER

The eminent domain clause of the Fifth Amendment of the U.S. Constitution states that "Nor shall private property be taken for public use, without just compensation." This clause allows private property to be taken for public use, but requires "fair" compensation. The clause raises three major questions: What is "public use"? What is "fair compensation"? And is the principle of eminent domain desirable in a modern economy? I briefly discuss all three questions.

Public Use. The recent 5–4 Supreme Court decision in *Kelo v. City of New London,* 545 U.S. 469 (2005), elaborated on the Court's interpretation of "public use." The majority argued that it meant "public purpose," even if the project is undertaken primarily by private companies and individuals, as long as it produces general benefits in the form of increased economic development, greater tax revenue, and the like. The minority opinion written by Justice O'Connor considered this interpretation to be excessively broad, and argued for a narrower interpretation, but her opinion did not provide a clear criterion for narrowing it. The Institute of Justice, representing the fifteen homeowners who opposed the city's plan to raze their homes, wants to limit the clause to situations with actual ownership or use by the public. Examples acceptable to the Institute include construction of roads or public utilities, although courts in the past have allowed a much broader interpretation of the right to eminent domain.

It is difficult to establish a simple dividing line between what is and what is not a public use. Since private companies are involved in building roads, running electric power plants, and other public use projects, why is that fundamentally different from using eminent domain to authorize construction of private baseball stadiums, or private business redevelopment in a poor neighborhood?

Although the majority opinion by Justice Stevens argues the reasonable position that the decision-making power in specific instances should be left to state and local governments, the power to condemn property allows a government to avoid the need to demonstrate that a planned development will actually raise economic value or other benefits. The best judge of this is the market test of whether the new owners could fully compensate the old owners and still benefit, yet the right to eminent domain means that a public project can avoid having to pass this test.

Fair Compensation. To me, the only reasonable interpretation of "fair compensation" is the worth of property to the present owners. This often is greater than the highest bids for the property in the marketplace. For example, one of the fifteen homeowners who objected to selling her home to the city of Bridgeport was born there eighty-seven years ago. Clearly, the house was worth more to her than the city's assessment. Why should she be forced to sell at a price that could be way below its full value to her?

A second problem with the fair compensation test is that large property owners usually do better in the litigation over compensation than do small owners. The reason is that larger owners hire better attorneys and spend in other ways to increase their compensation. In the *Kelo* case, the Institute of Justice, a libertarian public interest law firm, came to the defense of the fifteen small property owners, but that usually does not happen. A Ph.D. study years ago by Professor Patricia Danzon of Wharton showed that smaller property owners generally receive lower compensation relative to market assessments of value than do large owners. The true picture is probably much worse since she did not have data on the subjective value of having lived in a home for a long time.

Is Eminent Domain Desirable? In addition to analyzing where to draw the line in deciding what is legitimate "public use," we should ask whether the line should be allowed at all. Is eminent domain a desirable principle in the twenty-first century? In the eighteenth, nineteenth, and early twentieth centuries, governments did rather little, so there was not much to fear from great abuse of the eminent domain constitutional clause. In fact, the first real eminent domain case was not decided until 1876. Now, however, government at all levels do so much that the temptation is irresistible to use eminent domain condemnation proceedings to hasten and cheapen their accumulation of property for various projects, regardless of a project's merits.

Without the right to eminent domain, governments would have to buy property in the same manner that private companies often accumulate many parcels to create shopping centers, factory campuses, and building complexes, like Rockefeller Center. There are difficulties involved in combining separate parcels into a single more extensive property, but why should that be made too easy, as through a condemnation proceeding?

To be sure, property owners may have incentives to free ride and hold out, particularly when their homes or businesses help complete a larger property, as in the property needed to construct a road. But usually a road can take competing paths, a power plant can be built in different locations, and so forth, so that buyers, government or private, can use the leverage from competition among sites to reduce the advantage of holding out. And sometimes they can build around stubborn holdouts, as happened when the property to build the privately accumulated Rockefeller Center was put together.

I am not claiming that a system without eminent domain would work perfectly—it would not. But modern governments have more than enough power through the power to tax and regulate. Although eminent domain can be considered just another (but highly intrusive) form of regulation, condemnation is too powerful and easy a regulatory form. "Power corrupts" is an old saying, which explains why condemnation has indeed been frequently abused (see Martin Anderson's classic study, *The Federal Bulldozer* [1964]). It allows governments to avoid the market test of whether a proposed project adds value in the sense that a project is worthwhile even after owners of property are bought out through regular market proceedings.

Eliminating the eminent domain clause from the Constitution is obviously not feasible in any foreseeable time frame. But it is still useful to discuss the benefits and costs of this clause, or to question whether it is desirable. A negative answer might help provide guidance to judges, legislatures, and voters in determining how far they want to push the privileged position of property accumulation for an alleged public benefit.

THE KELO CASE, PUBLIC USE, AND EMINENT DOMAIN—POSNER

The Fifth Amendment permits the use of eminent domain, in which government takes private property without negotiation but must pay the owner the market value of the property, only if the taking is for a "public use." (The Fifth Amendment is applicable only to action by the federal government, but the Fourteenth Amendment, which applies to state and local government action, has been interpreted to incorporate the "public use" limitation on eminent domain.) In *Kelo* the city took private residential property as part of a redevelopment plan under which the property would be turned over to private developers for office space and parking.

Whether the case was "correctly" decided depends on one's theory of constitutional adjudication, which might in turn point one to the origins of the "public use" provision and to the Supreme Court's precedents. I want to abstract from the legal questions and ask three practical questions: When if ever is eminent domain proper? Is it ever proper when the private property taken is going to be transferred to another private entity rather than being kept by the government for some governmental use, such as a post office or an army base? And is the power granted local municipalities by the Kelo decision likely to be abused?

Generally, government should be required to buy the property it wants in the open market, like anyone else. If it is allowed to confiscate property without paying the full price, it will be led to substitute property for other inputs that may cost less to society to produce but that are more costly to the government (a private rather than social cost) than land because the government has to pay the full price for them. This assumes that government in its procurement decisions tries to minimize dollar costs rather than full social costs, but the assumption is realistic.

When the government does take property by eminent domain, it has to pay the owner the market value of the property, but that value will be less than the owner values the property—otherwise he would sell it to the government at market value and there would be no need for the government to incur the cost of eminent domain proceedings. Generally, property is worth more to the owner than the market price (which is why it's owned by him rather than by someone else), because it fits his tastes or needs best as a consequence of its location or improvements (which is why he bought it rather than some other piece of property) or because relocation costs would be high. Real estate is a heterogeneous good and so a particular parcel in the hands of a particular owner will generally yield him an idiosyncratic value that is on top of the market value. Eminent domain operates to tax away that value; if market value is $X and total value (including idiosyncratic) is $1.2X, then if the government takes it by eminent domain it pays for it in effect by spending $X out of the government's own coffers and $.2X out of the owner's pocket. This is an arbitrary form of taxation and one that, as I said, creates the illusion that an input is cheap because its money price is less than its social cost, and as a result causes a misallocation of resources.

The only justification for eminent domain is that sometimes a landowner may be in a position to exercise holdout power, enabling him to obtain a monopoly rent in the absence of an eminent domain right. The clearest example is that of a right of way company, such as a railroad or a pipeline, which to provide service between two points needs an easement from every single one of the intervening landowners. Knowing this, each landowner has an incentive to hang back, refusing to sell to the right of way company except for an exorbitant price. Each hopes to be the last holdout after the company has purchased an easement from every other landowner—easements that will be worthless if it doesn't obtain an easement from that last holdout.

Most right of way companies are private, which answers my second question: the rationale for eminent domain is unrelated to whether the party exercising the eminent domain power is the government or a private firm.

Right of way companies are not the only private enterprises that can make an argument for the use of the eminent domain power. The argument is available in other cases in which a large number of separately owned contiguous parcels have to be acquired for a project that will create greater value than the parcels generate in their present use. It is impossible to tell from the opinions in the *Kelo* case whether that was the situation. Pfizer had decided to build a large research facility adjacent to a ninety-acre stretch of downtown and waterfront property in New London, and the city hoped that Pfizer's presence would attract other businesses to the neighborhood. The plaintiffs' residential properties were on portions of the ninety-acre tract earmarked for office space and parking, and it might have been impossible to develop these areas for those uses if the areas were spotted with houses (the plaintiffs owned fifteen houses in all in the two areas).

The Court, however, did not discuss whether there was a holdout problem; it thought it enough to justify the taking that the city had a bona fide and reasonable belief that the planned redevelopment would generate net benefits for the city and its residents as a whole, although the plaintiffs of course would lose any idiosyncratic values that they obtained from their property. However, in the absence of a holdout problem, there is no need for eminent domain—private developers will rush in without need for city assistance if indeed the property would be worth more in a different use from the present ones. The Court was mindful of the possibility of abuse of the eminent domain power; it made clear that there would not be a public use if all a municipality did was take property from one person and give it to another, with no showing of an increase in overall value. But the Court did not consider whether development plans such as New London's actually on average increase value for the municipality that undertakes them, or rather are usually the product of rent-seeking political deals. Thus the actual impact of the Court's decision on economic welfare cannot readily be determined.

It is possible that what really motivated the Court was a simple unwillingness to become involved (or to involve the lower courts) in the details of urban redevelopment plans; a flat rule against takings in which the land ends up in the hands of private companies would, as I have explained, be unsound. Another practical defense of the decision is that the more limitations are placed on the private development of condemned land, the more active the government itself will become in development, and that would be inefficient. If the city of New London had built office space, parking, etc., on land condemned from private owners, a challenge based on the "public use" limitation would be unlikely to succeed—unless the Court confined public use to holdout situations and was prepared to try to determine, case by case, whether a genuine holdout situation existed.

8

PHARMACEUTICAL PATENTS

December 12, 2004

PHARMACEUTICAL PATENTS—BECKER

The pharmaceutical industry is under attack once again for its high prices, because of a belief that it pays insufficient attention to safety, and allegedly that sometimes the industry hides damaging information about its drugs. The industry is no paragon of virtue, but during the past fifty years it has become a major contributor to the dramatic declines in mortality and increases in the quality of life. Reforms that undervalue these contributions are likely to do far more harm than good.

Some of the industry's important products include aspirins, antibiotics, blood-pressure-lowering medications, cholesterol-lowering drugs, AIDS cocktails, drugs that slow the progress of breast and prostate cancer and Parkinson's disease, effective sleeping pills, and antidepressants that enable many mentally troubled persons to live reasonably normal lives. Although the cost of producing these and other drugs is typically quite low, enormous amounts are usually spent trying to discover and develop them.

In 2003, American drug companies spent over $30 billion on research and development, which includes the very expensive clinical trials required by the FDA and government regulatory bodies in other countries. This is not very far behind the federal government's spending on basic and other medical research. The average number of new molecular entities approved during the past five years averaged about fifty. So American drug companies are spending some $600 million (=$30 billion/50) per new molecular entity. This heavy R&D burden explains why stock prices of drug companies have not performed especially well during the past five to ten years, despite very high prices for a few blockbuster drugs. Biotech companies as a whole probably even lost money over this period.

The low cost of producing drugs once discovered creates the impression that drug companies are gouging seriously ill cancer, AIDS, and other patients. But these companies cannot recoup their huge R&D spending without charging for a number of years much more than the cost of producing their drugs. The patent system provides protection against generic competition for about twenty years from the date of first filling for a patent. However, competition from chemically similar entities usually appears years before patents expire, and the extensive testing required by the FDA considerably shortens effective patent lengths. Still, without patents or similar protection, other companies can reverse engineer most drugs to discover how they are made, and then sell them at much lower prices since they do not have the burden of heavy R&D costs.

To be sure, a patent system creates a tension between the effect that prices well above costs of production have in reducing the use of drugs by sick persons, and the effect of high prices in helping companies recoup their large R&D spending. This tension is the cause of the increasing attacks on drug companies as more blockbuster drugs have been introduced during the past couple of decades. So an important public policy question is whcther we can do better than the present patent system? I believe we can improve how the system operates in many ways, but some suggestions are likely to make matters worse rather than better.

One tempting idea is to have the government buy out patent rights and place them in the public domain available to all producers. Competition would then insure they would be sold to consumers at the cost of production. Recently, the Harvard economist Michael Kremer revived this old idea in sophisticated form. Kremer suggests that the government use auctions to decide how much patents on new drugs are worth. The value of a winning price would be paid not to the winner, but to the discoverer and patent holder—who can refuse the government's offer and hold on to the patent. The winner of an auction only provides a measure of the drugs' worth, and would not receive exclusive rights, even if the discoverer accepts the government's offer, except in "a small proportion of patents." But if this proportion is really small, the incentive to provide serious bids is greatly weakened. I also believe such a system might create a bureaucratic nightmare, but his proposal is worth more attention.

State governments and other groups are exerting great pressure to allow imports from Canada and online pharmacies, where drugs are much cheaper. But Canadian drug prices are cheap in good part because they impose price controls. In essence, Canada (and most other countries) free ride on the profits collected from the higher prices in the American market. The United States could also impose price controls if it wanted to do so, but these would be counterproductive because they would discourage discovery of new drugs. Moreover, if many drugs begin to be reshipped from Canada, drug companies would cut the amounts supplied to Canada, and prices there would rise. That is why Canada is beginning to crack down on online pharmacies that resell to the American market.

Perhaps patent lives should be shorter, but they were lengthened in the 1990s because clinical trial procedures take so long due to the requirement of three clinical stages: the first to determine safety, the second to determine efficacy, and the third to check safety and efficacy through randomized trials.

It has been estimated that perhaps 40 percent of all R&D costs are spent on these trials. I have proposed elsewhere that the FDA trust patients more, and allow them more freedom to use new drugs by granting approval without the efficacy and randomized stages—this was the situation prior to 1962. At the same time, the FDA can tighten up safety standards, especially by putting resources into following more closely possible side effects over long time periods. Were my suggestion implemented, R&D costs would go down considerably, patent length could be considerably reduced, and yet companies would have more incentive to invest in finding new drugs.

I do not like the hype and some other salesmanship of big pharma and biotech companies, but this industry has made enormous contributions to raising world health. It is likely to become even more important in the future as drugs are developed to match individual genetic differences. One does not want to kill this goose that is laying golden eggs by ill-thought-out and counterproductive "reforms."

PHARMACEUTICAL PATENTS—POSNER

I agree that no adequate, feasible alternative to patents exists for encouraging R&D by manufacturers of pharmaceutical drugs. But my agreement should not be understood as indicating approval of the present U.S. patent system.

Patents are a source of great social costs, and only occasionally of commensurate benefits. The social cost of patents that was traditionally emphasized by economists is the wedge that a patent drives between price and marginal cost. Generally, we expect that competition will compress price to marginal cost and that this is efficient because it means that no one willing to pay the marginal cost of a good is deflected to a substitute that might cost more to produce, yet look cheaper simply because the price of the good was above marginal cost. By preventing duplication, a patent reduces competition and so may enable the producer to charge such a price. But the objection to patents that is based on the wedge is superficial because the producer may have incurred costs that do not affect his marginal cost. Suppose the cost of R&D that the producer must incur to bring a drug to market is $100 million, but the marginal cost (the cost added to total costs by each unit of output) is a constant $1 a pill. Then no matter how many pills the producer sells at $1, he will never recover his upfront investment.

The real concern about patents is the costs imposed on inventors themselves. There is the cost of searching the records of the patent office to make sure you're not going to be infringing a patent, but more important is the transaction cost involved in obtaining a license from an existing patentee. Invention is a cumulative process; a new invention is usually an incremental improvement on an existing one.

So the more patents that are "out there," the greater are the costs involved in negotiating for a license from every patentee whom the new inventor may arguably be infringing. Because a patent can be obtained without even a prototype, because patent examiners are overworked and it takes less work to approve than to reject a patent application, and because the U.S. Court of Appeals for the Federal Circuit, which reviews patent validity, is extraordinarily pro-patent, the number of issued patents has grown steadily in recent decades. There is concern that some fields are so blanketed with patents (which may be owned by firms that do no production at all—whose business plan centers on demanding license fees under threat to sue for patent infringement) that innovation is actually being impeded. Most firms don't actually want patents; for those firms, the costs involved in obtaining licenses from patentees are not offset by the prospect of obtaining license fees on their own patents. There are many alternatives to patents for protecting one's investment in R&D, and they are often cheaper and more effective. They include trade secrecy; the advertising value of, and the consumer loyalty generated by, being the first to produce a popular product; the fact that marginal cost may increase steeply with output, so that a price equal to marginal cost may cover the fixed costs of invention after all; the fact that it may be costly and time consuming for competitors to duplicate the invention exactly; and, related to the last point, the learning curve—if costs of production fall over time as the producer learns more about how to make the product at least cost, the first firm in the market will tend to have a cost advantage over competitors, who arrive later. But if other companies are busy getting patents, you may have to patent defensively, and the patent thicket thickens.

The pharmaceutical drug industry is the industry that can make the strongest case for needing patent protection. The investment required to bring a new drug to market is very great, in part because of the many "dry holes." And it may take years before the new drug can be sold, which shrinks the effective term of the patent (if it takes eight years to bring the drug to market, the effective term of a twenty-year patent is only twelve years). This not only reduces the revenue from the patent; but because the costs of the upfront investment are incurred years before revenues commence, those revenues must, because of the time value of money, exceed the upfront costs in order to be fully compensatory. In addition, once the drug is in production, it is easily duplicated by competitors, and the marginal cost is very low at all feasible output levels, so that with free entry the original producer would not be able to recoup his R&D investment.

That said, I am skeptical about the length of the patent term for pharmaceuticals. Congress has tacked on to the normal twenty-year patent term (which until 1995 was only seventeen years) an additional term of up to five years for the time it takes a pharmaceutical manufacturer to get a new drug approved by the Food and Drug Administration. In addition, the expiration of a pharmaceutical patent does not extinguish the patentee's ability to obtain a higher price than the generic substitutes that come on line when his patent expires, because there may be substantial consumer and physician goodwill attached to the trademark of the patented drug—consumers, even physicians, may distrust generics and prefer the original brand even at a higher price. Indeed, there is evidence that when a patent expires the ex-patentee will actually increase price, ceding the low-price end of the market to the generics. His overall profits will be lower but may still be substantial.

Against this it may be argued that the fact that the drug companies apparently do not have excess profits shows they need every bit of patent protection they have. Not necessarily. Competition for a profit opportunity may transform expected profits into costs. Suppose the drug companies believe that the invention of some new drug will yield the successful inventor a $1 billion net profit. The prospect will induce heavy expenditures on being first (the aggregate expenditures may actually exceed $1 billion). The result is that none of the companies, or the industry as a whole, may have abnormal profits. Now suppose that as a result of a shortening of the patent term, the prospect for the successful inventor is for making only an $800 million profit. Less will be spent on the patent race. Yet consumers as a whole may be better off, because the investment saved may have greater value elsewhere in the economy. The entire patent "prize" goes to the firm that crosses the finish line first, and so a firm might spend a huge amount of money to beat its nearest rival by one day even though the value to the public of having the invention one day earlier might be negligible. This danger is greater the bigger the prize. Shortening the patent term would reduce this potential waste by reducing the revenue from a patent; it would also reduce the transaction costs of licensing, because more inventions would be in the public domain.

9

GROKSTER, FILE SHARING, AND CONTRIBUTORY INFRINGEMENT

July 3, 2005

THE GROKSTER CASE—POSNER

On the last day of its term, the Supreme Court decided *MGM Studios, Inc. v. Grokster,* 545 U.S. 913 (2005), holding that the court of appeals had erred in affirming summary judgment for Grokster, a company that distributes free of charge software that enables computer owners to form "peer-to-peer" networks whereby a copy of a file in one computer can be transmitted to another computer. (There was another defendant as well, but I'll ignore that detail.) As explained in the Court's majority opinion,

> On the FastTrack network opened by the Grokster software, the user's request goes to a computer given an indexing capacity by the software and designated a supernode, or to

some other computer with comparable power and capacity to collect temporary indexes of the files available on the computers of users connected to it. The supernode (or indexing computer) searches its own index and may communicate the search request to other supernodes. If the file is found, the supernode discloses its location to the computer requesting it, and the requesting user can download the file directly from the computer located. The copied file is placed in a designated sharing folder on the requesting user's computer, where it is available for other users to download in turn, along with any other file in that folder.

Grokster was sued by owners of music and film copyrights, who complained that Grokster was facilitating the infringement of their copyrights. Instead of buying a CD or DVD, the owner of Grokster software could search the network composed of other owners of the software for a computer file containing the copyrighted music or film and if he found it, copy the file. This would be infringement, and the Supreme Court ruled that there was enough evidence of "contributory infringement" by Grokster to warrant a trial. The Court was unanimous, but there are several opinions, and they are long and labored. The basic principles are simple, however, and a single, much shorter opinion would have sufficed.

A contributory infringer is someone who facilitates infringement. By making the contributory infringer liable, the law reduces the cost of enforcing copyright, since it would be very costly for copyright owners to sue every person who is engaged in file sharing.

The general approach is not limited to copyright law. For example, someone who sells burglary tools to a burglar is guilty of aiding and abetting if the burglar uses the tools to commit a burglary. And someone who induces a breach of contract is liable to the victim of the breach, even though the victim could just have sued the other party to the contract for breach of contract.

But difficulties arise when a product has both lawful and unlawful uses. It would be ridiculous to hold sellers of butcher knives liable civilly or criminally if a purchaser used the knife to commit a murder, unless the seller knew that that was the intended use. And even when the seller knows that the use will be illegal, he may not be liable. A standard example is the dress shop that sells a dress to a woman whom the shop knows to be a prostitute planning to wear the dress in soliciting customers. The idea is that at least in the case of minor crimes, we don't want to put sellers at risk of civil or criminal liability for aiding and abetting because it would make them too careful about inquiring into the uses of their wares; the added transaction costs would exceed the benefits in reduced social costs of crime.

In the case of Grokster and other companies that offer file-sharing services (or, in Grokster's case, just software, for unlike earlier file-sharing facilitators, such as Napster, Grokster does not copy files onto its own servers or use its servers to facilitate file sharing—it merely provides the software that enables computer owners to establish a network among themselves for sharing), there are potential lawful uses. This possibility was enough to convince the lower courts that Grokster was not a contributory infringer. Not all musical recordings or films are copyrighted (the copyrights might have expired); and in addition some producers of copyrighted works, especially if the producers are new and trying to establish a reputation (a new rock and roll band, for example), may want their works distributed as rapidly and as far as possible even at the sacrifice of royalties. In effect, these producers are willing to grant royalty-free licenses to the users of Grokster software.

Nevertheless, the Court cited evidence indicating that most of the file sharing enabled by Grokster's software is, as Grokster well knew, infringing, just as most sales of burglar tools are to burglars, though some are to people who want to be able to break into their own house if they lock themselves out and others are to the police, or to the curious, or to would-be burglars who get cold feet before they commit their first burglary with the new tools. Contributory infringement would be an empty box if any lawful uses, however trivial in relation to the unlawful, enabled the contributory infringer to get off the hook on all uses of his product even though he knew that the vast majority were infringing.

But that is not the end of the analysis. Some infringements, paradoxically, may actually benefit a copyright holder, yet he may refuse to grant a royalty-free license because he thinks he can extract a royalty and thus have his cake and eat it too. People will pay more for a CD if they think they can share it with others over a peer-to-peer network, because then the CD becomes a form of currency for arranging advantageous swaps and even "buying" new friends. Then too, if you travel a lot and bring your computer with you, with file sharing you don't have to drag your favorite CDs along; file sharing in such a situation merely gives you better access to a product that you paid for—and you will pay more, if you have that better access, just as you would pay more for a cell phone that you could use in any country in the world. In addition, through file sharing you might develop a taste for a particular band or composer whose recordings you wouldn't have bought without the free exposure to them; this is file sharing as advertising of copyrighted recordings for the copyright owner.

But again, the mere possibility that infringement may confer benefits on copyright owners can't suffice to defeat a suit for contributory infringement any more than it could defeat a suit for direct infringement, as it is always possible to conjure up such possibilities.

If the Grokster case is tried, the trial will provide an opportunity to compare the revenue loss to the copyright owners against the possible gains that I have listed. Unfortunately, subjecting providers of file-sharing software to the threat of trial places them at substantial risk, which may drive many of them from the market.

The final argument against imposing liability on Grokster and similar enterprises without bothering with a trial is a kind of "infant industry" argument. The software industry is dynamic, and there is concern that imposing liability on software producers may retard innovation, since even if the only or major current use of some type of software is to facilitate copyright infringement, the software may turn out to have important lawful uses if only it isn't strangled in the cradle. This is hard to credit in the case of file-sharing services and software, however, since there is an immense lawful demand. File sharing of noncopyrighted materials is fundamental to the Internet, and for that matter to the intelligence system—the Intelligence Reform Act passed last fall ordains the creation of an "Information Sharing Environment" to facilitate the sharing of data across the many databases used by federal intelligence agencies. Also, any diminished innovation due to contributory-infringement liability must be traded off against the enhanced innovation that can be expected if intellectual-property rights are strongly protected by the law.

Grokster relied heavily on a case that the Supreme Court had decided many years ago involving Betamax, a predecessor to the VCR. At the time, the principal use of Betamax was to record television programs for later viewing. Insofar as the recording merely shifted the program to a more convenient viewing time, it clearly benefited the owners of the copyrights on the programs; but insofar as it enabled the viewer to erase the commercials, it hurt the copyright owners, whose remuneration depended on advertising revenues. The Supreme Court held that, given this dual-use situation, Sony, the manufacturer of the Betamax, was not a contributory infringer. The decision turned out to be fortunate for the film industry, because within a few years the sale and rental of home video recordings became a major channel of film distribution, which the studios had not anticipated. And so it is argued that file sharing of copyrighted music and film may also turn out to have unexpected benefits for the copyright owners themselves (beyond the modest benefits suggested earlier). But the logic of this argument is that there can never be liability for contributory infringement because the possibility can never be excluded that the product or service offered by the alleged contributory infringer, even if it is used exclusively by infringers, will turn out in the future to have substantial noninfringing uses.

There is a possible middle way that should be considered, and that is to provide a safe harbor to potential contributory infringers who take all reasonable (cost-justified) measures to prevent the use of their product or service by infringers. The measures might be joint with the copyright owners. For example, copyright owners who wanted to be able to sue for contributory infringement might be required, as a condition of being permitted to sue, to place a nonremovable electronic tag on their CDs that a computer would read, identifying the CD or a file downloaded from it as containing copyrighted material. Software producers would be excused from liability for contributory infringement if they designed their software to prevent the copying of a tagged file. This seems a preferable approach to using the judicial system to make a case by case assessment of whether to impose liability for contributory infringement on Grokster-like enterprises.

GROKSTER AND THE SCOPE OF JUDICIAL POWER—BECKER

Grokster is a company that distributes software free of charge that enables copies of files on one computer to be transferred to another computer. Grokster was sued by MGM and other owners of copyrighted music and films with the claim that Grokster was facilitating the infringement of their copyrights. The Supreme Court decided unanimously that the evidence of contributory infringement by Grokster was sufficient to warrant a trial.

I do believe the case deserves a trial, and primarily for this reason I signed (without any compensation) an amici curiae brief submitted by several economists to the Supreme Court against Grokster. The arguments about infringement are set out in that brief and in Posner's discussion. This software has few other uses so far other than to copy files from one computer to another, which often is a violation of copyright protection on the files copied. Although Grokster is not per se violating any copyright by producing this software, its software unquestionably facilitates these violations. It is also much more efficient to litigate against the contributory infringement of Grokster than to litigate against every college student and other individuals who are actually engaged in transferring files illegally.

The courts have held in the past that it is not contributory infringement if a company produces a product with sufficient sales for legitimate uses, even though it is sometimes used to violate either copyright or other laws. For example, it is legal to produce box-cutters, even though they have been used to commit terrorist acts. Posner gives other examples along similar lines.

But several things concern me about the issues raised by this and related court decisions. I basically do not trust the ability of judges, even those with the best of intentions and competence, to decide the economic future of an industry. Do we really want the courts determining when the fraction of the total value due to legal sales is high enough to exonerate manufacturers from contributory infringement? Neither the wisest courts nor wisest economists have enough knowledge to make that decision in a way that is likely to produce more benefits than harm. Does the fraction of legitimate value have to be higher than 50 percent, 75 percent, 10 percent, or some other number? Courts should consider past trends in these percentages because new uses for say a software—legal or illegal—inevitably emerge over time as users become more familiar with its potential. Must courts have to speculate about future uses of software or other products, speculation likely to be dominated by dreams and hopes rather than firm knowledge?

Posner suggests requiring software producers to prevent the copying of CDs or other files with nonremovable electronic tags placed on them by copyright owners. Unfortunately, this suggestion merely shifts the problem one stage backward by providing incentives to other innovators to produce software that removes such tags!

My other concern is more strictly economic. The burglar using tools to pry open doors, safes, or windows, the good example Posner uses, is almost invariably producing harm through his activities. It is much less clear that the harm exceeds the benefits when someone buy files and then shares them with friends, and in many similar violations of intellectual property. A person might pay more for files that he expects to share with friends partly because to gain their goodwill, or partly because he can then share their files. Individuals may jointly pay for files if there is software that can be used to share them. In addition, free use of some files due to copying may encourage purchase of additional ones because the music or film copied whets the appetite for certain types of music, films, or other copyrighted material.

These points are not simply intellectual exercises, for at least some of the serious studies of the effects of copying and other apparent violations of intellectual property on sales do not show any strong negative effects, and sometimes even claim to find positive effects. Posner gives the example of Betamax, a losing competitor to the VCR. The movie industry opposed Betamax because they thought it would help destroy the sale of movies, but it failed to appreciate the eventual importance of videos to their overall market. There may also be conflicts among companies with copyrights, so that the majority might gain from a freer market and prefer to do nothing, while a few companies sue because the copying of their materials hurts them.

Experience and theory tells us that it is best to let markets rather than courts determine the evolution of industries—just remember the mess made of the telephone industry by Judge Greene. I increasingly believe that this principle applies also to alleged violations of intellectual property through contributory infringement. This form of legal remedy should be used but rarely.

10

ORPHAN DRUGS, INTELLECTUAL PROPERTY, AND SOCIAL WELFARE

November 20, 2005

ORPHAN DRUGS—POSNER

A pair of excellent articles by Geeta Anand on the front page of the *Wall Street Journal* for November 15 and 16, 2005, discusses the little-known but very costly Orphan Drug Act of 1983. The act is designed, mainly by providing expanded intellectual-property protection (there are also tax incentives and research subsidies, but they are considered less important), to encourage the creation of drugs for the treatment of rare diseases, defined as diseases that afflict no more than two hundred thousand Americans at any given time. Partly because different cancers are classified as different diseases, an estimated 25 million Americans have a rare disease as defined by the act.

A company that is first to obtain the Food and Drug Administration's approval to sell such a drug has the exclusive right to sell it for seven years. Although this is shorter than the term of a pharmaceutical patent (normally twenty years), establishing patent eligibility is a far more difficult and protracted undertaking and a patent once obtained is subject to court challenges that often succeed in invalidating it.

The expansion in intellectual-property rights brought about by the Orphan Drug Act makes the following economic sense: The incentive to create an intellectual work is a function of the size of the potential market for it. The reason is that, by definition, the principal costs of such a work are fixed costs, incurred before the first sale is made; in the case of orphan drugs, they are the cost of R&D plus (what is often greater) the cost of clinical testing, and they greatly exceed the costs of actually producing the drug. The larger the market, the lower the fixed costs per sale, and so the less the seller has to charge in order to recover those costs. If fixed costs are 100 and variable cost (the cost of producing one unit of the product) is 1, then if there are 10 customers the producer must charge each at least 11 (100 divided by 10, plus 1) to break even, but if there are 100 customers he can break even at a price of 2 (100 divided by 100 plus 1). Hence the rarer a disease, and thus the smaller the potential market for a drug to treat it, the higher the price that the producer must charge in order to break even. His ability to charge that high price will depend on his ability to exclude competition; a producer allowed to duplicate the new drug could undercut the price charged by the original producer yet make a large profit because he would not have borne any R&D costs. The higher the break-even price and therefore the greater the profit opportunity for a competitor, the likelier that competition will quickly erode the price and prevent the original producer from recovering his fixed costs. Giving the original producer more than the usual protection against competition that the law provides to creators of intellectual property is thus a method of increasing the incentive to create drugs that have only a small potential market because relatively few people suffer from the diseases that the drugs treat.

This is not just a theoretical point. The fixed costs of a new drug are indeed high, even if the industry-sponsored figure of $800 million is, as I believe, an exaggeration. This means, moreover, that even without the threat of competition, the incentive to develop a new drug that would have very few buyers would often be insufficient to induce that development. Suppose a drug cost $500 million to develop and had only 50 potential customers. Then each would have to pay (over his lifetime) $10 million (actually more, because of discounting to present value) to enable the producer to cover its fixed costs. Health insurers might be unwilling to pick up such a tab.

The success of the Orphan Drug Act in encouraging the creation of orphan drugs (more than two hundred such drugs have been approved since the act was passed, compared to only ten in the preceding decade), which in 2003 had total worldwide sales estimated at roughly $28 billion, confirms the economic analysis and shows that intellectual-property protection can have important incentive effects. But has the act produced a net gain in economic welfare? That is less certain. Of course many people have benefited from the drugs. But the costs per benefited person are frequently astronomical; that is implicit in the rationale for giving producers of such drugs increased protection against competition. The costs are especially high for those orphan drugs, apparently the majority, that alleviate symptoms or prolong life but do not cure the disease, so that the patient has to take them for the rest of his or her life. The *Wall Street Journal* articles give an example of a woman who suffers from Gaucher's disease and spends (or rather her health insurer spends) $601,000 a year for the drug, Ceredase, and its administration. Because by definition the percentage of people who suffer from rare diseases is small, it is feasible for health insurance to cover such extraordinary expenses, provided the insurance pool is large. And Ceredase is at the high end of orphan drug expense.

Resources for medical research are finite. The Orphan Drug Act sucks large research expenditures into creating treatments for rare diseases. Without the act, those resources would be channeled by the market into other investments that might produce a higher social return. The English economist Arnold Plant pointed out many years ago that if the law protects some monopolies, as by granting patents or equivalent intellectual-property protection, the profit opportunities that such protection creates (Ceredase generates an estimated 25 percent annual rate of return on investment for its producer, Genzyme Corp.), which are not generally available in the economy, may attract into the monopoly markets resources that would produce greater consumer welfare if invested in production in competitive markets. As a result of competition, the price of television sets is much less than the price that people would be willing to pay if the sale of television sets were monopolized; the difference is "consumer surplus" and is a measure of the net value that the industry creates. For all one knows, the consumer surplus that would be generated if the resources now devoted to developing orphan drugs were channeled into competitive markets would exceed the net benefits of those drugs, bearing in mind that there are few beneficiaries. The number of people who take orphan drugs is far fewer than the total number of people with rare diseases. Indeed, apparently only two hundred thousand Americans are taking such drugs. Assuming that most global expenditures on orphan drugs are for Americans (I'm just guessing—I do not have U.S. figures), this would be an average expenditure of $100,000 ($100,000 times 200,000 equals $20 billion). Few people would be willing, if only because few people would be able, to spend anywhere near this much on drugs.

As the economist Tomas Philipson points out, however, if people who do not suffer from rare diseases derive a benefit from orphan drugs—whether because they are altruistic or because they fear that they or members of their families might develop such a disease—then the total social surplus created by the Orphan Drug Act may exceed the consumer surplus. Yet if the R&D expenditures induced by the act were channeled instead into developing drugs for equally serious but much more common diseases, this might well be preferred by most people.

COMMENT ON ORPHAN DRUGS AND INTELLECTUAL PROPERTY—BECKER

I agree with most of Posner's discussion that as usual is presented very clearly. But I appear to differ on one issue that I believe is important.

The Orphan Drug Act of 1983 greatly expanded research on rare disease that has resulted in the discovery of many more drugs that successfully treat such diseases. Yet R&D spending on these drugs still takes only a small share of total spending on R&D by biotech and pharmaceutical companies. This is why I doubt, but cannot prove without much additional research, whether the R&D spending on orphan drugs stimulated by this act significantly affected spending on finding treatments for more common diseases. It probably mainly increased total spending on medical R&D by a modest amount.

If this conclusion is correct, is it a mistake to have the Orphan Drug Act give greater intellectual-property protection for drugs that treat rare diseases because these diseases would attract little research effort without better protection? I follow Posner initially and ignore the tax benefits and research subsidies provided by the act. Suppose that only because of the better patent protection provided for seven years, a biotech company develops a drug that treats a rare disease with a small market, and charges a high price—as in some examples given in the *Wall Street Journal* articles. Assume to start the analysis that persons with the disease treated by this drug pay for treatments from their own resources, and enough of them can pay so that the biotech company can cover, perhaps more than cover, their development and production costs.

Surely not only the biotech company, but also persons with the disease are better off that the drug was developed due to the act, even though they have to pay a lot. If they were not better off, they would not be willing to pay the high price demanded. Since it is a win-win situation, in such cases it is obviously helpful to persons with rare diseases to have an act that stimulates the development of drugs that treat their diseases.

The analysis is not greatly different if private health insurance providers voluntarily cover rare diseases, as discovered with great effort by the woman with Gaucher's disease chronicled by the *Wall Street Journal*. As Posner indicates, insurance companies might be willing to cover rare diseases since such coverage does not raise premiums very much for other persons who are insured. This would be a strictly business decision by the insurance industry if made without political pressure. So voluntary private insurance coverage of persons with rare diseases does not materially change my favorable evaluation of the Orphan Drug Act.

The hard cases arise when the high prices charged for drugs that treat rare diseases are paid not by persons with the diseases, but by the government through Medicaid, Medicare, or other publicly funded health programs. Then taxpayers rather than persons with these diseases or private insurance companies may foot most of the cost of developing drugs that treat rare diseases. Should taxpayers be asked to pay $100,000 per year (Posner's estimate of the average cost of the drugs developed for rare diseases) for drugs that can keep persons with rare diseases alive for many years? The answer is not obviously yes, although, as Tomas Philipson has argued, government coverage might be justified if taxpayers are concerned about the welfare of persons who are unfortunate to have these diseases, or as a way to provide insurance protection against the risk of being born with rare genetic defects.

Medicare pays enormous sums to hospitals, nursing homes, and drug companies to keep elderly persons alive sometimes for only a few additional months. Yet the justification for doing this seems weaker than using government funds to pay for expensive drugs that enable young persons with rare diseases to live fairly normal lives for many years rather than dying at young ages. Perhaps Medicare should not pay a lot to keep elderly persons alive for a short period, but I do not believe the case for government payment of the cost of treating persons with rare diseases can be analyzed in isolation from a more general consideration of what type of health care should be provided out of government funds.

The act also would look less favorable if, as is likely, biotech and other drug companies sometimes reclassify the markets for new drugs to help them qualify for the act's benefits. I also have doubts about the wisdom of the provision that allows drug companies to immediately write off their R&D spending on orphan drugs.

So an overall evaluation of the Orphan Drug Act is not easy. Still, it might well be desirable to give stronger patent protection to drugs with small markets that treat rare diseases in order to induce the development of such drugs.

11

ORGAN SALES

January 1, 2006

SHOULD THE PURCHASE AND SALE OF ORGANS FOR TRANSPLANT SURGERY BE PERMITTED?—BECKER

There were about fifty thousand persons on the waiting list for kidney transplants in the United States in the year 2000, but only about fifteen thousand kidney transplant operations were performed. This implies an average wait of almost four years before a person on the waiting list could receive a kidney transplant. The cumulative gap between demand and supply for livers was over ten thousand, which implies an average wait for a liver transplant of a couple of years.

In 2000, almost three thousand persons died while waiting for a kidney transplant, and half that number died while waiting for a liver transplant. Many also died in other countries while on the queue waiting for an organ transplant. Some of these people would have died anyway from other causes, but there is little doubt that most died too early because they were unable to replace their defective organs quickly enough.

If altruism were sufficiently powerful, the supply of organs would be large enough to satisfy demand, and there would be no need to change the present system. But this is not the case in any country that does a significant number of transplants. While the per capita number of organs donated has grown over time, demand has grown even faster. As a result, the length of the queue for organ transplants has grown significantly over time in most countries, despite exhortations and other attempts to encourage greater giving of organs.

In recent years the United States has taken several steps to improve the allocation of available organs among those needing them, such as giving greater priority to those who could benefit the most. These steps have helped, but they have not stopped the queues from growing, nor prevented large numbers of persons from dying while waiting for transplants. Some countries use an "opt out" system for organs, which means that cadaveric organs can be used for transplants unless persons who died had indicated that they did not want their organs to be so used. Alberto Abadie and Sebastian Gay, "The Impact of Presumed Consent Legislation on Cadaveric Organ Donation: A Cross Country Study," 25 *Journal of Health Economics* 599 (2006), finds that opt out systems may yield somewhat more organs for transplants than the "opt in" systems used by the United States and many other nations, but they do not eliminate the long queues for transplants.

To an economist, the major reason for the imbalance between demand and supply of organs is that the United States and practically all other countries forbid the purchase and sale of organs. This means that under present laws, people give their organs to be used after they die, or with kidneys and livers also while they are alive, only out of altruism and similar motives. In fact, practically all transplants of kidneys and livers with live donors are from one family member to another member. With live liver transplants, only a portion of the liver of a donor is use, and this grows over time in the donee, while the remaining portion regenerates over time in the donor.

If laws were changed so that organs could be purchased and sold, some people would give not out of altruism, but for the financial gain. The result would be an increased supply of organs. In a free market, the prices of organs for transplants would settle at the levels that would eliminate the excess demand for each type of organ. In a paper on the potential of markets for live organ donations, Julio Elias of the University of Buffalo and I estimate that the going price for live transplants would be about $15,000 for kidneys and about $35,000 for livers. Gary S. Becker and Julio Jorge Elias, "Introducing Incentives in the Market for Live and Cadaveric Organ Donations," *Journal of Economic Perspectives,* Summer 2007, p. 3. We recognize, however, that the data are too limited to be confident that these numbers would be close to equilibrium prices that equate supply and demand—they may be too high or too low. But even if our estimates were only half the actual equilibrium prices, the effect on the total cost of transplants would not be huge since current costs for live transplants in the United States are in the range of $100,000 for kidney transplants and $175,000 for liver transplants.

An open market in organs would sharply curtail the present black market where some persons in need of transplants have them in poorer countries like Turkey where enforcement against selling organs is slack. Since the quality of the surgeons and hospitals in these countries is much lower than in advanced countries, this often greatly reduces the quality of the organs used and how well they are matched to the organ types of recipients.

Still, despite these strong arguments in favor of allowing commercial markets in organs, I do not expect such markets to be permitted any time in the near future because the opposition is fierce. Some critics simply dismiss organ markets as immoral "commodification" of body parts. More thoughtful critics suggest that allowing organs to be bought and sold might actually reduce the total number of organs available for transplants because they claim it would sufficiently lower the number of organs donated from altruistic motives to dominate the increase due to those sold commercially. That scenario, however, is extremely unlikely since presently only a small fraction of potentially useable organs are available for transplants. Compensating persons either for allowing their organs to be used after their death, or for kidneys and livers to be used while they are alive, would enormously widen the scope of the potential organ market.

Another set of critics agree with me that the effect on the total supply of organs from allowing them to be purchased and sold would be large and positive, but they object to markets because of a belief that the commercially motivated part of the organ supply would mainly come from the poor. In effect, they believe the poor would be induced to sell their organs to the middle classes and the rich. It is hard to see any reasons to complain if organs of poor persons were sold with their permission after they died, and the proceeds went as bequests to their parents or children. The complaints would be louder if, for example, mainly poor persons sold one of their kidneys for live kidney transplants, but why would poor donors be better off if this option were taken away from them? If so desired, a quota could be placed on the fraction of organs that could be supplied by persons with incomes below a certain level, but would that improve the welfare of poor persons?

Moreover, it is far from certain that a dominant fraction of the organs would come from the poor in a free market. Many of the organs used for live liver or kidney transplants are still likely to be supplied by relatives. In addition, many middle-class persons would be willing to have their organs sold after they died if the proceeds went to children, parents, and other relatives. Although this is not an exact analogy, predictions that a voluntary army would be filled mainly with poor persons have turned out to be wrong. Many of the poor do not have the education and other qualifications to be acceptable to the armed forces. In the same way, many poor persons in the United States would have organs that would not be acceptable in a market system because of organ damage due to drug use or various diseases.

Still another criticism of markets in organs is that people would be kidnapped for their organs, and that totalitarian governments would sell organs of prisoners. This would happen, but not likely on a significant scale since the source of organs offered for sale could be determined in most cases without great difficulty.

A criticism particularly of a commercial market for live transplants is that some persons would act impulsively out of short-run financial needs, and that they would regret their decision to sell a kidney or allow their liver to be used for a transplant if they had taken more time. I do not know how important such impulsive behavior would be, but it could be sharply reduced by having a month or longer cooling off waiting period between the time someone agrees to supply an organ and the time it can be used. They would be allowed to change their mind during the interim.

Many of the arguments against the sale of organs indirectly stem from an influential book in 1971 by the British social scientist Richard Titmuss, *The Gift Relationship: From Human Blood to Social Policy.* He argues against allowing blood to be sold for transfusions, and compares the British system, which did not allow the purchase of blood, with the American system, which did allow its purchase. Titmuss basically ignored that the American system in fact was getting more blood per capita than the British system. Instead, he concentrated on the quality of the blood. Since a significant fraction of the American blood came from individuals with hepatitis and other diseases that could not be screened out, the blood given under the British system tended to be healthier. In the absence of effective screening techniques, perhaps shutting down the commercial market was an effective way then to improve blood quality.

But that is no longer the case as highly effective methods have since been developed to determine whether blood is contaminated with various types of hepatitis, HIV, and other transmittable diseases. Under present screening technology, a market in blood yields much more blood, and with enough diligence its quality can be maintained at a high level.

My conclusion is that markets in organs are the best available way to enable persons with defective organs to get transplants much more quickly than under the present system. I do not find compelling the arguments against allowing the sale of organs, especially when weighed against the number of lives that would be saved by the increased supply stimulated by financial incentives.

ORGAN SALES—POSNER

The case for organ sales argued by Becker is compelling. The shortages, queuing, black market, cumbersome nonmarket allocation schemes, and quality problems that he describes are the classic symptoms of price controls: in this case a zero price limit for the sale of an organ.

I have just a few brief thoughts to add.

A puzzle is that "opt out" systems, used, for example, in France, whereby cadaver organs are automatically available for harvesting for transplant purposes unless an individual indicates (for example, when receiving his driver's license) that he doesn't want that, yield a significant increase in donations compared to our "opt in" system. The cost of opting out is trivial; why then could a shift from opt in to opt out have any significant effect? Yet the Abadie and Gay study that Becker cites indicates, after correcting for other factors, that an opt out ("presumed consent") system increases cadaver donations by 25 to 30 percent. (I believe that in later work Gay has reduced this estimate, but I cannot find a reference to that work.) As the authors point out, however, an increase in cadaver donations would presumably reduce the number of donations from living people, so the net effect on donations is uncertain. As the authors also realize (and attempt to correct for, while recognizing the difficulty of succeeding in the attempt), the adoption of an opt-out system may reflect, rather than cause, a propensity to donate organs.

One possible reason the weak default rule appears to have a significant effect is public ignorance. The probability that one's organs will be harvested for use in transplantation must be very slight—so slight that it doesn't pay to think much about whether one wants to participate in such a program. When the consequences of making a "correct" decision are slight, ignorance is rational, and therefore one expects default rules to have their greatest effect on behavior when people are ignorant of the rule and therefore do not try to take advantage of the opportunity to opt out of it. In this regard, it is perhaps significant that the countries with high rates of organ donation tend also to be countries with abnormally high traffic fatalities.

Becker mentions that in an effort to minimize the bad effects of the shortage of organs for transplantation, the U.S. government has given priority to the patients who would benefit from the transplant the most, as determined by medical personnel. This is an ambiguous and questionable criterion. The patient who is deemed to benefit the most from a transplant might be someone who was in such poor health that the transplant would merely prolong his life by a few months, whereas another patient, who was in better health, might gain added years from a transplant but without one would die soon—sooner than the unhealthy patient, who might therefore be thought the one who would benefit the most from the transplant.

The legal ban on the sale of organs is part of a broader social policy of limiting "commodification," or propertization, of many valuable goods and services: or in other words of limiting the scope of the free market. Among such limitations that command essentially universal assent in our society: people may not agree to engage in gladiatorial contests in which they fight for the death, to sell themselves into slavery, to agree to have their knees broken if they default on a loan, to buy certain mind-altering drugs, to buy or sell sex, or to sell their parental rights. The grounds that are offered for these various limitations on the free market often have a certain plausibility, but do not seem adequate to explain the revulsion that the idea of the prohibited transactions arouse in most people. The transactions may have third-party effects or be the product of ignorance, shortsightedness, or lack of self-control, but this is true of many transactions that are permitted, such as drinking alcohol and gambling. It seems that the prohibited transactions are prohibited because they are highly offensive to nonparticipants; why they are highly offensive remains to be explained.

One form of organ commodification that remains to be considered is an enforceable contract to bequeath one's organs upon death to an organ depositary. Then the donor would receive money up front without having to give up his organ until death. The price would undoubtedly be low. The problem is enforcement: there would need to be a mechanism by which to inform the depositary promptly of the donor's death. But this problem should not be insuperable; the name and address of the depositary could be indicated on the donor's driver's license or (together with the donor's name) on some central registry to which police and paramedics would have access. Moreover, the existence of such a depositary is probably presumed by any market system in organs; one would not expect the patient to be negotiating directly with a potential donor, rather than dealing with an intermediary.

12

TRAFFIC CONGESTION

February 12, 2006

THE SOLUTION TO TRAFFIC CONGESTION—BECKER

An iron law of economics states that demand always expands beyond the supply of free goods to cause queues. There is no better illustration of this law than the traffic congestion in virtually every major city and also in many smaller cities that has resulted from allowing city roads to be used without paying any fees. During much of the day, traffic moves slowly not only in New York, Los Angeles, Chicago, and many other American cities, but also in Mexico City, São Paulo, Paris, Rome, London, Tokyo, Beijing, Shanghai, and Bombay.

Congestion has greatly increased over time, and traffic has become congested not only during morning and evening rush hours on commutes into and then out of cities, but also during rush hours in the opposite direction as well. That is, traffic is heavy and progress is slow also going out of cities into suburbs during the morning rush hours, and back into a city during evenings. The direct cause of the growth in road congestion in developing countries like Brazil,

China, India, and Mexico is the huge increase in the number of cars. The number of cars also rose in the richer countries, partly due to the increase in the labor force activities of married women who drive to work.

Despite the greater traffic congestion on roads, most men and women still choose to drive since that gives them greater flexibility about the times to travel for leisure or working. In addition, cars have become more comfortable, reliable, and safer with power steering, four-wheel drive, improved tires, air conditioning, cell phones, and advanced audio equipment. Opposition to the building of additional highways on environmental and other grounds slowed down the construction of highways in many countries to accommodate the growing number of cars on the road.

The Texas Transportation Institute estimated that the extra time and fuel spent in driving as a result of traffic congestion in 1994 was worth over $75 billion. They assumed about one and one-quarter persons per car, and that the average value of time per person was $11 per hour. The increase in congestion and in the value of time since then would suggest that a comparable figure for 2005 would likely exceed $150 billion, or more than 1 percent of American GDP. Moreover, these estimates do not account for any pollution damage caused by the excessive driving that causes congestion.

Like the weather, everyone talks about traffic—Google lists over 11 million Web sites that discuss traffic congestion—but aside from some new roads and public transportation system, little has been done to reduce this congestion. Congestion is inevitable when people live in cities and in highly built up suburbs. But there is a fundamental reason why the amount of traffic congestion is greater than the efficient amount. When a person decides to drive to work during rush hours, he takes into account any extra time it will take because of congestion on the roads at those times. But he generally does not take account of the effects of his driving on the congestion faced by others.

Economists call this increase in the congestion he causes others a negative externality. Of course, each person that decides to drive during a congested period only imposes a very small harm on others since he only increases traffic times by a tiny amount. But adding up all these small externalities over thousands of cars sums to a large aggregate externality, and a large increase in traffic congestion, that does not enter in any individual's decisions about whether to drive or not, or whether to avoid rush hour traffic.

The optimal way to induce drivers to take account of the congestion they cause to others is to charge them fees for driving during congested periods that would vary with the degree of the congestion. So these fees would be higher during rush hours than during other hours of the day, and they would be lower on weekends when traffic is generally lighter than on weekdays. Fees should be greater when it is raining or snowing since congestion is greater with bad weather, in part because driving is slowed down by the weather, and in part because more people decide to drive rather than walk or take public transportation when it rains.

No city has such a sophisticated form of congestion pricing. But interestingly, it took a left-wing mayor of London, Kenneth Livingstone (sometimes called "Red Ken"), for London to become the first really large city to introduce an extensive congestion road tax, although Singapore pioneered this approach with a license system that began in 1975. In 2003, Livingstone implemented a pricing system for cars entering the central part of London during business hours. Owners of cars that cross the cordon around central London were initially charged £5 for each time their cars crossed; that fee was raised in 2005 to £8. Cameras record the license plates of cars as they cross, and anyone who is caught trying to avoid paying their accumulated charges is fined. This simple system has done much better than some analysts expected, although economists know from many other examples that people find ways to substitute for any good or activity that becomes more expensive. This fundamental law of demand applies to driving during peak hours as well. Car traffic in the central city of London has fallen by about 20 percent, average traffic speed in the center has increased from about eight to eleven miles per hour, and both car and bus delays during peak traffic periods have fallen by even larger percentages.

People adjusted by using public transportation, carpooling, bicycling, or walking into central London instead of driving. More people ended up switching to buses rather than trains because bus travel became a lot faster due to the reduced congestion on central city streets as the number of cars competing with buses for space on the central city streets dropped a lot. In the long run, this toll would induce some companies and shops to move their offices and stores outside the central part of London.

The London system is rather effective, but it is still a crude pricing system since the amount charged for entering the central city does not vary during the business day, even though congestion does vary, due sometimes to changes in the weather. The deputy mayor of London told me that they are contemplating introducing a more sophisticated system. Anyone who enters the central city would need to have a device on his car, a tracking system, that would transmit information to electronic toll collectors on the locations of the car at different times. The charge to an owner would then depend on the degree of congestion at the times his car was in the central city. At the end of each month, car owners would be assessed the congestion charges accrued during the prior month.

Such a more sophisticated pricing system would have all the advantages of the present system plus some additional ones since it would raise the tax when traffic was moving more slowly, and lower it when traffic flowed more quickly. Such congestion based tolls would, in addition, encourage some companies to stagger their opening and closing times to avoid the peak rush hours when fees were greater. It would encourage weekday shoppers to wait until rush hours were over before going into the central city, and to leave before traffic became heavy at the end of the working day.

A toll on cars is more efficient than others ways of reducing congestion. Some cities allow cars to enter the central part only on alternative days, an approach that takes no account of the different values placed by different drivers on the advantages of entering every day. A tax on gasoline reduces driving and in this way helps to reduce congestion, but it takes little account of the greater effect on congestion of driving during heavy traffic periods than the effect of driving when traffic is light.

A few weeks ago Mayor Michael Bloomberg of New York rejected the imposition of a tax on cars that passed a cordon imposed around New York's downtown area. Apparently, the city administration gave no attention at all to a more sophisticated form of congestion taxing. New York's decision is not unusual since many other cities have considered and then rejected imposing tolls to help relieve the terrible congestion during business hours in order to speed up traffic. Partly, the opposition comes from businesses and shops in the downtown area that might have fewer customers and have to pay more for employees. The opposition comes also from car owners and some conservatives who see this as just another tax to raise government revenues.

I certainly have no desire to increase the already heavy tax burden in cities and elsewhere. Ideally, I would like any increase in revenue from congestion tolls to be offset by reductions in other taxes—that is, to be revenue neutral. However, congestion is a tax too, but a hidden tax on the time of people rather than on their pocketbooks because it increases the amount of time wasted in heavy traffic. This tax on time from congestion is a very inefficient tax because it is not paid to anyone, but in effect just throws away time, the most valuable resource that people have. Unless the government would do great damage with the revenue collected from congestion tolls, these tolls are much more efficient than the current taxes on time that result from traffic congestion.

TRAFFIC CONGESTION—POSNER

Traffic congestion is a classic negative externality. As Becker explains, a driver does not consider the effect of his driving on the other users of the road, but only on himself. The standard method of reducing congestion—building more roads—is not only very costly but to a degree self-defeating, since by reducing congestion (and thus the time cost of driving) it attracts more traffic.

Despite much road building, congestion measured by average commuting delays has increased substantially in recent years. Becker makes the important point that the average per-hour private cost of commuting by car has fallen with the substantial improvements in automobile comfort. But it probably has not fallen enough to fully offset the increased delay.

The usual recommendation by economists for dealing with negative externalities is to tax the activity that produces them. The London solution described by Becker—a fee for driving into central London during weekdays—is a step in that direction, with impressive results, such as a 20 percent reduction in London vehicle traffic. But it is doubtful that this success can be duplicated in the United States. Before the imposition of the London commuting fee, 85 percent of the commuters were already using buses and other forms of public transportation rather than commuting by car. This indicated both that most commuters thought such transportation a good alternative to driving (though of course the 15 percent might not) and, more important, that the public transportation system could easily absorb additional commuters. A 20 percent decline in commuting by car translates into only a 3 percent shift to public transportation if commuters by car are only 15 percent of the total number of commuters before the fee is imposed. True, there are other methods of economizing on driving besides switching to another mode of transportation, such as carpooling, but carpooling has the same features that cause people to dislike public transportation: less privacy and flexibility than driving by oneself.

I believe that among major U.S. cities, only New York has comparable figures—some 80 percent of commuters to downtown Manhattan get there by means of public transportation, mainly subway, rather than by car. All cars entering Manhattan pay heavy bridge or tunnel tolls, however, so there would doubtless be stiff resistance to the imposition of a commuting fee. Mayor Bloomberg considered such an imposition but has backed off.

Resistance to a commuting fee would be much greater in cities that do not have good public transportation alternatives. The reason is that in such cities, heavy commuting fees would reduce the number of commuters, hurting downtown businesses. On average, only about 2 percent of American commuters use public transportation.

Notice also that by reducing congestion and hence the cost of commuting by car, a stiff commuting fee may have only a modest effect on congestion. Indeed, the fee will induce some commuters to substitute driving, if they have a high time cost, for public transportation.

The political obstacles to commuting fees have persuaded the traffic economist Richard Arnott that more attention should be paid to substitute methods of reducing traffic congestion. A good deal of congestion is due to commuters hunting for parking places and to trucks blocking streets while unloading, as well as to bad driving (for example, leading to more accidents), increased vehicle size (for example, SUVs), poor road surfaces, road repairs, poor road design, weather, and bottlenecks. The problem is that any measure that reduces congestion without imposing any additional cost on the commuter will, as I mentioned, tend to increase the amount of traffic as commuters and other drivers switch from public transportation to cars or make less effort to avoid rush-hour traffic.

A frequent suggestion for combating traffic congestion is staggered work hours. A favorite suggestion of economists that would have a similar effect would be to make the commuting fee vary by time of day, so that it would be higher during rush hours. But these suggestions involve a hidden cost: by reducing the overlap of working hours, they reduce one of the principal economies of urban business districts—the dense network of face-to-face interactions that such districts enable.

I conclude that until traffic congestion gets significantly worse, little will be done, and perhaps little should be done, to try to reduce it. But I am not pessimistic. In the long run what will reduce traffic congestion will be the continued digital revolution, which will not only increase the amount of telecommuting but also lead to a substantial substitution of virtual for face-to-face interactions in business, shopping, and even socializing. The business district of the future and the mall of the future may be located in cyberspace.

The digital revolution has altered my own commuting. With high-speed Internet access I work at home much more than I did when I started as a judge twenty-four years ago, and rarely have occasion to drive during rush hour.

13

PRIVATIZING HIGHWAYS

June 20, 2006

PRIVATIZING THE NATION'S HIGHWAYS, AND OTHER INFRASTRUCTURE—POSNER

The state of Indiana has just (June 29, 2006) leased the Indiana Toll Road—a 157-mile-long highway in northern Indiana that connects Illinois to Ohio—to a Spanish-Australian consortium for seventy-five years for $3.8 billion, to be paid in a lump sum. The lease is complex, imposing many duties on the lessee (such as to install electronic toll collection, in which Indiana has lagged). A key provision is that the consortium will not be able to raise toll rates until 2016 (for passenger cars—2010 for trucks) and then only by the greatest of 2 percent a year, the consumer inflation rate (CPI), or the annual increase in GDP. (On the eve of the lease, Indiana raised toll rates—which hadn't changed since 1985—significantly.) Two years ago Chicago made a similar lease of the Chicago Skyway, an eight-mile stretch that connects Chicago to the Indiana Toll Road, for $1.8 billion. There is considerable interest in other states as well in leasing toll roads to private entities.

The idea of privatizing toll roads is an attractive one from an economic standpoint. Private companies are more efficient than public ones, at least in the limited sense of economizing on costs. I call this sense of efficiency "limited" because there are other dimensions of efficiency, for example, the allocative; a monopolist might be very effective in limiting his costs, but by charging a monopoly price he would distort the allocation of resources. Some of his customers would be induced by the high price to switch to substitutes that cost more to make than the monopolist's product but that, being priced at the competitive rather than the monopoly price, seemed cheaper to consumers. (This is the standard economic objection to monopoly.) The reason for the superior ability of private companies to control costs is that they have both a strong financial incentive and also competitive pressure to do so—factors that operate weakly or not all in the case of public agencies—and that their pricing and purchasing decisions, including decisions regarding wages and labor relations, are not distorted by political pressures and corruption. There is a long history of price fixing in highway construction and maintenance, attributable in part to bidding rules that, in endeavoring to prevent corruption, facilitate bid rigging. For example, if to prevent corruption contracts are always awarded to the low bidder, a bid-rigging conspiracy will always know whether one of its members is cheating, if the low bidder, who gets the contract, was not the bidder that the conspiracy assigned to make the low bid. If cheating on a conspiracy is readily detectable, cheating is less likely and therefore the conspiracy more effective.

The problem of allocative efficiency looms when, for example, there are externalities; but the solution to the problem rarely requires public ownership. One significant externality associated with vehicular transportation is the congestion externality: no driver is likely to consider the effect of his driving on the convenience of other drivers, because there is no way in which he can exact compensation from drivers for not driving or driving less and therefore improving their driving time. That externality is internalized by a toll road, because congestion reduces the quality of the driving experience and so the amount each driver is willing to pay in tolls; the owner of the toll road will trade that willingness to pay against the reduction in the number of drivers as a result of a higher toll.

Another externality, however, will not be internalized by the toll-road operators. That is the contribution that driving makes to pollution and global warming. But public ownership is not necessary in order to internalize this externality. The government can force its internalizing by imposing a tax on driving.

There is, however, in the toll-road setting another source of allocative inefficiency, and that is monopoly, which I have mentioned already. Drivers who do not have good alternatives to using the Indiana Toll Road can be made to pay tolls that exceed wear and tear, congestion effects, social costs of pollution, and other costs of the road, engendering inefficient substitutions by drivers unwilling to pay those tolls. To an extent, the toll-road operator may be able to discourage substitution by price discrimination, but this is unlikely to be fully effective and indeed can actually increase the allocative inefficiency of the monopoly.

The monopoly issue raises the question: what exactly was Indiana selling when it leased the toll road for $3.8 billion? The higher the tolls and the greater the lessee's freedom to raise the tolls in the future, the higher the price that the state can command for the lease. If the lease placed no limitations on tolls, the state would be selling an unregulated monopoly. If the lease could constrain the lessee to charge tolls just equal to the cost of operating the toll road (including maintenance, repairs, snow removal, lighting, and the collection of the tolls), the market price of the lease would be significantly lower. To the extent that the state wants to maximize its take from the lease, it will be creating allocative inefficiency by conferring monopoly power on the lessee.

It is difficult to determine whether the $3.8 billion price tag for the Indiana Toll Road is closer to the competitive or the monopoly price level. On the one hand, the lessee cannot raise tolls until 2010 or 2016 (depending on the type of vehicle), and increases after that are capped. On the other hand, the tolls were raised significantly just before the lease, and allowing the operator in 2010 to begin raising toll rates annually by the increase in GDP may confer windfall gains, since the cost of operating the toll road may not increase at so great a rate. One would have to know a great deal more about the economics of operating a highway than I do to figure out whether the terms of the lease confer monopoly power on the lessee.

I do not regard the monopoly concern as a strong objection to the leasing of the toll road, however. The reason is that most, maybe all, taxes have monopoly-like effects, in the sense of driving a wedge between cost and price. Suppose the lease price would have been only $2 billion had the state imposed more stringent limitations on toll increases. Then the state would have $1.8 billion less in revenue and would presumably make up the difference by increasing tax rates or imposing additional taxes, and these measures would have allocative effects similar to those of higher tolls charged by the lessee of the toll road. If the monopoly issue is therefore considered a wash, the principal effect of the lease will be the positive one of reducing the quality-adjusted cost of operating the toll road and the lease is clearly a good idea.

Toll roads are more attractive candidates for privatization than nontoll roads because it is easy to charge user fees; tolls are user fees. It would be harder to charge for the use of city streets, though no longer impossible, given electronic technology for monitoring drivers. Privatizing certain security services pose special problems as well, as Becker and I discussed in our May 28 posts about security contractors in Iraq. But public services the costs of which are defrayed in whole or significant part by user fees are good candidates for privatization, including Amtrak, the postal service, building and restaurant inspections, veterans' hospitals, and federal, state, and local airports. The privatization movement has a long way to go before achieving an optimal mixture of public and private service providers.

Against all this it will be argued—and it is an argument emphasized by opponents of leasing the Indiana Toll Road—that privatization, at least when it takes the form of a sale or long-term lease of government property for a lump sum, beggars the future by depriving government of an income-producing asset. The argument, at least in its simplest form, is unsound, because the state is not disposing of an asset but merely changing its form: from a highway to cash. The subtler form of the argument is that, given the truncated horizons of elected officials, the state will not invest the cash wisely for the long term, but will squander it on short-term projects. This is a danger—how great a one I do not know. It would be an interesting study to trace the uses to which privatizing governments here and abroad have put the proceeds of sales of public assets.

ON PRIVATIZING HIGHWAYS AND OTHER FUNCTIONS—BECKER

There is a well-known conflict in privatizing a government enterprise between the desires to raise revenue from the privatization and to create an efficient enterprise. Government revenue is increased by giving the privatized company a protected position against competition, while allowing other companies to compete vigorously against the privatized company increases efficiency. Greater efficiency typically means lower prices for the privatized product, and hence lower bids for the enterprise to be privatized.

Governments often succumb to the desire to increase their revenue, which has caused the creation of monopolies in privatization programs all over the world. I differ with Posner in believing that the revenue from a monopolized privatization would not be fully raised elsewhere if not raised from the privatization because it is difficult to tap other sources of revenue to substitute for foregone revenues from privatizations. Put differently, governments end up with bigger total spending budgets when they increase their revenue from privatizations by giving privatized companies some monopoly power.

Still, I generally strongly support privatizations, even when privatized companies have monopoly power in setting prices and other conditions of the sale. The reason is that other companies are more likely to find ways to compete against private monopolies than against government ones. A very important part of this argument is that technological progress is faster with private monopolies than with public monopolies. For example, AT&T was a private regulated monopoly before the breakup of the Bells in the early 1980s into competing entities. The breakup was desirable, but still AT&T was much more efficient than were the government-run companies that dominated the telephone industry at that time in the rest of the world.

These and the arguments given by Posner strongly imply that highways, along with postal systems, trains, airports, ports, and other infrastructure, including even some security activities, should be privately rather than publicly operated. The main challenge arises when it is more difficult to stimulate competition for the privatized company because of so-called natural monopoly conditions in the industry. Due to economies of scale, it may not be efficient, for example, to have another highway built across Indiana to compete against the Indiana Toll Road. Yet even in that case, it would still be desirable to privatize the toll road, but controls could be imposed on the prices and other conditions that can be levied imposed on consumers by the privatively owned road.

Yet I believe that in the dynamic world we live in, natural monopoly considerations are less common than often supposed because new technologies and processes can bring competition to what appear to be protected markets if the profits are large enough. In this way, the supposed natural monopoly position of traditional telephone companies due to the large fixed costs of a network of telephone wires has been eroded by the development of cable and its alternative wired network, and of course by wireless telephony and the use of the Internet for phoning.

Roads and airports are examples of industries that pose greater challenges to create competition among private companies. However, smaller airports in a region, such as the one at Gary, Indiana, would be expanded to attract business from higher priced dominant airports in the same region, like O'Hare, if the dominant airport was charging excessive fees, and if both airports were privately run. Even a second private toll road would be built to compete against at least part of a privatized toll road that was charging excessive fees, especially over the most densely traveled portions of the privatized road.

The theory of the efficient allocation of resources is radically changed when dynamic competition with induced technological progress is the framework of analysis instead of the traditional static theory of competition. Dynamic competition analysis is more comfortable with accepting short-term monopoly power of privatized enterprises that are allowed to set their own prices. The reason is that the monopoly profits from high prices by the privatized enterprise would stimulate other entrepreneurs to find ways to compete against the enterprise, and in this way claim some of the monopoly profits through lower prices and better service. "Natural monopoly" looms large in the theory of static allocation of resources, but is considerably less important in the actual world because of technological progress that is induced by monopoly power and excessive profits.

When dynamic competition is effective, a public enterprise, like a toll road or the postal system, should be sold without any restrictions on future pricing, unlike what happened in the sale of the Indiana Toll Road. I do not go so far as to claim that dynamic competition always arises in a powerful way to compete against privatized roads or other privatized infrastructure that have no restrictions on pricing. But I do believe it is far more common and effective than in textbook discussions of competition and entry. If that is the case, it would then pay to privatize most of the public infrastructure of roads, communication, mail delivery, electric power generation, and the like, with few controls over the prices that can be charged to consumers. That would create some pockets of persistent monopoly profits, but it would take politics out of rate setting. It would also stimulate the development of different ways to compete against what appears to be an unassailable monopoly enterprise.

AFTERTHOUGHTS TO PART II

POSNER AFTERTHOUGHTS

Regarding the *Kelo* case, which authorized the condemnation of land for private development (as opposed to the more conventional forms of eminent domain, which either are designed to solve holdout problems, as when a railroad is permitted to condemn property for its right of way, or to procure land for a public facility, such as a post office or military base), by June of 2008, thirty-seven states had passed laws designed in various ways to limit the power of eminent domain authorized by the Supreme Court in *Kelo.* The significance of this development lies in its underscoring the difference between constitutional decisions that forbid and that authorize government action. The former, such as the recent *Heller* decision, curtailing the power of government to restrict private ownership of guns, replace democratic with judicial governance, and when applied nationwide stifle experimentation by the states with divergent solutions to social and economic problems. In contrast, a decision such as *Kelo* that reduces judicial control over state action invites, and has received, diverse responses to the gap in regulation that the decision creates or reveals. Those thirty-seven new state laws on eminent domain are notably diverse, and from a comparison of experience under them and with the laxer regulations in the remaining states we will eventually learn what the scope of the eminent domain power should be. Incidentally, as late as May 2008, the development in New London, Connecticut, to which the Supreme Court gave the go-ahead in *Kelo* had still not begun because the developers had not obtained the necessary financing. This and other evidence suggests that the states are wise to curtail eminent domain, because condemning land for private development does not seem to generate social value. Of course the bursting of the housing bubble is another reason to doubt the value of such condemnation.

I continue to be enthusiastic about the privatization of toll roads and other transportation infrastructure. (Recently, Chicago has decided to privatize Midway Airport.) Shortly after the Indiana Tollway was privatized, its electronic tollbooths were made compatible with E-ZPass and I-Pass, so that a subscriber to either can use his transponder for the Indiana Tollway as well. The continued deterioration of the interstate highway system underscores the need to bring business acumen to bear on the design and execution of optimal methods for maintaining the highways without imposing excessive construction delays on the users. Becker and I expressed concern about the monopoly power of a tollway owner, so it is interesting to note the proposal to construct a new highway to be called the "Illiana Expressway" that would run parallel to the Indiana Tollway and thus provide competition with it. Finally, continued advances in the technology of monitoring moving vehicles suggest that even electronic tollbooths, with the modest delays that they impose, will give way to billing methods that do not require any stopping or slowing and so will facilitate the privatization of roads other than just limited-access ones.

On the related subject of traffic congestion, there is no doubt that the most efficient method of control is a tax on congestion, which the billing methods just mentioned would enable. A tax on motor vehicles is inferior because most roads are not congested. But the defeat of Mayor Bloomberg's proposal to introduce congestion pricing in New York City suggests that such a tax is a politically unpalatable solution to the congestion problem. (It has worked in London, but in part this is because only 15 percent of London commuters drive to work.) That political resistance supports traffic economist Richard Arnott's suggestion that more attention be paid to substitute methods of reducing traffic congestion, much of which is due to commuters hunting for parking places and to trucks blocking streets while unloading, as well as to bad driving (for example, leading to more accidents), increased vehicle size (for example, SUVs), poor road surfaces, road repairs, and poor road design.

BECKER AFTERTHOUGHTS

I believe I may have too readily dismissed the negative effects of the development of cheap copying methods on the revenues of companies and individuals producing songs, music, and other intellectual property. Some studies have since indicated that demand for music has decreased significantly, in part because of the greater ease of making copies.

At the time I wrote the column on congestion pricing, New York City Mayor Bloomberg had opposed its introduction in that city. Later he backed the use of such pricing to reduce traffic jams in Manhattan. However, the proposal ran into much opposition from commuters and politicians outside Manhattan in other boroughs and suburbs. That is a shame since pricing the use of congested roads still is the most promising way to greatly lower the enormous amount of time wasted by Americans and drivers and passengers in cities in other countries when their progress is stalled during heavy traffic.

III

UNIVERSITIES

14

PLAGIARISM

April 24, 2005

PLAGIARISM—POSNER

Recent "scandals" involving charges of plagiarism by professors and other writers treat plagiarism as (1) a well-defined concept that (2) is unequivocally deserving of condemnation. It is neither. Take the second point first. The idea that copying another person's ideas or expression (the form of words in which the idea is encapsulated), without the person's authorization and without explicit acknowledgment of the copying, is reprehensible is, in general, clearly false. Think of the remarkable series of "plagiarisms" that links Ovid's *Pyramus and Thisbe* with Shakespeare's *Romeo and Juliet* and Leonard Bernstein's *West Side Story.* Think of James Joyce's *Ulysses* and of contemporary parodies, which invariably copy extensively from the original—otherwise the reader or viewer would not recognize the parody as a parody. Most judicial opinions nowadays are written by law clerks but signed by judges, without acknowledgment of the clerks' authorship. This is a general characteristic of government documents, CEOs' speeches, and books by celebrities.

When unauthorized copying is not disapproved, it isn't called "plagiarism." Which means that the word, rather than denoting a definite, well-recognized category of conduct, is a label attached to instances of unauthorized copying of which the society, or some influential group within it, disapproves.

In general, disapproval of such copying, and therefore of "plagiarism," is reserved for cases of fraud. The clearest example is a student buying an essay that he then submits for course credit. By doing this he commits a fraud that harms competing students and prospective employers. Another clear example is the professor, or other professional writer, who steals ideas or expression from another professor or writer, and by doing so obtains royalties or tenure or some other benefit that he would not have gotten were the truth known—again, a case of fraud. It is less serious than the student fraud, however, because it is more likely to be caught. A student essay is not published and so will not be widely read. A published work is quite likely to be read or brought to the attention of the author of the purloined work. The easier it is to detect a wrongful act, the lesser is the punishment required to deter (most of) it; this may be why—to the outrage of students—plagiarism by faculty tends to be punished less severely than plagiarism by students. Moreover, whereas student plagiarism has absolutely no social value, plagiarism in a published work may have such value. If what is plagiarized is a good idea, the plagiarism creates value by disseminating it further than the original author may have done. Moreover, the plagiarist may add his own input to the plagiarized idea and as a result produce a superior work.

I lumped together copying a professor's work and copying the work of another type of professional writer, say a writer of popular history. In both cases, the copying will probably be a copyright infringement. In both cases, too, the copying will be a form of fraud. What will differ in the two cases is the injury that the fraud inflicts. In the case of the popular writer, the injury will be a loss of royalties or other fees—and will usually be negligible, unless the plagiarist is trying to produce a substitute for the work, rather than just enhancing a noncompeting work with incidental material from another book. The academic writer will usually suffer no loss of royalties even if the plagiarized work is a direct substitute, because few academic writings generate royalties (textbooks are the principal exception). But he may suffer grievously nevertheless, because recognition of original contributions is the key currency of academic reward and that recognition is blurred when someone fails to acknowledge another's priority. The contrast in this regard with judicial opinions is very striking. Far from flaunting their originality, judges try to conceal it. They like to pretend that rather than making up new law, they are merely applying existing law made by others. So they do not complain at all if another judge or a law professor "steals" novel ideas that they have managed without acknowledgment to smuggle into some of their opinions.

Perhaps the most difficult current question about plagiarism concerns the "managed book," or more broadly the use of research assistants or other aides in the creation of a book. The term refers to a book in which the nominal author is actually an editor—an assembler and maybe a reviser—of work done by persons whom he has hired. He is much like a movie director. He presides over the composition of the work rather than being the composer. The phenomenon is not new; according to *An Unfinished Life,* Robert Dallek's recent (2003) biography of John F. Kennedy (a biography highly favorable to its subject, but not uncritical), *Profiles in Courage* was a "managed book" (not Dallek's term, though). Many judicial opinions are of this character. It seems likely that many multivolume treatises by (that is, nominally by) law professors are "managed books" in which most of the actual writing is done by student research assistants—though I am guessing; I have no actual evidence.

Let me say, as someone who has written a number of books, that the idea of writing a "managed book" is not to my personal taste. I think that the person who writes a first draft largely controls the final product, even if it is carefully edited by the "author" of the managed book. But the issue of plagiarism has nothing to do with the taste of particular writers. It is an issue of fraud. So the question regarding the managed book is whether failure to disclose that most of the actual writing was done by persons other than the nominal author misleads readers to their detriment. That depends mainly on the conventions, and hence expectations, of a particular field. A professional historian who "authored" a managed book without disclosure of the fact would be committing a fraud because his fellow historians would think he'd written it himself. At the opposite extreme, few lawyers care whether a judicial opinion is written by a law clerk or by the judge, provided they think it's the judge's decision (the bottom line, the outcome), which it almost always is. In between is the legal treatise—the American legal treatise, that is; for it has long been the norm in Germany and other European countries for academic law books to be written by the assistant to the professor under whose name the book will be published. That is not the norm in the United States. I believe without knowing that the delegation of the writing of extensive portions of such works is recent, and much of the profession, including the treatise author's colleagues, may be unaware of the trend—if there is a trend, of which I am not certain. It would be prudent, therefore, for such treatise writers to acknowledge the coauthorship or first-draft responsibility of their students, in order to avoid a charge of plagiarism.

COMMENT ON PLAGIARISM—BECKER

Posner correctly argues that there is no hard and fast line that separates plagiarism from accepted use of other people's written work. But wherever the line is drawn, plagiarism is the reverse of counterfeiting activities. Plagiarists try to take credit for the work of others, while counterfeiters credit others for their own work.

Both have been with us for a long time, but the Internet and other new technologies have made both plagiarism and counterfeiting easier. A potential plagiarist has access through the Internet to extensive written materials on any topic, while counterfeiters can discover designs and products to copy, and can find customers through e-mail and Web sites. It is also more difficult to detect plagiarists and counterfeiters since the number of potential sources for reports and other documents to the plagiarists is immense, as are the outlets for counterfeiters.

A well-recognized part of the theory of deterrence of illegal and other undesirable activities is that punishments should be greater when the likelihood of detection is smaller. So it follows that since these technologies have made plagiarism much easier, and its detection more difficult, punishments of plagiarists should be greater than in the past.

Posner discusses the damage from plagiarism by students and professors, and appears to conclude that punishment should be less severe on professors caught plagiarizing than on students. I share his concern about plagiarism, but do not agree with this conclusion. Plagiarism by professors and other writers makes greater use of the work of others than does plagiarism by students. As Posner notes, this provides an incentive for authors to discover professors and other writers who plagiarize since citations of one's work is the major way to gain a reputation in academic fields, and sales is the source of income to professional writers.

But the analysis of deterrence implies that punishment should be directly related both to the magnitude of the gain from an illicit activity, and the extent of knowledge about whether it is illicit. On both issues, professors are more culpable than students. A professor who succeeds in plagiarizing typically gains far more from this than a student who plagiarizes in preparing say a term paper. The student may get a higher grade, while the professor helps his chances of getting tenure, promotions, and raises. In addition, professionals know much more than students do about the distinction between plagiarism and simply relying on the contributions of others.

This is why I side with students who believe that professors discovered to have plagiarized are typically let off too easily. They should be fired for clear-cut and flagrant plagiarism. Unfortunately, that does not usually happen if they are in senior positions because that means revoking their tenure, which is usually vigorously opposed through litigation and other means.

In particular, the American Association of University Professors, a kind of union of professors, has opposed with almost a religious fervor all attempts to revoke tenure of faculty except for the most dismal behavior, defined in part by what is politically incorrect at the time.

To return to counterfeiting, companies that produce clothing with unauthorized labels of famous designers, watchmakers who falsely claim their watches are Rolexes or other expensive brands, or private producers of $20 bills pretend to be other producers in order to free ride on their reputations and markets. These and other examples of reverse plagiarism are clear violations of patent or copyright law even when the counterfeit product is just as good as the original, which it often is not.

I mentioned earlier that production of counterfeits has become easier because of the Internet and other technologies, while detection is more difficult also because of these technologies. Detection is also more difficult because markets have become more global. These changes imply that punishment of counterfeiters should be harsher than in the past. However, globalization often makes it harder to punish producers of counterfeit products since developing countries do not really want to enforce the copyright and patent protection on products made elsewhere.

15

TENURE

January 15, 2006

TENURED EMPLOYMENT—POSNER

Most Americans employed in the private sector do not have any job protection. They are what are known as "employees at will." They can quit or be fired at any time for any reason other than a reason forbidden by law, such as race. Unionized workers (now a very small percentage of the private-sector workforce) have some job protection; they can be laid off if their employer experiences a fall in demand and therefore doesn't need as many workers, but they can be fired only "for cause," normally some form of deficient job performance. In the public sector, most employees below the top political level have extensive job protection (including teachers), except in the military and other national security employment, such as the CIA. Generally, civil employees of the government can be discharged only for cause, which often is very difficult to prove. The Supreme Court has largely abolished, in the name of free speech, the "spoils" system whereby state and local government jobs were given to the political supporters of the party in power. Federal judges can be removed (barring physical or mental disability) only by the cumbersome process of impeachment by the House of Representatives and conviction by the Senate. An important category of job-protected workers that bridges the public and private divide is tenured professors, who cannot be fired without cause. Finally, in Europe most workers have far more extensive job protections than American workers do.

The question I wish to address is whether this pattern makes any economic sense. One way to pose the question is to ask why—since employment at will is the cheapest form of employment contract—aren't all employees employees at will? In the otherwise dissimilar cases of unionized workers and public employees protected by the Supreme Court's interpretation of the First Amendment against political firing, tenure (employment protection) is imposed from the outside. Employers would like greater flexibility, but outsiders—unions or judges—impose tenure for their own reasons. Unions worry that without tenure protection, employers will pick off the union's supporters; the Supreme Court worries that without tenure protection public employees will be afraid to express political views opposed to those of their superiors, and so freedom of expression will be curtailed. But surely the curtailment would be slight, since few public employees will engage in public disagreement with their superiors even if they can't be disciplined for doing so. Moreover, there is a trade-off between professional competence and personal loyalty. A slightly less able employee who is loyal to his superiors because of political compatibility or even nepotism will work more harmoniously with them, and the reduction in friction may offset a (modest) competence deficit.

Tenure is an efficient system in what organizational economists call a "high commitment" workplace. Contrast two types of enterprise. In one, the contribution of the individual employee to the enterprise's output is readily measured. Ordinarily this will be a business firm. Revenues, costs, and ultimately profits provide objective measures of performance. The individual employee's contribution to those measures may be more difficult to measure, especially when employees work in teams. But reasonable estimates are usually possible—employees and their superiors negotiate reasonable goals for the coming year relating to sales, markups, and cost reductions and progress toward those goals is measured throughout the year. Employees can therefore be paid a salary or wage that approximates their marginal product. With their productivity continuously measurable, there is no need for job protection.

Or so it seems; for even in a firm, there may be some benefits to providing a degree of job protection. Suppose employees are in a position where by sharing their know-how they could increase the productivity of other employees. They may be reluctant to do this if they fear losing their jobs because they have helped the other employees become more productive than they. Some firms deal with this problem by making an employee's annual bonus depend not only on his own contribution but also on the overall performance of the firm that year. This is a more flexible method than giving workers tenure.

The sharing problem is sometimes offered as an argument for how unionization might actually increase productivity. But it is a weak argument. If tenure is an efficient employment contract, employers will institute it without union prodding. The steep decline of unionization in the private sector is a convincing "Darwinian" refutation of the argument one used to hear that unions actually promote efficiency.

Although performance measures are generally most feasible for business firms, some governmental or other noncommercial activities lend themselves to such measures. Criminal investigation agencies such as the FBI provide good examples. An FBI agent can be evaluated by the number of arrests he makes weighted by convictions (arrests that do not lead to convictions are not productive), with the convictions in turn weighted by the length of the sentence and the value of any property recovered as a result of the prosecution. Note that the measure here, as in a firm, is not a simple quantitative measure of contribution to output, but rather is a value measure.

In activities (some of which may be team production within business firms) in which performance measures are infeasible, usually because either the value of output or the employee's contribution to that output cannot be quantified, methods of employee motivation other than performance-based compensation must be sought. The "high commitment" workplace is a recognition that, fortunately, employees have other motivations for working productively besides the hope of salary increments, such as identification with the goals of the employer, as when judges and (other) civil servants internalize a "public service" ethic that induces them to work productively for a modest wage with limited hope of advancement. Tenure in such a setting both encourages sharing and discourages "influence activities," a term organizational economists use to refer to the kind of jockeying for position that occurs in the workplace when the absence of objective performance measures opens the door to worker competition based on personality, connections, and intrigue.

Even in a high-commitment environment, additional motivation may be provided by a tournament-style promotion system. Even if an employee's output cannot be measured with any precision, it may be possible to identify the best employee because the gap between his contribution and that of the next best may be large enough to be perceived without being quantifiable. Promoting the best employee to the next rank is therefore a method of incentivizing employees to do their best.

Both judicial and academic tenure are defended as needed to encourage independent thought and prevent political retaliation for unpopular views. This rationale is more persuasive in these contexts than in that of ordinary public employees, but it is not very satisfactory. In most nations, including nations that we consider our peers, the judiciary is insulated from political pressures, but the judicial career is much like that of other employees. Judges start at the bottom rung of the judiciary when they are appointed and work their way up by impressing their superiors. The U.S. federal judicial system (also the British judiciary, and that of the other former British possessions) is unusual in being a system of lateral appointments (from practice or the academy, generally) with very limited promotion. The difference may be due to the fact that the Anglo-American and especially the U.S. legal system gives much more discretionary authority to judges than other foreign systems do, so that identifying the "best" for promotion is difficult and even arbitrary.

I do not think tenure makes a great deal of sense any longer in the academic setting, and I expect to see it gradually abandoned. (It has already been abandoned in England, for example.) If a university wishes to offer its faculty protection against political retaliation for unpopular views, it can do that by writing into the employment contract that politics is an impermissible ground for termination. Tenure is no longer needed because of an absence of performance measures. These measures exist in abundance. Quality of teaching is readily measurable by student evaluations, provided care is taken to prevent teachers from courting popularity by easy grading and light assignments and student evaluations are supplemented by faculty observation of the classroom. Quality of research is readily measurable by grants, prizes, and above all by citations to the professor's scholarly publications, weighted by the quality of the journal in which the citations appear.

In some fields, such as mathematics, there is generally a significant falling off in academic output at a young age, and there is fear that without tenure these faculty would be turned out to pasture long before retirement age. But this is no different from the situation in professional sports, modeling, and other youthful occupations, where it is handled by an alteration in the wage profile. If a career in mathematics entails a sharp falloff in market wages after, say, age forty, the academic market will compensate by offering disproportionately high wages to young mathematicians; otherwise, talented mathematicians will choose professions, such as economics, in which math skills are valued but productivity does not decline steeply with age.

One reason for the superior productivity of U.S. compared to European workers is that tenure encourages laziness by reducing the cost of laziness to the worker. But that is not the principal problem. Tenure removes the stick but not necessarily the carrot. More productive professors can be paid more and, even if their university has a lockstep compensation system, can obtain prestige and outside income by outstanding performance. The greater cost of tenure is simply in forcing retention of inferior employees. The eighty-year-old mathematician may be working hard, but he may be incapable of achieving the output of the twenty-five-year-old mathematician who would take his place were it not for tenure. Note how governmental prohibition of compulsory retirement at a fixed age aggravates the inefficiency of tenure—and is no doubt contributing to its eventual abandonment.

Perhaps the strongest argument for academic tenure is that without it academics would be reluctant to undertake promising projects with a high risk of failure. But the situation is no different in "knowledge" firms such as software and pharmaceutical drug producers, which encourage their scientists to undertake high-risk projects—and do not think it necessary to offer tenure. If most good new ideas are produced by young academics, then an institution that raises the average age of faculty, namely tenure, seems likely to reduce academic productivity. An interesting empirical project, therefore, would be to study the effect of England's abolition of tenure on the average age and productivity of English university faculties.

COMMENT ON TENURE—BECKER

The traditional justification for academic tenure is that otherwise professors would be unwilling to express unpopular views for fear of being fired. This argument for academic tenure is extremely weak in the United States where several thousand colleges and universities compete for professors. In fact, tenure only became common at American universities in the 1920s. It is possible for academics with extremely unpopular views to gain an appointment with tenure at different institutions, as seen from the tenure of faculty who deny the Holocaust, or a Ward Churchill at the University of Colorado with outrageous views on terrorism and other issues. The case for tenure is stronger in countries where governments control all universities, and can block academics with unpopular opinions from gaining and keeping appointments. Yet even that argument has become weaker with the rapidly growing international market for good academics.

Are there other persuasive arguments for academic tenure? Some have been made in the economics literature, including the alleged difficulty in judging the quality of teaching and research, the nonprofit nature of universities, and still others. I have not found any of them persuasive—for example, there is rather widespread agreement in most departments about which are the good teachers, and also to a large extent about who has produced the more influential research.

The U.S. Constitution gave federal judges lifetime tenure so that they would be free to decide cases without fear of political reprisals for unpopular decisions. I have argued (see posts in Part V of this book) against the lifetime tenure of judges as encouraging judges to remain too long, especially now when they are likely to live into their eighties and into their nineties within a couple of decades. A single long term of between fourteen and twenty years would entirely eliminate any political influence over their decisions due to any fear of losing their positions. It would also weaken the opposition to the appointment of judges with strong views since they would not be deciding cases for thirty years or more.

Civil servants have tenure because of similar political considerations, but top-level government officials do not have tenure presently, and are selected by the administration in power. It is hard to see why low-level government employees should have tenure either since they do not make any politically sensitive decisions. Perhaps tenure would be justified at certain intermediate levels, but that would at best cover only a small fraction of all government officials.

Companies often give de facto tenure to employees who have worked for them for a long time, except when the companies get into financial difficulties. This is readily explained since long-term employees usually have made significant investments in what is called firm-specific human capital. This term means knowledge and skills of employees that are more valuable at the company where they have worked for many years than at other companies. In order to encourage such investment, and to discourage inefficient quits, companies give a combination of implicit tenure and higher wages to their long-term employees.

Note that tenure alone would not be sufficient to encourage these investments and discourage quits.

It has to be combined with higher earnings to long-term employees. Indeed, high enough earnings to employees with much firm-specific investment would be sufficient to discourage quits without tenure. But bargaining between workers and employees should lead to at least de facto tenure because that is more efficient if employees are more productive at this firm than at other firms. It is efficient because both workers and companies would be better off if workers with much relevant firm-specific investment stayed at the companies where they have worked for many years.

Firm-specific investment provides some of the "commitment" that Posner discusses since employees are obviously more committed to companies where they are more productive. Similarly, the company would be more committed to these employees than to other employees. Commitment is also related to loyalty to an organization and to employees. Loyalty in any organization is extremely important, both loyalty from employees to the organization, and from the organization to its employees. That can be encouraged by higher earning as performance improves, and by good and considerate treatment of employees. It would be in the self-interest of organizations to keep their loyal employees, so no explicit tenure rule seems desirable to encourage the retention of loyal members of an organization, no matter what work or profession they engage in.

Since de facto tenure is in the self-interest of companies as well as workers, the value of tenure does not provide justification for laws against firing older workers, or laws that require costly severance pay to long-term employees. Union contracts that make long-term employees less subject to layoffs may in some circumstances provide useful codifications of implicit tenure. However, this could be inefficient when more senior union members have a disproportionate influence over union bargaining. In any case, one would expect companies without unions to have an incentive when it is efficient to codify hiring and firing rules. In fact, most large nonunion companies already have these rules.

16

FOR-PROFIT COLLEGES

January 22, 2006

FOR-PROFIT COLLEGES—BECKER

An article in yesterday's *New York Times* discussed the moratorium imposed last week by the New York State Board of Regents on new for-profit or commercial colleges in that state. Commercial colleges have been growing rapidly nationally, and the *Times* article discusses problems that have been found with some of them in New York and elsewhere. Despite various abuses, I believe that for-profit colleges and universities fill an important need, and the moratorium imposed by New York is unwise and should be lifted.

Government-run schools dominate higher education in most countries, including the United States where some 70–75 percent of undergraduates attend public colleges and universities. To be sure, private nonprofit colleges and universities make important contributions in some countries, such as the University of Chicago, Stanford University, and Swarthmore College among many others in the United States, Keio University and numerous other little known schools in Japan, and Insead in France. During the past thirty years, the number of for-profit colleges and universities has grown rapidly from negligible numbers, especially in the United States but also in China and elsewhere in Asia. The Career College Association, an association of for-profit postsecondary institutions, lists over two thousand members, and that association does not even include the best-known for-profit colleges, the University of Phoenix and DeVry University. Phoenix is the largest accredited private university, and among the oldest of the for-profit universities. It was founded in 1976, enrolls one hundred thousand online students, even more students at 170 campuses in over thirty states, and it is publicly listed with a market capitalization of several billion dollars.

According to the *Times* article, commercial colleges enroll about 7 percent of students in higher education in New York State. This is even without the University of Phoenix, which has not yet been allowed to enroll students in that state. Other states also have rapidly growing enrollments in for-profit colleges, although I do not have figures on their enrollment shares.

What explains the boom in commercial colleges, given the difficulties in competing against highly subsidized taxpayer-financed institutions, and private nonprofit institutions with considerable endowments, and exemption from property and income taxes? To me, the obvious answer is that commercial colleges are meeting a need not met by these other institutions. For-profits generally enroll lower income and older students who are disproportionately African American and from other minority backgrounds. They offer specialized programs with classes that often meet in the evening and at other convenient times. Such opportunities are usually less available at cheaper government-run colleges and nonprofit institutions.

In addition, for-profit institutions have taken the lead in providing online education that offers the greatest flexibility for working students. Students can take online courses in the evening, weekends, before they start working, or at other times that are convenient for them. Online courses do not allow direct interaction among students and faculty available in classrooms, but virtual classrooms provide opportunities to chat with other students no matter where they are located. In addition, they often provide direct and immediate access to faculty who answer questions and provide other information. No wonder that hundreds of online for-profit institutions continue to operate even after the crash several years ago of Internet-based companies. Some of these online institutions offer degrees, including advanced degrees, while most offer specialized training in particular areas, or refresher courses for out-of-date professionals.

Students at certified for-profit colleges have long been eligible for federal-backed loan programs, and are also eligible for most state programs that provide financial assistance, such as New York State's extensive tuition-assistance program. Since for-profits enroll relatively many students from poor backgrounds with modest earnings, it is no surprise that their students take a disproportionate share of federal-backed loans and state grants. For example, according to the *Times* article, they get 17 percent of the tuition assistance provided by New York while enrolling only 7 percent of the students.

The *Times* concentrates on a few examples of corrupt practices uncovered in New York State and elsewhere. In addition, it is well known that students who went to proprietary colleges have higher rates of default on federal-backed loans than students who went to state or nonprofit institutions. For-profit institutions have been accused of false advertising about their programs, very low standards for admission, and even changing student answers to make them eligible for state aid.

However, no one to my knowledge has conducted a good study that analyzes the frequency of misleading advertising, or deceptive and dishonest practices, at commercial institutions of higher education compared with state and private nonprofit institutions. Many of the private and public nonprofit colleges and universities are guilty of shoddy teaching, misleading claims in their handbooks and advertising about what students would learn at their institutions, taking students in Ph.D. programs where jobs are almost impossible to find upon graduation, and other false, misleading, or immoral practices. The late George Stigler, a Nobel Prize– winning economist, wrote a humorous essay entitled "A Sketch of the History of Truth in Teaching," reprinted in his collection of essays *The Intellectual and the Marketplace* (1962), in which he basically argues that if traditional universities were held to the same standard of truth as private companies, they would be subject to large and numerous lawsuits.

Some economists have argued that nonprofit organizations perform better from a social perspective than for-profit firms when customers have difficulty assessing various hidden qualities of the services provided. But that argument does not seem important in comparing performances of nonprofit and for-profit institutions of higher education. Students can usually quickly evaluate the type of teaching they receive, and they can also learn whether graduates of their institution get good jobs. Many students at commercial institutions may overestimate their abilities and the job market they would have upon graduation or finishing a program, but that is also likely with students who major at the most prestigious universities in subjects where few jobs are available, such as Icelandic literature or medieval European history.

Commercial colleges have grown rapidly in a highly competitive industry where other colleges are greatly subsidized. This suggests that they generally are filling a useful niche inadequately covered by traditional colleges and universities. Sure, lying and cheating by these institutions should be attacked by private and public lawsuits, but government moratoriums and other orchestrated attacks should not be the way nonprofits are allowed to fight off new and tough competitors.

FOR-PROFIT COLLEGES AND UNIVERSITIES—POSNER

I agree with what Becker has written on this important subject. I want to approach the subject from a slightly different angle, however, which is to consider why higher education in the United States is dominated by public and nonprofit-private institutions (abroad, almost all education is government operated) and what this implies about the reasons for the growth of the profit-making institutions.

A nonprofit enterprise is one that (1) enjoys an exemption from taxation and (2) operates under a nondistribution constraint—that is, any surplus of revenues over expenses cannot be distributed as profits to the firm's "owners." The points are related. To enjoy a charitable exemption from taxes, an institution must not only have a purpose deemed worthy (such as promoting education, health, religion, the arts, and so forth), but must also devote all its resources, including income on endowment, to its charitable purpose.

The nondistribution constraint is indeed constraining, because it means that the institution cannot raise money in the equity markets. It can compete with profit-making competitors only if it can attract investment from donors. Generally, this requires that it have many affluent alumni, as they are the principal donors to colleges and universities (partly out of gratitude, partly for the less altruistic reason that they derive prestige from having attended a distinguished institution and they want to help it maintain its distinction). There is a chicken and egg problem. To attract children of well-to-do families, and other children who have good earning prospects, the school has to offer an attractive program, good living and athletic facilities, and a distinguished faculty, but all those things cost money, which is hard for a nonprofit institution to raise unless it already has wealthy alumni. This may be why the very successful nonprofit colleges and universities tend to be quite old. They have had a long time to "grow" alumni who make generous contributions. Brandeis University, founded in the 1940s, is one of the few prominent private universities that is not very old—and it has had great trouble building up an endowment (though in part this is because of the elimination of Jewish quotas at other prominent universities—those quotas were one of the major factors in the decision to create Brandeis).

The result is a tendency for nonprofit colleges and universities to be quite expensive. Access to them by kids who are not well off and do not have good earnings prospects is further restricted by the practice of "legacy admissions," an important part of the fund-raising strategy of the classy nonprofit institutions.

Public colleges and universities take up much of the slack by subsidizing tuition; there are also federal and state loan programs for college tuition. But tuition expenses at public institutions have been rising, at the same time that these institutions have begun angling for more affluent students by becoming semiprivate—sometimes more than semi: for example, the University of Michigan, though state owned, now derives only about 10 percent of its revenue from the state.

The rise of the profit-making college and university, described in Becker's post, can therefore be interpreted as a response to the increasing scarcity of places in nonprofit and public colleges and universities for students who for whatever reason do not have good prospects as high earners, which would make them attractive to and able to afford the tuition charged by the nonprofit and public institutions. Not being able to rely on future alumni donations from such students, the capital required for their education must be raised from nonaltruists, i.e., profit-making investors; hence the increasing adoption of the for-profit form. Nonprofit institutions catering to the low end of the market have also emerged in recent years, but they may be at a competitive disadvantage vis-à-vis profit-making firms, as they may find it difficult to raise capital without an alumni base.

Is fraud and other malfeasance more likely in the new profit-making institutions? I think so, for two reasons. First, the consumers served by these institutions are less sophisticated than the consumers (the students and their families) of the educational services provided by the established institutions. Second, established institutions have more "reputation capital" at stake than a new enterprise; hence fraud or other misconduct is more costly to them and so they make greater efforts to prevent it. This has nothing to do with any differences in "greed" across different organizational forms, but merely with differences in the cost of engaging in misconduct, which is greater for the nonprofit and public institutions because of their clientele and reputation. But reputation capital is as important to established profit-making institutions, such as the University of Phoenix, as to nonprofit ones. However, the rapid growth in the number of profit-making colleges and universities means that a disproportionate number of these institutions are new and therefore not yet established, and that would suggest that fraud may indeed be on the increase, as the New York authorities believe.

Even so, that is no reason to shut down the profit-making educational sector, which may have discovered a demand for college education that the nonprofits had overlooked. Given the private as well as social return to higher education, the contribution of for-profit colleges and universities should not be disparaged.

17

RANKING HIGHER EDUCATION

March 4, 2007

THE ECONOMICS OF COLLEGE AND UNIVERSITY RANKINGS—POSNER

The choice of a college or a professional or graduate school to attend is of course an important one, and also a difficult one because of the great differences across colleges and universities in prestige, programs, facilities, faculty, amenities, location, and expense. Most of these differences translate into differences in the value of attendance at a particular school to the student. It is easy enough to determine whether the school has nice facilities and a charming location, but difficult to determine what contribution attending it will make to one's human capital, which is the principal product of education. As a result, education, including higher education, is what economists call a "credence" product, in the sense that its value cannot be determined by inspection or other reliable means before purchase, but must, in a broad sense, be taken on faith in the producer.

One might think that because most colleges and universities (for the sake of brevity, I'll generally use "college" to refer to any institution of higher education) are nonprofit institutions, they can be trusted to be candid in their marketing, but that notion is naive. Institutions of higher education are highly competitive, and if anything less scrupulous in their marketing than commercial sellers because they are less subject to legal sanctions for misleading advertising (it is harder to prove that one's college experience did not "work" than that the camera one bought didn't work) and because of the illusion of moral and intellectual superiority to which college faculty and administrators can easily succumb. Concern with reputation cannot be relied upon to keep colleges from making exaggerated claims of their "value added," because it is very difficult for the graduates to determine, even after a lifetime, how much of their human capital is due to their college experience. There is some market control, however. In particular, colleges that depend very heavily on alumni donations have stronger incentives than colleges that do not to avoid exaggerated claims that may cause disillusionment on the part of students after they graduate.

The combination of credence goods and unreliable sellers (in the sense of sellers not adequately deterred by legal or reputational concerns from engaging in misleading marketing efforts) produces a demand for third-party evaluations, on the model of *Consumer Reports.* In the case of higher education, the traditional evaluations provided by high school guidance counselors (and by college professors and college guidance counselors with respect to professional and graduate schools) has now been supplemented by the rankings published annually by *U.S. News & World Report* since 1983. These rankings are at once influential and (among academics and academic administrators) controversial.

The rankings raise several interesting economic questions: the effect of rankings on information costs, in general and with particular reference to higher education; the manipulability of rankings by the colleges themselves; the effect of the rankings on education; and why *U.S. News & World Report'* s annual rankings, though fiercely criticized by prominent universities (such as Stanford), face little competition. (There are, however, some competing ranking systems, particularly for business schools.)

There is a trade-off in communications between information content and what I'll call absorption cost. Ranking does very well on the latter score—a ranking conveys an evaluation with great economy to the recipient; it gives the recipient an evaluation of multiple alternatives (in this case, alternative schools) at a glance. But a ranking's information content often is small, because a ranking does not reveal the size of the value differences between the ranks. One reason that disclosing the ranks of students has lost favor at elite colleges is that meritocratic standards for admission from a large applicant pool tend to create a student body most of which is rather homogeneous with respect to quality. The quality difference between number 1 and number 2, or between the top 10 and the bottom 10, may be very great, but the quality difference between number 100 and number 200 may be small, at least relative to the appearance created by such a large rank-order difference.

The information content of college rankings, as in the case of *U.S. News & World Report'* s rankings, is particularly low because these are composite rankings. That is, different attributes are ranked, and the ranks then combined (often with weighting) to produce a final ranking. Ordinarily the weighting (even if every subordinate ranking is given the same weight) is arbitrary, which makes the final rank arbitrary. *U.S. News & World Report* ranks fifteen separate indicators of quality to create its composite ranking of colleges.

The rankings, moreover, are manipulable by the schools, depending on the attributes that are ranked. A common attribute is the ratio of applications to acceptances. Both components of the ratio are manipulable—the number of applications by injecting a random element into acceptances, so that students who do not meet the normal admission criteria nevertheless have a chance of admission, which may motivate them to apply; and the number of acceptances by rejecting high-quality applicants who seem almost certain to be admitted by (and to accept) a higher-ranking school.

The effect of college ranking on the education industry is unclear, but my guess is that it is negative. The principal information conferred, given the information limitations of ranking in general and composite ranking in particular, is simply the rank of the college. But that is important to students (and their parents). And rightly so. Given the high costs of actually evaluating colleges, employers and even the admissions committees of professional and graduate schools are likely to give weight to a school's rank, and this will give applicants an incentive to apply to the highest-ranking school that they have a chance of being admitted to (if they can afford it). The result will be to increase the school's rank, because SAT scores and other measures of the quality of admitted students are an important factor in a college's ranking. That increase in turn will attract still better applicants, which may result in a further boost in the school's rank. The result may be that a school will attract a quality of student, and attain a rank, that is disproportionate to the quality of its teaching program. As a result, the value added by the college experience may be smaller than if rank were based solely on the quality of the college's programs, and so the students are getting less for their money than they could elsewhere. However, this conclusion must be qualified in the following important respect: the clustering of the best students at a handful of highly ranked schools may, regardless of the quality of the schools' programs, contribute to the human capital formation of these students by exposing them to other smart kids and embedding them in a valuable social network of future leaders. This may be a significant social as well as private benefit.

A final question is why, given the imperfection of *U.S. News & World Report'* s college ranking system, yet the boost that publishing its rankings has given the magazine's circulation, no significant competitor has appeared on the scene, at least for the magazine's college and law school rankings (the latter are particularly influential). I conjecture that the market for other commercial ranking systems for colleges would be weak, because the publisher of a new system could not make a convincing case that the new system was better than the established one. It could not do that because the quality of a ranking system is even more difficult to evaluate than the quality of the education provided by a given college. College applicants and their parents would thus have little incentive to consult the second system.

SOME ECONOMICS OF RANKINGS—BECKER

Rankings of educational programs, hospitals, physicians, cars, and other goods and services have become increasingly popular during the past twenty years. There is a robust market for various rankings because of the difficulty students, patients, and other consumers have in getting sufficient information about the numerous attributes being offered, such as quality of other students and faculty, size of classes, earnings of graduates, or mortality rates of hospital patients. I believe that on the whole rankings convey useful information about quality, although there are obvious problems in getting reliable rankings.

Perhaps the most serious problem with rankings is that institutions "game the measure." So if the ratio of admissions to acceptances were used, then as Posner indicates, schools might tend to admit applicants who do not have good alternatives. If hospitals are ranked partly by the death rate among patients, then hospitals have an incentive to shy away from admitting terminally ill patients, or those with difficult-to-cure conditions. Yet schools and other organizations respond to their ranking position not only by gaming the measure, but also by improving what they provide. In this way, some business schools and colleges ranked low in the amenities and other characteristics of the learning experience provided students have responded by improving physical facilities and the guidance offered to students, reducing class size, and increasing networking. The issue in determining whether measures have on balance positive or negative value to consumers is whether the good information provided exceeds the misleading information, due in part to "gaming."

The difficulty for consumers is that not only do colleges, business schools, and hospitals provide credence products, but also that there is little or no repeat business since students do not go to the same college more than once, and few patients have multiple spells in the same hospital. Still, applicants to colleges (and/or their parents), and sick persons choosing hospitals tend to recognize that institutions have an incentive to game the measure. That weakens the quantity of information they believe they get from rankings based on particular measures, but it does not generally make the information worthless.

Any conclusion that rankings make the information available to consumers worse does not do justice either to the difficulty of making sensible decisions about education programs and medical help in the absence of ranking information, nor to the competitive search for different criteria to use in rankings of schools and medical care. A more accurate conclusion would be that the great interest in rankings, and the rapid expansion in the number of magazines, newspapers, and nonprofit groups that provide rankings of schools, hospitals, doctors, and other goods and services suggests strongly that consumers believe they do get useful information from rankings. How much information they get varies with their access to other information.

Those profit and nonprofit organizations that provide rankings compete by emphasizing different criteria. For example, the several newspapers and magazines that rank MBA programs weight differently evaluations of business recruiters, earnings of graduates, the increase in earnings of graduates compared to what they earned before enrolling, the amenities provided, the research of faculty, the attention to globalization issues, and so on. That rankers compete by using different criteria and weightings strongly suggests that significant numbers of applicants to schools consider how rankings are determined.

To be sure, there are ways to improve the basis of rankings that make them less vulnerable to gaming by the institutions being ranked. See the discussion of hospital rankings in Mark McClellan and Douglas Staiger, "Comparing the Quality of Health Care Providers," 3 *Forum for Health Economics and Policy,* Article 6 (2000), and other papers by these authors, for example, McClellan and Staiger, "Comparing Hospital Quality at For-Profit and Not-for-Profit Hospitals," in *The Changing Hospital Industry* 93 (David Cutler ed. 2000). For example, MBA programs can be compared not by earnings of graduates, but by the increase in earnings of graduates compared to what they earned before entering an MBA program. This shift in the earnings measure would help control for the quality of students in a program (the *Financial Times'* rankings of MBA programs are based partly on this measure of value added). To help determine what benefits students actually get from an MBA program or college, one should not only interview current students, but also those who graduated three, five, or ten years ago. After several years of working or additional study, the effects of attempts to influence student evaluations through superficial amenities should have been replaced by a consideration of longer-term benefits.

The obvious interest in rankings by consumers suggests that they consider the rankings of schools and programs, or health care, or automobiles to be valuable. These rankings can be, and are being improved, but that they have survived the test of the marketplace indicates that consumers believe they are useful enough to be willing to pay for them.

AFTERTHOUGHTS TO PART III

POSNER AFTERTHOUGHTS

The primary focus of the blog posts in this part of the book is higher education, and developments since those posts can be summed up in one word: commercialization. For good or for bad, colleges and universities are behaving more and more like business firms. They are more competitive, and therefore more focused on minimizing costs and maximizing revenues. As I said in a later post (October 7, 2007):

> The leading universities are becoming giant corporations with multi-hundred-million dollar (or even billion dollar) budgets. As they grow, they need, and so they hire, professional management. Professional university management, in turn, takes its cues from its peers in the business sector. So we have universities deeply involved in hedge funds, greedy for supra-competitive investment returns, engaged in the commercialization of scientific research, angling for applications for admission by the children of the rich, manipulating their statistics in order to move up in *U.S. News & World Report'* s college rankings (for example, by fuzzing up their admissions criteria, so that they get more applicants and therefore turn down more

and so appear more selective), exaggerating the job prospects of their advanced-degree graduates, bidding for academic stars by offering high salaries and low teaching loads, and, related to the bidding wars, creating a two-tier employment system with tenured and tenure-track faculty on top and tenure-less, benefit-less graduate students and temporaries on the bottom to do the bulk of the teaching.

A sign of the times is the recent decision by the Harvard and Stanford law schools to move toward a system of pass-fail grading, rather than letter or number grades. This is a blow to employers; as a judge who has been hiring law clerks for the last twenty-seven years, I can attest that letter grades, or, preferably, number grades, provide valuable information to a prospective employer. But grading is (somewhat mysteriously) disfavored by students at elite law schools. Yale Law School gets the best students on average, and it is believed that the fact that Yale has (essentially) pass-fail grading is a significant factor in student preference. The fact that other leading law schools are following suit illustrates the transformation of students from educational subjects to customers because of high tuition and the dependence of universities on alumni donations—and in a commercial system, the customer is always right.

A number of comments on my plagiarism post suggested that I am "soft" on plagiarism, especially when it is committed by professors and other "grown-up" writers, as distinct from students. I adhere to my heretical view that student plagiarism is a more serious offense. The student who plagiarizes not only advances his career at the expense of his honest fellow students; he doesn't learn anything from plagiarizing, whereas a professor who "steals" ideas or even phrases and incorporates them into his own work not only produces a better product, to the benefit of his readership, but may well improve his own skills. Of course the author should acknowledge the copying; it is the failure to do so that is the wrong; my point is only that the plagiarizing work may gain extra value by virtue of the plagiarism. Because faculty copying is more likely to be detected (the copy will be contained in a published work) and because exposure of a professor or other professional writer as a plagiarist is in itself a powerful shame sanction, and because as several comments point out, computer search engines make detection of plagiarism ever easier, I continue to believe that the sanction of expulsion should probably be reserved for students.

My views on plagiarism are set forth in greater length in my short book *The Little Book of Plagiarism* (2007).

IV

INCENTIVES

18

FAT TAX

October 8, 2006

TAXING FAT—BECKER

There is growing concern in rich countries, especially in the United States, about the increase in consumption of fats and sugar, and the related increase in obesity. These trends are particularly noticeable among teenagers and even younger children, who consume large quantities of fast foods and soft drinks. Some localities, like New York City, and countries like Denmark, have proposed to either phase out or restrict sharply the use of trans fats in french fries, margarine, and other foods. The concern goes far beyond trans fats, however, and includes proposals to restrict the sale of foods high in saturated fats, such as Big Macs.

One proposal receiving some attention is to impose a tax on foods that contain high quantities of saturated fat in the hope of cutting down consumption of these foods. The basic law of demand states that a tax on saturated fat would raise the price of fatty foods, and thereby would reduce their consumption. A good analogy is with other "sin" taxes, such as the very heavy tax in most countries on cigarettes, or the large tax in many countries on alcoholic beverages. These taxes have greatly raised the price of these goods and reduced their consumption. For example, it is estimated that every 10 percent increase in the retail price of cigarettes due to higher taxes cuts smoking by about 4 percent after the first year, and by a considerable 7 percent after a few years. Responses are greater in the longer run because more people decide over time not to start smoking (or drinking), and many of those who were smoking (or drinking) eventually manage to quit or cut down the amounts used.

I do not know of any estimates of the responsiveness of the consumption of bad fats to higher fat prices, but I am confident it would be reasonably large, particularly for teenagers and lower income families who have the highest rates of obesity, and are more sensitive to these prices. I also believe it would be possible to define a fat tax that would effectively target foods that are high in saturated fat content. Yet I would like to express some doubts about whether that would be good public policy.

First of all, public policy should not ignore the pleasure consumers get from cheeseburgers, french fries, and other high-fat foods, or for that matter from soft drinks, smoking, alcoholic drinks, and other such "sins." Good policies require that these pleasures are more than offset by strong negative public consequences.

Although the growing obesity of teenagers and of adults too during the past twenty-five years may be partly related to the greater consumption of fats, a stronger factor seems to be the increased time spent at sedentary activities, and a corresponding reduced time spent exercising and at other active calorie-burning activities. These sedentary activities include watching television, surfing the Internet, playing computer games, communicating on chat rooms and through instant messaging, and listening to music on iPods and other devices. For a careful analysis of the growth in weight of teenagers that concludes that increased sedentary activities is the main culprit, see the 2006 Ph.D. thesis by Fernando Wilson in the Economics Department of the University of Chicago.

The reduced exercise rate of teenagers is not mainly because they are too fat to have the energy to be active, but rather due to technological developments, such as the Internet, computer games, iPods, television, and the like. Put differently, lack of exercise has caused obesity (to a large extent) rather than that obesity has caused reduced exercise. I doubt if there would be much of a call for taxes on computer games, or iPods, or use of the Internet in order to reduce obesity. Dr. Michael Roizen has pointed out, however, that certain types of computer games do require manual dexterity and other exercise.

Suppose, however, that increased fat consumption is the major cause of the gain in weight. Is this enough reason to justify active public interventions? I raise this question not only because of the pleasure received from eating foods with saturated fats, but also because doubts have been raised about the connection between excess weight and medical problems like cardiovascular diseases, diabetes, cancers, and other serious diseases. Of course, no one denies that extreme overweight is dangerous to health, such as a body-mass index (BMI) of over 45. This would mean that a male of average height weighs over three hundred pounds, and less than 1 percent of the American male population is that heavy relative to their height. And often an important distinction is drawn between overall weight and how much is concentrated in the belly, the later being much more hazardous to health.

A possibly more important consideration than the connection between fat consumption and weight may be that the consumption of fats crowds out diets richer in fruits and vegetables. Diets heavy on fruits and vegetables appear to reduce the incidence of various serious diseases, such as colon cancer and heart attacks. If such diets were to be encouraged, a more direct and powerful approach than taxing fat consumption would be to subsidize fruits and vegetables. Yet teenagers, the group that elicits greatest concern, are likely to have weak responses to lower prices of fruits, and of vegetables like broccoli.

Even if excess weight and bad diets are very unhealthy in light of present medical knowledge, is it irrational for teenagers and other young persons to ignore the recommendations of nutritionists and medical associations, and to consume diets heavy in fats and gain weight? Not necessarily if young persons recognize the trade-off between present pleasures and future harms. Of course, some teenagers may not be aware of this tradeoff. An additional and highly important consideration that is almost never mentioned is that the next twenty to thirty years will probably bring at least as much improvement in medical knowledge and new drugs as the past several decades did. We now have drugs that greatly reduce the potential health hazards of high (bad) cholesterol, drugs to lower blood pressure greatly, drugs to reduce the consequences of mental depression, and many other important drugs that were unavailable a few decades ago.

The not so distant future will very likely see big advances in fighting various cancers, colon and lung cancer included, in preventing or better controlling adverse effects of diabetes, in preventing or slowing Alzheimer's disease, and in reducing still further the risks of strokes and heart attacks. The many teenagers who are unaware of these medical trends, and are inactive, gain weight, eat few veggies, and consume much fat will still benefit from these medical advances during the next several decades.

Yet suppose medical progress slowed down, and that heavy saturated fat consumption significantly would raise the probability of contracting a major disease in the future. Are public policy interventions then justified? A common affirmative answer relies on the fact that overweight people who get serious diseases use health resources that are partly financed by taxpayers. This argument has some merit because of heavy taxpayer involvement in health spending.

But the major flaw is in the health payment system that would be largely corrected by providing stronger incentives to economize on health spending through encouraging health saving accounts and requiring compulsory private catastrophic health insurance. These important changes in the health delivery system would give individuals much greater incentive then they have at present, partly due to greater insurance company pressure, to reduce their health spending by getting into better shape, eating better diets, and in other ways. To be sure, if the health delivery system were not greatly improved, the health spending "externality" from consuming fat would become more relevant.

I believe that aside from this externality argument about the use of taxpayers' monies, there is little reason for governments to intervene in eating decisions, with some important exceptions. The main ones might include policies to give greater publicity to the health advantages of better diets, and policies that kept unhealthy foods and possibly soft drinks out of school cafeterias and school vending machines. Perhaps a "say no" campaign against saturated fats would work, but I am dubious about its effectiveness.

Sometimes I wonder whether much of the public outcry over the gain in weight of teenagers and adults stems mainly from the revulsion that many educated people experience when seeing very fat people. Surely, though, this should hardly be the ground for interventionist policies!

THE FAT TAX—POSNER'S COMMENT

I share much of Becker's skepticism about a "fat tax" (see my article with Tomas J. Philipson, "The Long-Run Growth in Obesity as a Function of Technological Change," *Perspectives in Biology and Medicine,* Summer 2003 Supplement, p. S87), though I would look favorably on a tax on soft drinks; I would even consider a ban on the sale of soft drinks to children, as I explain later.

The case for a fat tax, as an economist would be inclined to view it, is that a high-calorie diet contributes to obesity, which contributes to bad health, which imposes costs that are borne in part by thin people (thin taxpayers, in particular). I do think, despite skepticism in some circles, that obesity, even mild obesity, has negative health consequences, including diabetes, high blood pressure, joint problems, and certain cancers, and that much of the cost of medical treatment is externalized. But as Philipson and I emphasized in our article and Becker emphasizes too, lack of exercise is also an important factor in obesity. Moreover, the significance of an externality lies in its effect on behavior, and I am dubious that people would consume fewer calories if they had to pay all their own medical costs rather than being able to unload many of those costs on Medicaid, Medicare, or the healthy members of private insurance pools.

Indeed, if as I believe obesity is positively correlated with poverty, reducing transfer payments to people of limited income might result in more obesity. Indeed, high-caloric "junk food" might conceivably though improbably turn out to be the first real-world example of a "Giffen good," a good the demand for which rises when the price rises because the income effect dominates the substitution effect. A heavy tax on high-caloric food might so reduce the disposable income of the poor that they substituted such food for healthful food, since fatty foods tend to be very cheap and satisfying, and often nutritious as well. However, this is unlikely because food constitutes only a small percentage (no more than 20 percent) of even a poor family's budget.

A fat tax would not only be regressive; to the extent it induced the substitution of more healthful foods (as opposed to the Giffen effect), it would as Becker notes reduce the utility (pleasure) of the people who love junk food. This assumes that the junk-food lovers are rational and reasonably well informed, so that they trade off the pleasure gains of eating such food against the health costs. Here I begin to have doubts. I don't think the fact that obesity is correlated with poverty is due entirely to the fact that fatty foods tend to be cheap as well as tasty and satisfying. I suspect that many of the people who become obese as a result of what they eat do not understand how, for example, something as innocuous as a soft drink can produce obesity. I also suspect that producers of soft drinks and other fatty foods are ingenious in setting biological traps—designing foods that trigger intense pleasure reactions caused by brain structures formed in our ancestral environment (the prehistoric environment in which human beings attained approximately their current biological structure), when a taste for fatty foods had significant survival value. (The producers of soft drinks and other junk food also place vending machines in schools, when permitted.) I am doubtful, however, that much can be done about this problem. I do not think, for example, that a campaign of public education would be effective, because it could be neutralized by industry advertising (which, however, would have the indirect effect of a tax—it would increase the food producers' marginal costs) and because the people who most need the education are probably the least able to absorb it.

However, the consumption by children of soft drinks that contain sugar presents a distinct and perhaps soluble social problem. Soft drinks have virtually no nutritional content (unlike foods rich in cream or butter), and recent studies indicate that they are a significant factor in obesity, as well as a source of caffeine dependence and dental problems. They also have good substitutes in the form of drinks sweetened artificially rather than by sugar. And while generally parents know better than government what is good for their children, many parents who permit their children to drink soft drinks do not. Banning the sale of soft drinks to children could not have a Giffen effect and would not be much more costly to enforce than the ban on the sale of cigarettes to children, and might well be a justifiable policy measure.

Now any measure for improving public health has the following limitation: if people are healthier and live longer, this does not necessarily reduce their lifetime expenditures on health care. Most of those expenditures are incurred in the last six months of life, and no matter how long people live, they will eventually enter that terminal phase. However, the longer their healthier lives, the lower their average lifetime health-care expenditures and the greater their productivity, as well as the greater their utility since poor health reduces utility. (Besides its health effects, obesity reduces physical comfort and attractiveness.) I would therefore expect a ban on sale of soft drinks to children to yield a modest net increase in social welfare.

19

TRANS FATS BAN

December 17, 2006

THE NEW YORK CITY BAN ON TRANS FATS—POSNER

New York City's Board of Health has decided to ban trans fats in food sold in restaurants (also in food sold by catering and meal services), the ban to become fully effective in mid-2008. The ban raises a fundamental issue of economic policy.

Trans fats are largely synthetic fats widely used in fried foods and baked goods. There is substantial medical evidence that they are significant contributors to heart disease (perhaps increasing the incidence of heart disease by as much as 6 percent) because they both raise the cholesterol that is bad for you (LDL) and lower the cholesterol that helps to protect your arteries against the effects of the bad cholesterol (HDL). About half of New York City's twenty thousand restaurants use trans fats in their cooking; and roughly a third of the caloric intake of New Yorkers comes from restaurant meals.

A strict Chicago School economic analysis of the ban would deem it inefficient. The restaurant industry in New York is highly competitive, and so if consumers are willing to pay a higher price for meals that do not contain trans fats, the industry will oblige them; to force them to shell out more money, rather than leaving it to their decision, is thus paternalistic, indeed gratuitous. Restaurants catering to health-conscious eaters will advertise that they do not use any trans fats in their meal preparations, or will state on the menu the amount of trans fats in each item. Other restaurants will cater to diners who prefer a cheaper meal to a healthier one. The ban thus forces people who want to eat in restaurants to pay higher prices even if they would prefer to pay less and take the risk of an increased likelihood of heart disease. Some of these would be people who eat in restaurants rarely, and avoid trans fats when they cook at home, so that the health risk to them of a restaurant meal containing trans fats is small. Others would be people who disbelieve the medical opinion—and such opinion often is wrong—or think that trans fats improve the taste of food or that the ban is the result of political pressure from producers of substitutes for trans fats, such as corn oil, or from the restaurants that have voluntarily abandoned the use of trans fats and don't want to be put at a competitive disadvantage by restaurants that have lower costs because they do use trans fats. Moreover, the enforcement of the ban will increase the costs of New York City government, resulting in higher taxes on an already heavily taxed population. Since half the restaurants in New York City continue to use trans fats, this shows that a majority of consumers would not support the ban.

What is missing in this analysis is a cost that, ironically, a great Chicago economist, George Stigler, did more than any other economist to make a part of mainstream economic analysis: the cost of information. It might seem, however, that the cost of informing consumers about trans fats would be trivial—a restaurant would tell its customers whether or not it used trans fats, if that is what they're interested in, and if it lied it would invite class action suits for fraud. But there is a crucial difference between the cost of disseminating information and the cost of absorbing it. If gasoline stations in the same neighborhood charge slightly different prices for the same grade of gasoline, the reason may be that the price difference is smaller than the time (and gasoline!) cost to the consumer of driving to the different stations to see which has the lowest price. But if the consumer did bother to conduct that search, he would have no difficulty in understanding the information that he obtained. It is different with trans fats. Many people have never heard of them; many who have don't know that they are (very probably) harmful to health; and, above all, almost no one outside the medical and nutrition communities knows how harmful trans fats are, and in what quantity. That is, they do not know what a dangerous level of trans fats is, what their own consumption of trans fats is relative to that level, and how much their restaurant-going increases the total amount of trans fats that they consume. They have, in short, no idea of the benefit of avoiding trans fats in restaurants. And except for a few hypochondriacs and people who already have heart disease, no one wants his restaurant experience poisoned by having to read a menu that lists beside each item the number of grams of trans fats it contains and indicates (perhaps with a skull and crossbones) the danger created by consuming the item. Actually the danger would be impossible to explain to diners, because it would depend on the diner's average daily consumption of trans fats, which neither the diner nor the restaurant knows.

In such a situation, even those of us who distrust government regulation of the economy should be open to the possibility that the ban on trans fats would produce a net improvement in the welfare of New Yorkers by satisfying a preference that most of them would have if the cost of absorbing information about the good in question were not prohibitive.

A very crude cost-benefit analysis suggests that this possibility is real. Proponents of the ban estimate that it will reduce the annual number of heart attack deaths in New York City by five hundred. That can be taken as an upper-bound estimate. It seems high to me, as the total annual number of deaths from heart disease in New York City is only twenty-five thousand, and it seems unlikely that removing trans fats from restaurant meals alone would cause a 2 percent drop in the heart disease death rate. If that five hundred figure holds up, then if one uses the consensus economic estimate of the value of an American life (an estimate based on behavior toward risk, behavior that reveals the cost that the average American is willing to pay to reduce the risk of death), which is $7 million, a saving of five hundred lives confers a benefit of $3.5 billion. (This figure is too high, but I will adjust it later.) On the cost side, although the restaurant industry is up in arms about the ban, and although the ban's proponents cannot be correct that the industry would incur no cost at all to substitute other fats for trans fats—for if there were no cost, the substitution would have been made years ago, when trans fats began to be implicated in heart disease—I have not seen evidence that the cost would be great. Remember that half the restaurants in New York City have already phased out trans fats, without anyone noticing a big jump in restaurant prices. And the manufacturing cost of the substitutes for trans fats does not appear to be higher—the only advantage of trans fats is that they increase the shelf life of foods somewhat. This is important to restaurants, by enabling them to economize on spoilage costs, but surely not critical.

The New York City restaurant industry has annual sales of $9.5 billion. I do not know what percentage of those sales is accounted for by the restaurants that have already phased out trans fats, so let me assume, conservatively, that the restaurants that have not done so account for $6 billion of the $9.5 billion. Suppose the ban would increase their costs by 1 percent—which seems too high, however, since the major costs of a restaurant are wages, which would be unaffected, and the cost of food, which would be affected only slightly (the shorter the shelf life, the more food must be bought relative to the amount that can be sold). Apparently the substitutes for trans fats do not affect the taste of food.

One percent of $6 billion is $60 million. My $3.5 billion benefit figure is obviously much greater than my $60 million cost figure, and probably it is too great. Many of the five hundred deaths may be of people who have advanced heart disease and thus a truncated life expectancy and impaired value of life, quite apart from trans fats. Most of the deaths are of elderly people (only about 12 percent of deaths from heart disease in New York City are of people below the age of 65), whose value of life may be below average, though most elderly people cling pretty tenaciously to life, consistent with studies that find that elderly people are on average actually happier than young people. I suspect too that the figure of five hundred deaths due to trans fats in restaurant food is too high. But suppose I slash it to one hundred, and assume that the average value of life in this group is only $1 million; this still yields a benefit figure, $100 million, that comfortably exceeds the cost figure, comfortably enough to cover the cost of enforcing the ban. Moreover, the benefit figure excludes the benefit to people who have heart disease but do not die of it (or have not yet died of it). Heart disease causes suffering even when it does not kill the sufferer.

I have also excluded from the benefit figure any external benefit, that is, a benefit to people who do not have heart disease (or perhaps never eat in restaurants), but subsidize the medical expenses of those who do, through Medicare, Medicaid, and risk pooling by private insurance companies. I exclude it because I'm not sure it's a net external benefit. Even a total elimination of heart disease might not significantly reduce aggregate expenditures on health care, because it would result in an increase in illness and death caused by other diseases, such as cancer. (Diseases in effect compete with each other; if a person is saved from one disease, this increases the "market" for another disease.) It would also increase the average age of the population, which might result in greater transfer payments and hence heavier taxes.

My cost-benefit analysis is, necessarily, highly tentative. However, it inclines me to a sympathetic view of the trans fats ban. I anticipate strong opposition from libertarians.

COMMENT ON THE NEW YORK BAN ON TRANS FATS—BECKER

Posner gives an excellent analysis of the possible risks from consuming too much trans fats, but I believe he reaches the wrong conclusion about whether the New York ban of trans fats in restaurants is warranted. In my view this ban is a further example of the tendency for local and federal government in the United States and other countries to act as nanny states. They presume with insufficient evidence that consumers are typically too ignorant to make decisions in their own interests, particularly regarding health, but in other areas as well.

Posner provides a well-presented case for what he calls the "Chicago" argument for why such an ordinance as New York's is unnecessary and undesirable. Perhaps it is no surprise to many readers that I find his argument unconvincing. He rejects these arguments because of his belief about consumer ignorance of trans fats. Posner does not mainly argue that restaurant-goers do not know which restaurants use trans fats, or even that they may be bad for you, or that restaurants possess private information not known to consumers about the adverse effects of trans fats.

His main concern is what he considers to be the great difficulty consumers have in "absorbing" information about trans fats. Posner gives a few reasons why he believes absorbing trans fat information is particularly difficult: that there is still considerable ignorance about the health risks of trans fats, that consumers do not know their total intake of these fats, and that consumers are unaware that alternatives are often claimed to be more or less equally tasty. In short, according to Posner, consumers do not absorb the alleged fact that the benefits of avoiding or cutting down trans fats far exceed their costs.

As far as I can judge, the evidence is rather strong that trans fats contribute to heart disease, but the degree of harm from different levels of these fats is still to be determined. The best summary of the scientific evidence that I know of is Darius Mozaffarian et al., "Trans Fatty Acids and Cardiovascular Disease," 354 *New England Journal of Medicine* 1601 (2006). The authors carefully review many studies, including several with quite small random samples. The estimated mean effects of common levels of trans fats on cardiovascular disease are typically large, but one of the best data sets that they analyze cannot reject (at the 95 percent confidence interval) the conclusion that there is either no effect of trans fats on this disease, or only a small one. So I have only modest confidence from the studies analyzed that typical trans fats consumption levels have large effects on cardiovascular disease.

To be sure, evidence cannot disprove Posner's claim about consumer ignorance of, and inability to process, information about trans fats. However, the fact that about half of all New York City restaurants did not use trans fats even prior to passing this ordinance—although these may be the restaurants where it was easier to eliminate trans fats—that many foods sold in ordinary supermarkets and other groceries have become trans fat free in a short period, that we do not know much about whether consumers who eat high–trans fat foods in restaurants eat little of these fats at home, that young persons are the primary consumers of heavy trans fat diets, and other unknown and relevant variables should make us skeptical of the ignorance argument. Indeed, it is remarkable how fast the food industry and restaurants have responded to the greater evidence during the past few years that trans fats in sufficient quantities contribute to heart disease. The article I cited earlier appeared only about eight months ago.

There is evidence in other areas that consumers respond quickly to health news. For example, studies have documented the rapid reduction in salt intake and growth of low-salt foods in response to evidence in the 1980s—now considered exaggerated—that high salt levels have been an important source of high blood pressure.

The prominence of young persons among the big consumers of trans fats, cholesterol, and calories in foods like french fries and Big Macs may not be due to ignorance. Rather, they may have an unarticulated awareness that when they reach older ages where heart disease and other diseases are more common, drugs are likely to have been developed that offset the negative consequences of what appears now to be unhealthy diets. Lipitor and similar drugs have greatly reduced the consequences of high levels of "bad" cholesterol, and drug companies believe they will pretty soon have drugs that will raise levels of "good" cholesterol. So even if prolonged consumption of trans fats has sizable negative health consequences in today's knowledge environment, that is likely to change many years down the road when today's youth are at risk for heart disease. Taxpayers may pay for a good share of their future expenditure on such drugs, but that is a wholly different and more complicated issue.

On Posner's assumptions, one might expect either that restaurants would be pressured to eliminate trans fats, or that eliminating trans fats would cause consumers to be worse off. Posner's first order estimate of the benefits from eliminating trans fats in New York City restaurants is $3.5 billion, and he takes $60 million as a generous estimate of the cost to restaurants from becoming trans fat free. Then the cost of trans fat consumption would exceed the expected benefits from lower prices in restaurants with trans fats, even for quite but not completely ignorant consumers who attach no more than a 2 percent chance to the likelihood that these fats have serious consequences for their health (0.02×$6.5 billion exceeds $100 million). These largely ignorant consumers too would only go to restaurants that are trans fat free; hence other restaurants would have to adjust or go out of business.

Posner also gives a kind of lower bound estimate of the benefits as $100 million, and also suggests a much lower cost to restaurants of becoming trans fat free—I take this as $30 million. With a small taste benefit from the use of trans fats—the *New England*

Medicine Journal article I cited earlier does admit positive effect of trans fats on "palatability"—the total cost of the ban would equal or exceed total benefits. For example, suppose 1 million persons on average eat two hundred meals per year in New York City restaurants with trans fats. If they value the taste of trans fats in their foods only by thirty-five cents per meal, the taste cost to consumers of the ban would be $70 million per year. Then the total cost of the ban would equal the benefits from the ban.

Does one really want to go down the road of a ban on trans fats when the net gains to consumers are dubious, and probably negative, and when reversing directions is politically difficult? As an example of the difficulty in adapting politically, new evidence indicates that requiring child car seats may increase their risk of injury in accidents, yet there is no movement to reverse these laws.

These and related calculations suggest that while city and other governments should continue to help provide the best information available about the effects of trans fats and other foods on health, market forces of supply and demand should determine the fats consumed. Otherwise, we encourage further attempts to legislate fat and calorie content of permissible foods not only in restaurants but also in foods consumed at home, and absurdities such as the new Italian ordinance that models cannot be too slim because it sets a bad weight example for young women. There are just too many opportunities for ill-considered attempts to override on limited evidence individual judgments about what they want to consume.

20

LIBERTARIAN PATERNALISM

January 14, 2007

A CRITIQUE—BECKER

Libertarians believe that individuals should be allowed to pursue their own interests, unless their behavior impacts the interests of others, especially if it negatively impacts others. So individuals should be allowed, according to this view, to buy the food they want, whereas drunk drivers should be constrained because they harm others, and chemical producers should be prevented from polluting as much as they would choose because their pollution hurts children and adults.

Modern research argues that sometimes individuals may not have enough information to effectively pursue their interests. In these cases, it may be suggested that government regulations and rules help guide individuals to the better pursuit of interests they would have if they had additional information. A few weeks ago Posner and I debated the role of information in interpreting New York City's recently enacted ban on the use of trans fats in restaurants.

A libertarian paternalist is happy to accept information arguments for government regulation of behavior, but typically stresses other considerations. One of the best statements of this view argues that "Equipped with an understanding of behavioral findings of bounded rationality and bounded self-control, libertarian paternalists should attempt to steer people's choices in welfare-promoting directions without eliminating freedom of choice. It is also possible to show how a libertarian paternalist might select among the possible options and to assess how much choice to offer." Cass Sunstein and Richard Thaler, "Libertarian Paternalism Is Not an Oxymoron," 70 *University of Chicago Law Review* 1 (2003); for a strong response, see Daniel Klein, "Statist Quo Bias," 1 *Econ Journal Watch* 260 (2004).

If not literally an oxymoron, the term "libertarian paternalism" is, I believe, awfully close to it. Before trying to show why, let me illustrate what this expression might reasonably mean—Sunstein and Thaler give some innocuous examples like the placement of desserts in cafeterias that raise no significant issues. Suppose a person smokes, but has an internal conflict between his stronger "self" who wants to quit, and his weaker "self" who continues to smoke whenever he feels under pressure, or in social situations. In effect, the weaker self does not stop smoking because he has limited self-control.

The goal of paternalism in this case is to help the more dispassionate self obtain greater control over the choices made by the conflicted individual because of his dual selves. Such paternalism may take the form of high cigarette taxes, so that even weaker selves would not want to smoke so much, or of ordinances to limit smoking in restaurants, bars, and other social situations to prevent weak selves from being tempted to smoke. The argument is that individuals would be "happier" if they were given a helping hand to exercise self-control. One study even claims to find that smokers are happier in states of the United States that heavily tax cigarettes than in seemingly comparable states that tax cigarettes more lightly because higher taxes help control the urge to smoke. If this evidence were valid, groups of smokers should lobby for higher cigarette taxes, yet to my knowledge there is not a single instance where this has happened. Indeed, if anything, they lobby for lower taxes, but perhaps one can claim—most anything goes in such a world—that they do not even know they have this conflict among their different selves!

Classical arguments for libertarianism do not assume that adults never make mistakes, always know their interests, or even are able always to act on their interests when they know them. Rather, it assumes that adults very typically know their own interests better than government officials, professors, or anyone else—I will come back to this. In addition, the classical libertarian case partly rests on a presumption that being able to make mistakes through having the right to make one's own choices leads in the long run to more self-reliant, competent, and independent individuals. It has been observed, for example, that prisoners often lose the ability to make choices for themselves after spending many years in prison where life is rigidly regulated.

In effect, the libertarian claim is that the "process" of making choices leads to individuals who are more capable of making good choices. Strangely perhaps, libertarian paternalists emphasize process when claiming conflict among multiple selves within a person, but ignore the classical emphasis on decision-making process that helps individuals make better choices.

Two other serious limitations of the libertarian paternalist approach further weaken its appeal. First, it is virtually impossible to distinguish such paternalism from plain unadulterated paternalism. How does one decide with objective criteria where "bounded rationality and bounded self-control" are important, and areas of choice where they are not? For example, models of rational addiction appear to do as well if not better than models of bounded self-control when applied empirically to smoking behavior. Why adopt models of bounded self-control in this case?

Or to take another illustration, is the weight gain of teenagers and adults since 1980 in much of the developed world, particularly the United States, due to bounds on rationality and control? If so, why did it not happen earlier, or why is the gain in weight so much greater in the United States than in most other countries? Are Americans less able than say the Japanese or Germans to exercise self-control? Often libertarian paternalism simply involves substituting an intellectual's or bureaucrat's or politician's beliefs about should be done with other peoples' time and money for the judgment of those choosing what to do with their own incomes and time. It is in good part because libertarians recognize the temptation in all of us to control choices made by others that they end up in favor of allowing people to make their own choices, absent clear negative (or positive) effects on others.

A serious problem arises if libertarian paternalism is not just considered an intellectual exercise, but is supposed to be implemented in policies that control choices, such as how many calories people are allowed to consume, whether adults are allowed to use marijuana or smoke, or how much they can save. Even best-intentioned government officials should be considered subject to the same bounds on rationality, limits on self-control, myopia in looking forward, and the other cognitive defects that are supposed to affect choices by us ordinary individuals. Can one have the slightest degree of confidence that these officials will promote the interests of individuals better than these individuals do themselves?

This is why classical libertarianism relies not on the assumption that individuals always make the right decisions, but rather that in the vast majority of situations they do better for themselves than government officials could do for them. One does not have to be a classical libertarian—I differ on some issues from their position—to recognize that the case for classical libertarianism is not weakened by the literature motivating libertarian paternalism. Indeed, when similar considerations are applied to government officials and intellectuals as well as to the rest of us, the case for classical libertarianism may even be strengthened!

LIBERTARIAN PATERNALISM—POSNER

The term is indeed an oxymoron. Libertarianism, as expounded in John Stuart Mill's *On Liberty,* is the doctrine that government should confine its interventions in the private sector to what Mill called "other-regarding" acts, which is to say acts that cause harm to nonconsenting strangers, as distinct from "self-regarding" acts, which are acts that harm only oneself or people with whom one has consensual relations authorizing acts that may result in harm. So, for example, if you are hurt in a boxing match, that is a "self-regarding" event with which the government has no proper business, provided the boxer who hurt you was in compliance with rules—to which you had consented—governing the match, and provided you were of sound mind and so could give meaningful consent.

Paternalism is the opposite. It is the idea that someone else knows better than you do what is good for you, and therefore he should be free to interfere with your self-regarding acts. Paternalism makes perfectly good sense when the "pater" is indeed a father or other parent and the individual whose self-regarding acts are in issue is a child. In its more common sense, "paternalism" refers to governmental interference with the self-regarding acts of mentally competent adults, and so understood it is indeed the opposite of libertarianism. The yoking of the two in the oxymoron "libertarian paternalism" is an effort to soften the negative connotation of paternalism with the positive connotation of libertarianism.

I would further limit the term "paternalism" to situations in which the government wishes to override the informed preferences of competent adults. The dangers of smoking are well known; indeed, they tend to be exaggerated—including by smokers. (The increased risk of lung cancer from smoking is smaller than most people believe.) Interventions designed to prevent smoking, unless motivated by concern with the effect of smoking on nonsmokers (ambient smoke, which is not much of a health hazard but is an annoyance to nonsmokers), are paternalistic in the sense in which I am using the term.

Thus I was not defending paternalism when I defended the ban on trans fats in New York City restaurants. If people are aware of the dangers of trans fats but wish to consume them anyway, the only nonpaternalistic ground for intervention, which I would be inclined to think insufficient by itself, is that they may be shifting some of the costs of their medical treatment for heart disease to taxpayers who forgo consumption of trans fats. If, however, people don't know the dangers of trans fats and it would not be feasible for them to learn those dangers (prohibitive transaction costs), and if as I believe the dangers clearly exceed any benefits from trans fats compared to substitute ingredients, then the ban can be defended on nonpaternalistic grounds, as I attempted to do. Another way to put this is that it is not paternalistic to delegate a certain amount of decision making to the government. There are some goods that government can produce at lower cost than the private sector, and among these is the banning of trans fats from food served in restaurants.

It might seem that the good could be produced just by competition-impelled advertising by restaurants that do not use trans fats. But such a suggestion ignores the difference between disseminating and absorbing information. If you have a peanut allergy, and the label on a package of cake mix says that the mix contains peanut oil, you know not to buy it; the cost of absorbing the information on the label is trivial. But if you are told that a restaurant does not use trans fats in its meals, determining the significance of that information to you would require you to undertake a substantial research project. You would have to learn about trans fats, somehow estimate the total amount of trans fats that you consume every year, estimate the amount of trans fats in the restaurant meals you consume relative to your total consumption of trans fats, and assess the significance of that consumption in relation to other risk factors that you have or don't have for heart disease. Few people have the time for such research, or the background knowledge that would enable them to conduct it competently. Given that trans fats have close substitutes in both taste and cost, it is not unrealistic to suppose that the vast majority of people would if consulted delegate to government the decision whether to ban trans fats.

One of the great weaknesses of "libertarian paternalism" is failure to weigh adequately the significance of the operation of the cognitive and psychological quirks emphasized by libertarian paternalists on government officials. The quirks are not a function of low IQ or a poor education; they are universal, although there is a tendency for the people least afflicted by them to enter those fields, such as gambling, speculation, arbitrage, and insurance, in which the quirks have the greatest negative effect on rational decision making. As Edward Glaeser has pointed out, the cost of these quirks to officials—who are not selected for immunity to them—is lower than the cost to consumers, because the officials are making decisions for other people rather than for themselves.

21

CHICAGO AND BIG BOXES

July 30, 2006

CHICAGO'S APPROACH TO BIG BOXES—BECKER

The City Council of Chicago recently passed an ordinance that makes Chicago the largest city in the United States to impose special wage and fringe benefit requirements for "big box" retailers. The ordinance requires that beginning next July, companies with more than $1 billion in annual sales and having stores in Chicago with at least ninety thousand square feet of space will have to pay Chicago employees a minimum of $9.25 an hour in wages and $1.50 an hour in fringe benefits, such as health insurance. By 2010 these will rise to $10 an hour in wages and $3 an hour in benefits. These minimums far exceed Illinois' minimum wage of $6.50 per hours. About forty existing stores in the city would be affected.

The ordinance was supported by thirty-five out of forty-nine alderman on the council despite the vehement opposition of Mayor Richard Daley, who in the past could dictate the council's policies. The mayor is right to be opposed, for it is indeed a bad ordinance, and will hurt the very groups, African Americans and other poor or lower-middle-class individuals, that supporters claim would be helped.

The ordinance will raise the cost of using low-skilled labor in Chicago by Wal-Mart, Target, Home Depot, and other big retailers with mega stores. Even without it, large cities are not attractive to mega retailers because space for large stores and for the parking they require is much more expensive in cities than in suburbs and smaller towns. These big box stores are much more common in suburbs of large cities than in the cities themselves partly for this reason, and partly because many suburban communities offer tax and other financial subsidies to these stores in order to induce them to locate there.

Even if retailers with mega stores were trying to cater at least in part to the Chicago market, this ordinance makes them more likely to open up in suburbs that could be reached by some Chicagoans as well as by those living in the suburbs. Large retailers that continue to operate in Chicago will reduce their use of low-skilled workers by replacing some of them by more skilled employees, and by machinery and other capital. Retailers will also try to avoid being covered by the ordinance by reducing their space to just below ninety thousand square feet.

In a city like Chicago the burden from these responses to the ordinance will fall disproportionately on African Americans and Latinos since fewer jobs will be available to workers in the city with less education and lower skills. In addition, prices in Chicago of items sold relatively cheaply by stores like Wal-Mart and Target will rise because fewer of these stores will open in the city. The mega stores that remain will raise their prices because their costs will go up. Since city customers of these stores are mainly families with modest incomes who seek low prices rather than elaborate service, they more than the affluent classes will be hurt by the rise in prices and reduced availability of big box outlets.

Who would favor such a bad ordinance that will harm the very groups it is claimed to help? Support for the ordinance from more conventional supermarket chains and clothing stores is easy to understand since the mega stores drain away customers and force prices down. The absence of opposition from low-income consumers who shop at these stores is not surprising since they are not well organized to exert political pressure on the city council.

The strong backing of the ordinance by Chicago unions is also to be expected. Unions always favor increases in minimum wages, even when as in this case the minimum only apply to some employers. Any increase in the minimum wage would raise the demand for unionized skilled workers who would substitute for the less skilled employees displaced by the minimum.

Unions have an additional reason to try to raise the costs of big box companies like Wal-Mart's since these companies do not have unions, and aggressively oppose them. Higher costs forced on nonunion companies reduce the competition they offer to unionized companies. Perhaps of even greater importance, this ordinance helps demonstrate that unions have the political clout that can make operations more costly and difficult for large nonunion retailers. To ward off further discriminatory ordinances, these companies could be forced to adopt a more favorable stance toward unionization of their employees.

It is more difficult to understand the aggressive support of the Chicago ordinance by most African American members of the council and other leaders of the African American community. However, it should be noted that some of those who represent predominantly African American communities voted against the ordinance, including Leslie Hairston who represents the Fifth Ward (where I live). Not only will fewer jobs be available for African Americans, but also the prices they pay for food, clothing, and many other retail goods would go up.

One explanation for why most African American leaders support the ordinance is that they are politically allied with unions and possibly other groups that benefit from this ordinance. These leaders may recognize that their constituents will generally be harmed by the ordinance, but in return for taking this hit they expect the support of unions on issues like more generous Medicaid support that help low-income families.

Clearly, this ordinance might raise serious federal constitutional issues because of its discriminatory treatment of large retailers. Since to my knowledge the city council has not offered any plausible reason for basing the ordinance on square footage of floor space, it is likely to be considered a violation of equal protection of the laws.

Still, ordinances like this one are dangerous not only because of their direct harmful effects, but also because they encourage future legislation that could apply similar and additional requirements to stores like McDonald's and other smaller stores. It also encourages interferences in other markets, such as the proposal now before the Chicago council that would require residential developers to include a certain percentage of "affordable" housing units in their developments. So Mayor Daley is right to oppose this ordinance, and he should veto it, even if the veto will be overridden.

THE "BIG BOX" MINIMUM-WAGE ORDINANCE—POSNER'S COMMENT

Becker's comprehensive analysis leaves me with little to add, especially as I am not permitted to comment publicly on the constitutionality of the "big box" ordinance because (if it does go into effect) its constitutionality is likely to be challenged, and in my court to boot.

The first-order economic analysis of minimum wage laws shows that they reduce employment by raising the price of labor; the law of demand teaches that an increase in the price of a good reduces the quantity of it that is demanded. A second-order analysis complicates the picture. Price affects supply as well as demand. An increase in the price of labor might attract into the labor force individuals who, at the existing price, prefer to go to school, engage in crime, work part time, or subsist on welfare. If, moreover, there is a large sector exempt from the law, the law's main effect may be to shift workers to the exempt sector rather than to reduce overall employment. The higher wages in the covered sector, by driving up employers' costs in that sector, will tend to reduce the demand for the products and services produced by those employers and to increase the demand for substitute products and services produced in the exempt sector, which in turn will increase the demand for labor in that sector.

What seems relatively clear, however, is that the brunt of the disemployment effect of the minimum wage will be felt by marginal workers. For example, some teenagers whose marginal product (that is, their contribution to the employer's profits) was just at or only slightly above the minimum wage will, if the minimum wage is raised, be replaced by slightly more productive teenagers from affluent households who were not attracted to working when the wage was lower.

The smaller the sector covered by the minimum wage law (and the coverage of the "big box" ordinance is very limited), the more dramatic the disemployment effects of the law are likely to be. The demand for labor as a whole is inelastic, but the demand for labor by an individual company or a small group of companies is likely to be quite elastic. Not because the company can easily substitute capital for labor, but because it cannot pass on increased costs to its customers if it has many competitors who have lower labor costs by virtue of being exempt from the minimum wage. Such a company, assuming it faces an upward-sloping average-cost curve (meaning that its average cost rises with its output—the normal assumption about a firm's cost structure in a market with many firms, because if its costs were invariant to its output it could expand indefinitely), can control its labor costs only by reducing its output and thus laying off workers. One especially draconian way of doing this is by relocating the firm's plants or other facilities from the jurisdiction imposing the high minimum wage to a jurisdiction that has a lower minimum wage. Becker points out that this may be a consequence of the Chicago ordinance because it does not reach Chicago's suburbs. It is a reason for believing that state minimum wages are likely to have fewer disemployment effects that local minimum wages, and the federal minimum wage fewer disemployment effects than state minimum wages.

At the current minimum wage in Illinois of $7.75 an hour, an employee who works two thousand hours a year (a forty-hour week with two weeks of annual vacation) and is paid the minimum wage earns only $15,500 a year. This is a pittance, though if the minimum-wage employee's spouse is employed at a significantly higher wage, the family's income may not be at a hardship level. Similarly, the minimum-wage employee may be an elderly person who receives social security and Medicare and may have a company pension in addition. These possibilities show that minimum wage laws, even if they had no disemployment effects, would be a clumsy instrument for combating poverty. A better approach than raising the minimum wage would be increasing the earned-income tax credit (negative income tax), which is a method of increasing the earnings of marginal workers without confronting their employer with a higher cost of labor and thus inducing the employer to discharge those workers whose marginal product is lower than the minimum wage. But this would be difficult for an individual city or even state to do; it would require federal action.

AFTERTHOUGHTS TO PART IV

POSNER AFTERTHOUGHTS

Chicago's "big box" ordinance that Becker and I criticize was vetoed by Mayor Daley, and the veto was sustained. New York City's ordinance banning trans fats in restaurants, which I support and Becker opposes, has been followed by a statewide ban in California. The trans fats bans exemplify one of three possible responses to the problem of high consumer information costs. The first is to require producers to provide more information; the second is to ban products on the basis of a judgment that if consumers knew the score they would not buy the product in question; and the third is to leave the burden of information on the consumer, thereby increasing his incentive to inform himself about the products he buys. Often the preferred ranking will be 2, 1, and 3. Banning the product eliminates information costs, though to justify so drastic a measure requires a high degree of confidence that informed consumers would not buy the product if they knew the facts about it. If as I believe trans fats have close and much more healthful substitutes that cost little more than trans fats, the attempt to ban trans fats in New York City restaurants made sense.

New York City took another step along the road of altering people's eating habits in July 2008, when, in an effort to reduce obesity (economic studies find that weight rises with lower relative prices of fast-food and full-service restaurants and the wider availability of such restaurants and hence the lower full price of eating at them), it began enforcing an ordinance that requires fast-food chains to post on menus and menu boards the number of calories in each menu item, in the same type size as the item itself. We blogged about the new ordinance on July 27, 2008. It illustrates solution 1 to the problem of high consumer information costs. My post noted the criticism of the ordinance as being at once unnecessary, because information about calorie content can be conveyed without requiring that it be printed in large type on the menu, and paternalistic, because people concerned about their weight have the incentive and ability to inform themselves about the number of calories they consume. But government programs designed to educate consumers in the causes and consequences of obesity have not been effective, and, partly because some of the costs of obesity are external, competition among restaurants or other food providers cannot be counted upon to optimize caloric intake; an obese person will not eat less in order to reduce the social costs of medical subsidies.

It is not even clear that competition will produce the caloric intake desired by consumers for purely selfish reasons of health, medical expense, and appearance. Firms are reluctant to advertise relative safety, because it alerts the consumer to the existence of danger. And food sellers have become adept at exploiting people's addictive tendencies, which have biological roots. In the "ancestral environment," to which human beings are biologically adapted, a taste for high-calorie foods had great survival value. Prominent display of calorie numbers might persuade consumers to avoid fast-food chains rather than to look for the chain with the lowest calorie numbers. The object in requiring that calorie numbers be printed next to the food items on menus and menu boards and in large type is less to inform than to frighten. Psychologists have shown (what is anyway pretty obvious) that people respond more to information that is presented to them in a dramatic, memorable form than to information that is presented as an abstraction or is merely remembered rather than being pushed in one's face; that is the theory behind requiring reckless drivers to watch videotapes of accidents and requiring cigarette ads to contain fearsome threats.

The effects of the new ordinance cannot be predicted. The argument for it is the argument for social experimentation generally: that it will yield valuable information about the effects of public interventions designed to alter lifestyles. I therefore favor the ordinance, though without great optimism that it will contribute significantly to a reduction in obesity.

BECKER AFTERTHOUGHTS

When I wrote the column on the opposition to big boxes in various American cities, the Chicago City Council had passed such an ordinance, and Mayor Daley had come out in opposition. He ended up vetoing the measure, and the council did not overturn his veto. It was a very silly ordinance that would have harmed poor consumers and less skilled workers, and the mayor was wise to oppose it.

V

JOBS AND EMPLOYMENT

22

JUDICIAL TERM LIMITS

March 12, 2005

JUDICIAL TERM LIMITS—POSNER

In examining the issue of judicial term limits (a perennial proposal but one being urged with renewed vigor these days), we are continuing the examination of governance that we undertook recently (February 27, 2005) with reference to the Larry Summers controversy. The judiciary, especially the federal judiciary, the judges of which are appointed, not elected, and appointed for life and removable only for serious misconduct or complete incapacity (due, for example, to senility), is another oddly structured institution, like a university, with which it shares the institution of life tenure now that mandatory retirement has been abolished for professors.

One can imagine a much more conventional organization of the judiciary. New graduates from law schools would be appointed to the judiciary, beginning as junior judges in traffic or domestic-relations or misdemeanor courts. Their performance would be evaluated by the administrators of the judicial system and if their performance was good they would be promoted through the ranks of the judges. This in fact is the system prevailing in most countries of the world, including the European nations (except the United Kingdom) and Japan. In contrast, in the U.S. federal judiciary, as in the English judiciary, judgeships are lateral-entry positions where promotion is rare and there is no systematic, official evaluation of performance. Most federal judges are appointed in their forties or fifties after a career in legal practice, prosecution, or law teaching. If they are appointed as district judges (i.e., trial judges), they will usually remain in that rank; promotion to circuit judge (i.e., to the court of appeals) is not wholly uncommon, but most district judges remain such for their career on the bench. Promotion of circuit judges to the Supreme Court is even less frequent. I was appointed a federal circuit judge from teaching in 1981, at the relatively young age of forty-two. I have thus been a circuit judge for twenty-three years and will remain in that job until I die or retire. And I am very difficult to remove from office!

At first glance, the U.S. federal system, in contrast to the European and Japanese, seems hopelessly devoid of incentives for good performance. Apart from the very limited promotion opportunities and the difficulty of removing federal judges, all judges at the same level (i.e., all district judges, all circuit judges, and all Supreme Court justices except the chief justice) are paid exactly the same salary and have only very limited opportunities to supplement their salaries with teaching or writing.

Nevertheless, the performance of federal judges (most state judges are elected, and for a variety of reasons this is an unsatisfactory method of judicial appointment, used nowhere else, as far as I know, in the world) is generally thought to be on a par with that of judges in Europe, Japan, and other countries that have a career judiciary. One reason is that when a person is appointed to the bench after another career, there is a good deal of information about his competence and work ethic; moreover, appointees are carefully screened by the FBI, the White House, and the Senate Judiciary Committee. It is commonplace when output is difficult to measure to monitor inputs instead. The output of the federal judiciary is difficult to measure because the complex and ambiguous character of much federal law makes it very difficult to determine when a judicial decision is erroneous. Nations that have career judiciaries generally have simpler, more cut-and-dried legal doctrines; that makes it easier to monitor judicial performance and so create a career ladder in which judges are evaluated for promotion by their superiors.

Whether in the academy or in the judiciary, life tenure is a formula for abuse. Basically, it eliminates any penalty for shirking; the salary structure of federal judges, noted above, eliminates the carrot along with the stick. This suggests the possible desirability of imposing term limits on judges—say, ten years (a common term for judges of constitutional courts in foreign countries). This would limit the length of service of the shirkers and also create an incentive for good performance because the judge would want to secure a good job after his judicial term expired. The downside (illuminated by the literature on term limits for legislators) is that judges would be distracted by having to make arrangements for another job at the expiration of their term; their decisions might be distorted by desire to curry favor with potential future employers; and more rapid turnover of judges would reduce legal stability. These might be compelling arguments were it not for the careful screening of judges, which eliminates from the appointment pool the candidates most likely to shirk. (I am assuming that judges would not be eligible for reappointment when their terms expired, as that would result in rampant politicization of the judiciary.)

An ingenious compromise is the institution of "senior status" whereby judges who reach the age of (voluntary) retirement, normally sixty-five, can continue to work, at no reduction in pay, as "senior" judges—provided they are willing to assume at least one-third of the normal workload. This is an attractive offer, which most eligible judges accept—but part of the deal is that a senior judge can be removed (though with no diminution of pay) from judging by the chief judge of his court or the court's judicial council; in effect, he no longer has tenure. This is a variant of the "buy out" schemes by which universities and other employers try to induce retirement.

The case for term limits for Supreme Court justices, as urged by Becker, is stronger. The Supreme Court is largely though not entirely a political court—almost a third branch of the legislature—and life tenure for politicians is profoundly undemocratic. The justices are ineligible for senior status, moreover, though if they retire they can sit in the lower federal courts if they want. With increased longevity, justices are likely to be serving very long terms into very old age. This strengthens the argument for Supreme Court term limits.

YES TO TERM LIMITS FOR SUPREME COURT JUSTICES—BECKER

I first expressed my support for judicial term limits in a column written for *Business Week* in 1990 and reprinted in Gary S. Becker and Guity N. Becker, *The Economics of Life* (1998). Over time I have become more convinced of that position, especially for Supreme Court justices. Still, I was pleasantly surprised to discover recently that a significant number of prominent law professors, practicing lawyers, and academics from both the left and right (not only conservatives) have signed on to a proposal to eliminate lifetime tenure for Supreme Court justices. I concentrate in these brief comments on the Supreme Court, and draw on my earlier column, and on the paper behind this proposal by two law professors, Paul Carrington of Duke University and

Roger Cramton of Cornell. See Paul D. Carrington and Roger C. Cramton, "The Supreme Court Renewal Act: A Return to Basic Principles," July 5, 2005, http://paulcarrington.com/Supreme_Court_Renewal_Act.htm (visited December 8, 2008).

Alexander Hamilton argued in the Federalist papers for lifetime tenure for judges in order to try to make their decisions independent from politics, and to encourage them to interpret the Constitution rather than to exercise "will." But the extraordinary expansion of government during the twentieth century has forced an aging Supreme Court to rule on problems of enormous significance: abortion, civil rights, taking of property, wrongful discharge, treatment of terrorists, and many other issues. What they decide makes a real difference, as seen from their rulings on abortion and many other issues. Perhaps this is inevitable, but most justices find it impossible not to follow their "will" rather than "interpretation."

There is no perfect system for handling these responsibilities of the judiciary, and the lifetime approach worked well enough during earlier times when far fewer issues came before the Court, and justices did not stay on for so long. But the average tenure of a Supreme Court justice has increased from about sixteen years to almost twenty-six years, and the average age at retirement grew from about seventy years old to eighty. The nine present justices of the Supreme Court have served together for the longest time in America's history, some ten years, with the last appointment made in 1994.

Given their desire to influence future Court decisions, presidents are appointing younger justices who will be able to affect judicial decisions for forty years or more. Moreover, the prestige and power of a justice is so great, and the workload so low—a typical justice writes about one opinion per month, and much of that is usually done by outstanding clerks—that they have little work incentive to retire before death or severe incapacity.

Do we really want eighty-year-olds, who have been removed from active involvement in other work or activities for decades, and who receive enormous deference, in large measure because of their great power, to be greatly influencing some of the most crucial social, economic, and political issues? My answer is no, and Posner seems to agree, at least for Supreme Court justices.

Carrington and Cramton propose a single eighteen-year term for Supreme Court appointees as an alternative to lifetime appointments. After their term expires, justices could serve on lower federal courts. That may be the best approach, although reasonable alternatives would be a single term of shorter length—such as the fourteen-year (although renewable) terms of Federal Reserve appointees—or perhaps even a ten-year term that is renewal once. With any of these approaches to term limits, Senate fights over confirmation would become less fierce and partisan since an appointee would then not be ruling for perhaps forty years on major legislation and other acts. There would also be less incentive for presidents to try to appoint very young justices.

Some of you might respond that I should first improve my own sector since academics like myself have lifetime tenure too. However, until the early 1990s universities forced professors to retire, usually at age sixty-five. I believe it was a mistake for Congress to eliminate forced retirement. Still, many universities do provide financial incentives to retire "early," and about one-third of the professors at major schools are taking such early retirement. In addition, sharp competition among universities induces higher compensation for professors who are doing well, and lower pay and other benefits for those who are slacking off. There is no comparable competition for members of the only Supreme Court.

Of course, it is far more difficult to change the tenure of Supreme Court justices and other federal judges since the Constitution guarantees lifetime tenure while in "office." But the proposal being advanced by Carrington and Cramton claims that "office" does not necessarily mean remaining as a Supreme Court justice, and could involve serving on lower federal courts, such as appellate courts.

I do not have a strong opinion on the optimal term limit, or whether a single term or two shorter terms is better. But I do believe that term limits for Supreme

Court justices (and perhaps other federal judges too) would be superior to the present lifetime system.

23

ECONOMICS OF THE REVOLVING DOOR

July 9, 2006

THE ECONOMICS OF THE REVOLVING DOOR—POSNER

Articles by Eric Lipton in the June 18 and 19 issues of the *New York Times* discussed the "revolving door" phenomenon with specific reference to the Department of Homeland Security. According to Lipton, although the department is only three and a half years old, already more than two-thirds of its senior executives have quit for jobs in the private sector, mostly working for companies that have or seek contracts with the department, which has an annual budget of some $40 billion. These executives, some of whom had come to the department from the private sector for brief stints in government service, are paid multiples of their government salaries when they leave to join or rejoin the private sector. Although departing government employees are forbidden to lobby their former government employer for a year, the prohibition is particularly porous in the case of the Department of Homeland Security because a former employee is permitted to lobby from the start any unit in the department for which he did not work. The department is a conglomerate of twenty-two formerly separate agencies, with overlapping responsibilities, and there are subunits with each of the agencies.

Should the revolving door be stopped or slowed? Two considerations favor the revolving door. First, people who have served in government have useful information about government's needs and procedures; that information can enable a better matching of government contractors with the agencies that purchase their services. Second, the opportunity for lucrative private employment after a stint of public service reduces the cost to the government of obtaining able employees. The compensation of government employees includes not only their government salaries but also the enhanced private earning capacity that they acquire by their government service.

But these points are persuasive only with regard to career government employees, in the sense of people who worked for the government—at a junior level initially at least—for many years. They accrue valuable knowledge over the course of their employment, and the prospect of eventual private-sector employment substantially increases in real terms their meager compensation as government employees. Not that there isn't a loss; many of the ablest and most experienced government employees leave government well before normal retirement age, while the least able stay until or beyond that age because of the difficulty of firing government workers.

The system can also produce transitional crises, as illustrated by the hemorrhaging of government security personnel in the wake of the September 11, 2001, terrorist attacks. The attacks caused a surge in private demand for security personnel, resulting in a sudden and substantial loss of experienced CIA, FBI, and other security officers to the private sector at greatly increased salaries. The increased ratio of private to government salaries represented a windfall for these officers because it had not been anticipated. In the long run, however, these windfalls become anticipations that will enable the government security services to hire abler people because they will foresee superior private-sector opportunities. In other words, as a result of the continuing concern with terrorism, working for government security agencies confers on one more human capital than before 9/11. Meanwhile, however, there is tremendous turnover in government security agencies, and a resulting decline in the quality of those agencies, as senior officers vacate their positions for the private sector and are replaced by inexperienced juniors. The impact on quality is aggravated by the disruptive effect of rapid turnover in any organization.

The exodus of officials of the Department of Homeland Security for the private sector, about which Lipton wrote, is a distinct phenomenon. Many of them are people who had come to work for Tom Ridge in the White House when he was the president's homeland security advisor and went with him to the department when it was formed in March of 2003 and he became the first head. Many did not have extensive or relevant government experience. Moreover, the department has from the outset been grossly mismanaged. The fault lies mainly in the design and structure of the department and in the haste with which it was created; but no one considers it, even given these constraints, a well-managed enterprise. The companies that have hired these officials do not care, however, because they are not hiring DHS officials for their managerial expertise. They are hiring them in the hope that it will facilitate the obtaining of contracts with the department.

The department needs contractors, of course, and its former officials doubtless have a good sense of how a contractor can make an attractive pitch to the department; otherwise the contractors would not have hired these officials at high salaries. But whether the officials are actually knowledgeable about the department's needs is another matter. Many of them were "birds of passage," who never became real experts on security. There is warranted suspicion that many of them got their high positions in the department by reason of political contacts, and those contacts may enable them to land contracts for their new employers that are not in the government's best interest. So the first reason I gave for why "revolving door" practices may serve the public interest is probably absent in the case of senior officials. And likewise the second. The prospect of subsequent reemployment by the private sector probably attracts few able nongovernment people to government jobs. It is disruptive to give up one's private job to work for government for a short time with the aim of then returning to the private sector at a higher level—a level one might well have attained in the ordinary course of promotions and job changes had one remained in the private sector.

Moreover, there is what economists call a "last period" problem that is more serious in the "bird of passage" case than in the case of the career government employee. An individual in the last period of his employment (or a company that is about to go out of business) is not restrained in his self-interested behavior by concern that his employer will fire him (or, in the case of the company, that its customers will desert it). Any government employee who has decided to seek private employment may be tempted to make decisions that will make him more attractive to prospective private employers; the added problem with the "birds of passage" is that their entire government service is last period because they know they are going to return to the private sector soon. All their decisions as government officials may be influenced by a desire to position themselves for as lucrative a reentry into the private sector as possible.

What might be done to alleviate the revolving-door problem? One possibility would be to restructure the civil service so that it paid better and, as important, reached higher in the government system. In the United Kingdom, civil servants occupy the highest posts in government just below the ministerial level. The opportunity to become a permanent undersecretary is an inducement to the ablest civil servants to remain in government service for their entire, or at least a very long, career. In our government quite junior officials, such as assistant secretaries of department and even many deputy assistant secretaries, are appointed from outside the ranks of the civil servants. These are, many of them, the "birds of passage"; and the diminished promotion opportunities for the civil servants makes a civil service career much less attractive for able and ambitious people than it would otherwise be.

The major exception of course is the military, a branch (realistically) of the civil service in which one can rise to a very high rank, because there is no lateral entry into the uniformed service. The CIA and FBI are other exceptions, since among their top officials ordinarily only the director himself is appointed from outside the agency staff.

Of course there would be costs in strengthening the civil service—one being that the able people it attracts might be more productive in the private sector. But the challenges faced by the American government at present are so acute that we must take steps to improve governmental efficiency, and reform of civil service may be one of them.

TURNOVER OF HIGH-LEVEL PUBLIC EMPLOYEES—BECKER

Quit rates of secretaries and other lower-level federal government employees are considerably below those of comparable workers in the private sector, while government officials quit at much higher rates than their civilian counterparts. What explains this difference, and is it good or bad?

The first part of the question is easy to answer: differences in quit rates are due to differences in the ratio of federal compensation to compensation in the private sector at low and high job levels. Federal employees at lower-level jobs may not make more than their civilian counterparts, but their economic situation is quite good when all other characteristics are taken into account. Government workers at these levels have great job security since they cannot be fired after a short probationary period, except for the grossest forms of misbehavior, such as frequent absences from work, racial or sexual remarks, etc. In addition, they get many holidays, good vacations, generous pensions and health benefits, and are usually not under much pressure at work. The full set of characteristics offered to these federal employees is very attractive, which is why lower-level jobs attract many applicants, and the jobs must be rationed through tests and in other ways.

By contrast, federal employees at higher-level jobs—including senior executives in the Department of Homeland Security that Posner discusses—are paid considerably below that of comparable private sector executives. In order to attract and keep high-quality employees, the federal government must provide enough compensating advantages in the form of prestige, power, working conditions, and in other ways. There is little turnover of federal judges presumably for that reason since most of these judges could earn much more as practicing lawyers, even judges who, unlike Judge Posner, are not particularly energetic.

For many high-level federal officials, government service is a short-term option that may provide interesting experiences, including learning about various policy issues. But after a while the much higher compensation in the private sector becomes too tempting—of course, their short stay in the government may have been anticipated—and many officials quit the federal government after only a few years (or less).

It would be possible to reduce turnover of federal officials by significantly raising their pay, so that it becomes closer to what they could receive in the private sector. As with federal judges, turnover might be low even with pay that remained considerable below that in the private sector, but not as much below as at present. Some talented men and women like working on public problems of great importance, the security of job tenure would appeal to some, and so on.

Members of Congress currently receive salaries of $165,200 per year—leaders in the House and Senate receives a little more—plus generous retirement and health benefits. That is a lot relative to the pay of most employees in the private sector, and there does not seem to be a shortage of men and women who want to be elected to Congress. Under present rules, it is not possible to pay senior officials in Homeland Security or other agencies more than members of Congress receive, even when higher pay is necessary to fight off the appeal of employment in the private sector. To pay top public officials much more than they already get would require a change in these rules, which would not be politically easy.

Yet for the sake of this discussion, suppose it were possible to cut down the turnover of federal officials in the Department of Homeland Security and elsewhere. Would that be desirable? I believe that having more experienced employees is as valuable to the federal government as it obviously is to the private sector. Turnover of executives with years of experience at the same private company is low—clearly much below that among federal employees—because these companies value that experience. Longtime executives accumulate useful knowledge about the organization and practices of the firms they have worked for over the years—what economists call firm-specific capital. I see no reason why such knowledge should be much less important in the federal government. As Posner indicates, Great Britain and some other countries do manage to retain high-level officials of good quality over much of their working lives.

Turnover of federal officials is undesirable for another reason that is not really applicable to the private sector. There is much "rent-seeking" by private companies that try to get special treatment and subsidies from the federal government as it spends huge resources. Hiring of former federal employees to top executive positions at private companies helps them improve their rent-seeking position vis-à-vis competitors. In particular, if competitors all hire former top executives of the Department of Homeland Security, that may simply augment their rent-seeking positions without adding social value. At the same time losing many top executives weakens this department.

So I favor higher pay for top federal officials in sectors that experience heavy turnover. However, without major changes in pay scales, I am skeptical about the advantages of developing much more stringent rules that prevent federal officials from going to work for suppliers of services or products to the agencies that employed them. The risk of such rules is that they eliminate one of the major present attractions of federal employment at high-level jobs. Adding such rules to the low pay would then make it even more difficult for federal agencies to attract able and honest top-level executives.

24

CEO COMPENSATION

May 14, 2006

ARE CEOS OVERPAID?—BECKER

The answer to the question of whether American CEOs are overpaid is clearly "yes" for those who earn large bonuses and generous stock options when their companies are doing badly, either absolutely or relative to competitors. *Business Week* has had an annual list of the most overpaid CEOs relative to the performance of the companies they head. A number of well-known companies usually top that list.

But the concern in the media and in Congress over CEO pay is not motivated by some bad apples like these, but by the huge increase in the typical CEO pay in the United States during the past twenty-five years. The total real compensation (that is, compensation adjusted for increases in the price level) of CEOs in larger publicly traded companies during this period grew a remarkable sixfold, where compensation adds together regular pay, bonuses, stocks awarded, the value of stock options, and payouts from longer-term pay programs. A big but not the only component of the increase is due to much greater use of stock options. Since median full-time real earnings during the same period only just about doubled, the gap between pay at the top and the average pay of employees widened enormously. It is hard to resist the widespread perception from these trends that CEOs and other top executives are being increasingly overpaid.

The case against the pay of American CEOs looks even more powerful by recognizing that the typical American company head receives greater total compensation than company heads in Great Britain, Canada, Japan, Spain, and in pretty much all developed countries. Clearly, American CEOs are much better paid than CEOs elsewhere, even when per capita incomes of the countries do not differ by very much.

Yet competition for top management can explain the rapid rise over time in the pay of the average American CEO. To understand how competition works in the management market, consider the strong and stable relation at any moment between the total compensation of CEOs at publicly traded companies, and the size of the companies they head. For every 10 percent increase in firm size, measured by the market value of assets, by sales, or by related variables, compensation increases by about 3 percent. This "30 percent" law held during the 1930s, and has held for every succeeding decade, including right up to the present. Note that stock options and other forms of compensation than salaries and bonuses were unimportant until the 1970s, so this relation is not due to the rapid growth of options and compensation through shares of stock.

The usual explanation given by economists for the positive relation between compensation and firm size is that the largest companies attract the best management. Therefore, bigger companies have to pay their CEOs better in order to discourage them from going to head smaller companies. It is also socially efficient to have the best mangers run the largest companies because their greater skills then have a bigger influence since they would manage a larger amount of labor and capital. The efficient combining of better managers with larger companies in a competitive market for top managers would imply a positive relation between firm size and the total compensation package. This analysis does not explain why the 30 percent rule holds, but it suggests that the relation between pay and size is likely to be sizable, even when top management in different-sized companies do not differ greatly in skills and abilities.

We need two additional facts to explain the sharp rise in pay over time, and the much higher pay in the United States than other countries. The first is that the average size of large American companies has grown in real terms about sixfold during the past twenty-five years, regardless of how "large" is measured, as long as the same measure is used consistently over time. The other important fact is that the largest fifty, one hundred, or five hundred

American publicly traded companies are much bigger than the largest companies in other countries.

Clearly, if large companies pay more, and if the average size of companies has grown sharply over time, average compensation would also grow, even if the value of the increasingly generous granting of stock options and equity shares were fully understood by stock markets and boards of directors. It is also possible to understand why average compensation grew about as rapidly as average company size, although the argument here is more complicated (for the details of this argument, see Xavier Gabaix [MIT] and Augustin Landier [NYU], "Why Has CEO Pay Increased So Much?" unpublished ms., April 17, 2006). The allocation of better managers to larger firms, and competition for these managers among companies of different sizes, means that companies in say 2006 would have to pay more for their CEOs than even the same-sized companies did in 1980, although much less than six times as much. The reasoning is that the 2006 companies of a given size are competing against relatively larger companies than comparable size companies did in 1980. Using this analysis, Gabaix and Landier are able to explain why total compensation of the average CEO of larger companies grew about sixfold along with the sixfold growth in average company size during the past several decades.

The same argument explains why compensation of American CEOs is much higher than that of CEOs in other countries. Since average firm size is much lower elsewhere, their pay would be more like that of pay in the United States in 1980 or 1990 than the pay of CEOs in today's much larger American firms. As the market for top executives becomes increasingly global, the pay of CEOs in other countries would rise, and that of CEOs in America might fall. For example, to attract Carlos Ghosn, a Brazilian working in France, to turn around Nissan, a seriously ailing company, Nissan had to pay him not at the low Japanese CEO levels, but at the much higher levels found in other countries.

I believe that the explanation based on the allocation of CEO talent largely is behind the explosion in compensation of American CEOs during the past several decades. Yet at the same time, some American CEOs are obviously grossly overpaid since they have mismanaged their companies and still receive exorbitant compensations. But mismanagement is not new and probably has not become so much more important over time. So I am suggesting that the rapid growth of compensation of American CEOs, and its premium over compensation of CEOs in other countries, is not mainly due to a growth in the degree of excess payment of executives in the United States. Rather, on this interpretation, the main cause of the increase in pay is the greater challenges and opportunities facing executives who manage much larger combinations of resources.

ARE CEOS OVERPAID?—POSNER

The media are full of stories about the compensation of chief executive officers of American companies. The theme of the stories is that CEOs are paid too much.

The economics of compensation are fascinating. In the simplest economic model, a worker, right up to the level of CEO, is paid his marginal product—essentially, his contribution to the firm's net income. But simple observation reveals numerous departures from the model. For example, wages vary across the employees of the same rank in the same company by much less than differences in their contribution to the company, and employees who do satisfactory work can expect real (that is, inflation-adjusted) annual increases in their wages throughout their career with the firm, even though their contribution will not be increasing at the same rate, and eventually not at all.

Let us see what sense can be made of the curious pattern of CEO compensation. American CEOs make much more on average than their counterparts in other countries—about twice as much. You might think that this is because Americans at all levels earn more than their foreign counterparts, but this is not so; the difference between U.S. and foreign wages is much smaller below the CEO level. In other words, wages are more skewed in favor of CEOs in American companies. The disparity is related to the fact that salaries are a much smaller fraction of American CEOs' incomes (less than half) than of foreign CEOs' incomes, with the rest consisting partly of bonuses but mainly of stock options. Both the fraction of CEO income that is nonsalary and total CEO income, have been rising, dramatically in the United States, over recent decades. But there is a recent tendency of foreign CEO compensation policies toward convergence with the American practice.

One can speculate about the causes of some of these differences. Stock options and other incentive-based compensation methods impart risk (variance) to CEOs' incomes, which reinforces the risk inherent in the fact that a CEO's human capital (earning capacity) may be specific to his firm, so that if he lost his job because his company had been doing badly (perhaps for reasons beyond his control), he would take a double hit—lower pay as the company declined and lower pay in his next job. Because business executives (as distinct from entrepreneurs) do not like risk, they demand a higher wage if the wage is going to have a substantial risky component. This may explain some of the difference between American and foreign CEO compensation, but surely not all or even much of it—especially since job turnover at the CEO level is actually greater in Europe than in the United States.

Another possible difference is that stock ownership tends to be more concentrated abroad than in the United States. The more concentrated it is, the more incentive shareholders have to monitor the performance of their firm's managers because they have more at stake. The more effective that monitoring is, the less need there is to create incentive-based compensation schemes: the stick is substituted for the carrot.

Cultural factors may also be important. European countries in particular are more egalitarian than the United States, suggesting that envy is likely to play a bigger role in compensation there. Astronomical ratios of CEO to blue-collar wages in the same company cause little resentment in the United States compared to what they would cause in Europe, though wide disparities between workers at the same level does engender resentment here even if the disparities track differences in productivity.

Envy might reduce average incomes at the same time that it reduces variance in incomes, if the more generous compensation of American CEOs merely reflects the greater contribution that they make to their companies' success. But there are two reasons to doubt this, and thus to suspect that American CEO incomes are padded to some degree. First, the most significant "incentive" component of these incomes—stock options—are not well correlated with the CEO's contribution to the value of his company and thus of the value of its stock. Many things move a company's stock besides the decisions of its CEO. To tie a CEO's income to the value of his company's stock is a bit like tying the salary of the president of the United States to the U.S. GNP.

Second, the choice of stock options as the principal method of providing nonsalary compensation to CEOs seems related to the fact that traditionally the income generated by these options, unlike salary or bonus income, was not reported as a corporate expense. Of course security analysts and stockholders large enough to follow closely the affairs of the companies in which they invest can calculate the expense of stock options, but the ordinary public cannot, and this is important because even in the United States envy is a factor that can influence policy and public opinion. A spate of recent articles has explained the ingenious devices by which CEO compensation that would strike the average person as grossly excessive is concealed from the public, and these articles, along with well-publicized corporate scandals, may place some downward pressure on CEO compensation. Companies cannot afford to ignore public opinion completely, because adverse public opinion can power legislative or regulatory measures harmful to a company or an industry.

It might seem that, provided the shareholders—the owners of the company—are made aware of the actual compensation received by the CEO, competition will drive that compensation down to approximately the level at which the CEO is just being paid his marginal product, with appropriate adjustment for risk. But given the size of companies, the cost to a major company of even a grossly overpaid CEO is so slight when divided among the shareholders that no shareholder (assuming dispersed ownership) will have an incentive to do anything about that excess expense.

What about the board of directors? Their incentive to minimize what from the overall corporate standpoint is only a minor cost is also weak, and may be offset by rather minor economic and psychological factors. The board is likely to be dominated by highly paid business executives, including CEOs, who have a personal economic interest in high corporate salaries and a natural psychological tendency to believe that such salaries accurately reflect the intrinsic worth of their recipients.

Becker in his comment on this post (below) cites an interesting paper by Gaibaix and Landier that argues the increase in CEO compensation is a function of the growth in the market value of firms. The basic idea is that the CEO of a more valuable firm is more productive, since if he increases value by say 1 percent, the increase in absolute value will be greater the more valuable the firm is. If there are two equally skilled managers and one manages a grocery store and one manages IBM, the manager of IBM is probably creating greater value.

The theory is too new to evaluate with any confidence. I am somewhat skeptical because rapid increases in CEO compensation should attract more talent to management, and the resulting greater competition for CEO positions should dampen the increase in compensation.

An alternative explanation for the correlation between firm value and CEO compensation, one that is consistent with the evidence that such compensation is often excessive from an efficiency standpoint, is that the greater the firm's market value, the easier it is to "hide" the compensation of the top executives. Suppose that a 10 percent increase in value is associated with a 3 percent increase in CEO compensation; then the percentage of the firm's value that is going to the CEO will have fallen. This may be one reason why many mergers fail to increase earnings per share, although the overall value of the enterprise will be greater after the merger (there will be more shares): the increase in overall value enables the CEO to increase his compensation regardless of whether he will be creating greater value as the manager of the larger enterprise.

25

INCOME INEQUALITY

April 23, 2006

IS THE INCREASED EARNINGS INEQUALITY AMONG AMERICANS BAD?—BECKER

Income inequality widened, particularly between urban and rural households after China began its rapid rate of economic development in 1980. At the same time, the fraction of Chinese men, women, and children who live on less than $2 a day—the World Bank's definition of poverty—greatly fell. Few would argue that the poor in China did not become much better off due to the rapid economic development, even though the gap between their incomes and those of the middle and richer classes widened by a lot. A similar conclusion would apply to India as the explosion in its general economic development during the past twenty years widened the gap between rich and poor, but raised the income levels of the very poor.

I make this observation in reaction to the great concern expressed by politicians and many others in the United States over the rather substantial increase during the past twenty-five years in earnings inequality among Americans. The China and India examples illustrate that whether rising inequality is considered good or bad depends on how it came about. I believe that the foundation of the growth in earnings inequality of Americans has mainly been beneficial and desirable.

The basic facts are these. There has been a general trend toward rising gaps between the earnings of more and less skilled persons. With regard to education, real earnings (that is, earnings adjusted for changes in consumer prices) of high school dropouts did not change much. Earnings of high school graduates grew somewhat more rapidly, so that the gap between dropout and graduate earnings expanded over time.

The main action came in the earnings of college graduates and those with postgraduate education. They both increased at a rapid pace, with the earnings of persons with MBAs, law degrees, and other advanced education growing the most rapidly. All these trends produced a widening of earnings inequality by education level, particularly between those with college education and persons with lesser education. I should also note that while an upward trend in the earnings gap by education is found for both men and women, and for African Americans and whites, the earnings of college-educated women and African Americans increased more rapidly than did those of white males. As a result, inequality by sex and race, particularly among college-educated persons, narrowed by a lot.

As the education earnings gap increased, a larger fraction of high school graduates went on to get a college education. This trend toward greater higher education is found among all racial and ethnic groups, and for both men and women, but it is particularly important for women. The growth in the number of women going to and completing college has been so rapid that many more women than men are now enrolled as college students. Women have also shifted toward higher earnings fields, such as business, law, and medicine, and away from traditional occupations of women, such as K–12 teachers and nurses. The greater education achievement of women compared to men is particularly prominent among blacks and Latinos.

The widening earnings gap is mainly due to a growth in the demand for educated and other skilled persons. That the demand for skilled persons has grown rapidly is not surprising, given developments in computers and the Internet, and advances in biotechnology. Also, globalization increased the demand for products and services from the United States and other developed nations produced by college-educated and other highly skilled employees. Globalization also encouraged a shift to importing products using relatively low-skilled labor from China and other low-wage countries instead of producing them domestically.

Rates of return on college education shot up during the past several decades due to the increased demand for persons with greater knowledge and skills. These higher rates of return induced a larger fraction of high school graduates to get a college education, and increasingly to continue with postgraduate education.

Some of you might question whether rates of return on higher education did increase since tuition grew rapidly during the past twenty-five years. However, increases in tuition were mainly induced by the greater return to college education. Pablo Pena in a Ph.D. dissertation in progress at the University of Chicago argues convincingly that tuition rose in part because students want to invest more in the quality of their education. Increased spending per student by colleges is partly financed by higher tuition levels.

This brings me finally to the punch line. Should not an increase in earnings inequality due primarily to higher rates of return on education and other skills be considered a favorable rather than unfavorable development? Higher rates of return on capital are a sign of greater productivity in the economy, and that inference is fully applicable to human capital as well as to physical capital. The initial impact of higher returns to human capital is wider inequality in earnings (just as the initial effect of higher returns on physical capital is widen income inequality), but that impact becomes more muted and may be reversed over time as young men and women invest more in their human capital.

I conclude that the forces raising earnings inequality in the United States is on the whole beneficial because they were reflected higher returns to investments in education and other human capital. Yet this is not a ground for complacency, for the responses so far to these higher returns is disturbingly limited. Why have not more high school graduates gone on for college education when the benefits are so apparent? And why did the fraction of American youth who drop out of high school, especially African American and Hispanic males, remain quite constant at about 25 percent of all high school students?

The answer to both questions lies partly in the breakdown of the American family, and the resulting low skill levels acquired by children in broken families. Cognitive skills tend to get developed at very early ages, while my colleague, James Heckman, has shown that noncognitive skills, such as study habits, getting to appointments on time, and attitudes toward work, get fixed at later, although still relatively young, ages. High school dropouts certainly appear to be seriously deficient in the noncognitive skills that would enable them to take advantage of the higher rates of return to greater investments in education and other human capital.

So instead of lamenting the increased earnings gap by education, attention should focus on how to raise the fraction of American youth who complete high school, and then go on for a college education. These pose tough challenges since the solutions are not cheap or easy. But it would be a disaster if the focus were on the earnings inequality itself. For that would lead to attempts to raise taxes and other penalties on higher earnings due to greater skills, which could greatly reduce the productivity of the world's leading economy by discouraging investments in human capital.

WHY RISING INCOME INEQUALITY IN THE UNITED STATES SHOULD BE A NONISSUE—POSNER

Becker explains the rising income inequality in the United States persuasively; I would add only that as society becomes more competitive and more meritocratic, income inequality is likely to rise simply as a consequence of the underlying inequality—which is very great—between people that is due to differences in IQ, energy, health, social skills, character, ambition, physical attractiveness, talent, and luck. Public policies designed to reduce income inequality, such as highly progressive income taxation and middle-class subsidies, are likely to reduce the aggregate wealth of society, and therefore should not be adopted unless rising income inequality is a social problem.

Is it? That depends, I think, on average income (and hence on the wealth of society as a whole), on whether incomes are rising (at all levels), and on the particular way in which the income distribution is skewed. The higher the average income in a society, the less likely is inequality to cause envy or social unrest. The reason is that, given diminishing marginal utility of income, people who are well-off do not have a strong sense of deprivation by reason of their not having an even higher income. If, moreover, their income is rising, they are more likely to derive satisfaction from a comparison of their present income to their former income than to be dissatisfied by the fact that some other people's incomes have risen even more. In my book *Frontiers of Legal Theory,* chapter 3 (2001), I present empirical evidence supporting a positive correlation between political stability on the one hand and average, and rising, income on the other hand.

It is true that progressive taxation and other income-equalizing policies are found in rich rather than poor countries. But that is partly because poor countries lack the governmental infrastructure for administering complex policies and partly because these societies have powerful social norms of equality. Studies of peasant societies find that "black" envy is widespread in them—that is, if your neighbor has a nicer barn than yours, you'd prefer to burn it down rather than to exert yourself to build an equally good barn. "White" envy, in contrast, better described as emulation, promotes economic growth.

As for the way in which a society's income distribution is skewed, if, though average income is high and rising, there is a very small, very wealthy, upper class, a tiny middle class, and a huge lower class, the society is likely to be unstable. Because the majority of the population will not be well-off, and the upper and middle classes small, there will be few defenders of the existing distribution.

The United States has a high average income, incomes are rising for most groups in the population—though more slowly than for the wealthiest—and most of the population is middle or upper class. It is therefore not surprising that rising income inequality has not generated noticeable social unrest or calls for return of heavy progressive taxation. Moreover, when nonpecuniary income is taken into account, there is less inequality than the income statistics suggest. In a democratic and rights-oriented society such as the United States, all citizens have a bundle of equal political rights (to the vote, to the free exercise of religion, to be free from unreasonable searches and seizures, and so forth) that are a form of income, and equal political duties that are a form of expense. Rich people as well as ordinary and poor are prosecuted for crime, and, as in the recent spate of corporate scandals, often punished very heavily.

What is more, income statistics do not record the enormous secular improvement in the quality of products and services, and hence in the utility that purchases confer on consumers. Think only of the extraordinary improvements in the quality of automobiles, medical care, and electronic products. Americans whose income has not increased faster than the rate of inflation are nevertheless living far better than they used to live. They know this, and it is one reason they are not clamoring for income redistribution.

A cultural factor that reduces the social tensions that might otherwise arise from a sharp and rising inequality of Americans' incomes is that the United States, unlike the countries of Europe, has no aristocratic tradition. There is no suite of tastes, accent, bearing, etc., that distinguishes the rich in America from the nonrich. The rich have more and better goods, but they do not act as if they were a "superior" sort of person, refined, well-bred, looking down on the average Joe. The rich play golf, but so do the middle class. The middle class follow sports, but so do the upper class.

Finally, rising income inequality in the United States is due in part to increased immigration, since immigrants, legal as well as illegal, tend to work for lower wages than citizens. Immigrants do not, however, compare themselves with wealthy citizens, but rather with the much lower wages they could expect to earn in their countries of origin. Rather than immigrants envying wealthy citizens, many citizens are hostile to poor immigrants!

The "problem" of income inequality should not be confused with the problem of poverty. The first, I have argued, is, at least in the United States at present, a pseudo-problem. Poverty is a genuine social problem, because by definition it signifies a lack of the resources necessary for a decent life. It is only tenuously if at all related to income inequality, since one could have zero poverty in a society in which the gap between the income of the worst-off members of society was huge—imagine if the poorest person in America earned $100,000 a year and the wealthiest $1 billion.

The more competitive and meritocratic a society, the more intractable the problem of poverty. The reason is that in such a society the poor tend to be people who are not productive because they simply do not have the abilities that are in demand by employers. It is unlikely that everybody (other than the severely disabled) can be trained up to a level at which there is a demand for his or her labor, and so there is likely to be an irreducible amount of poverty even in a wealthy society such as ours, unless we provide generous welfare benefits—which will discourage work.

26

CORPORATE SOCIAL RESPONSIBILITY

July 24, 2005

DO CORPORATIONS HAVE A SOCIAL RESPONSIBILITY BEYOND STOCKHOLDER VALUE?—BECKER

Do corporations have any responsibilities beyond trying to maximize stockholder value, adhering to contracts, implicit as well as explicit, and obeying the laws of the different countries where they operate? My answer is "no," although maximizing value, meeting contracts, and obeying laws help achieve many of the goals by those claiming corporations should be "socially responsible" by taking care of the environment, considering the effects of their behavior on other stakeholders, and contributing to good causes. Still, laws and contracts, and individual use of their own resources, rather than corporate behavior, should be the way to implement various social goals.

References to the behavior of corporations really mean the behavior of top management who are in essence employed by stockholders through their representatives—boards of directors. In most cases, it is rather obvious that management should try to increase stockholder value through their pricing policies, the products they offer, where they locate plants, and so forth. CEOs who fail to do this are subject to termination either through takeovers or by being fired. In fact, the tenure of corporate heads seems to have become shorter over time.

In many other situations, apparent conflicts between maximizing stockholder value and social goals disappear on closer examination. A corporation may give money to local charities, play up its contributions to the environment, and do other things that only appear to reduce shareholder value because that behavior sufficiently improves the government regulations that affect their profitability. Or a company may give to various public causes, like Ben and Jerry's ice cream company did in the past, because this attracts customers who want to support these causes partly by buying the products of companies that contribute to these causes.

Treatment of employees that on the surface appear to reduce profitability often are in fact consistent with the criteria of maximizing stockholder value while respecting laws and contract. For example, a company may raise the value to shareholders by keeping on older workers beyond the age where their productivity is sufficiently high to justify their earnings. Keeping older workers on attracts younger workers at lower wages since they expect too that they will not be let go when they get older. Or employees may invest in their on the job training because of an explicit contract or implicit agreement with their employers that their earnings will rise with their tenure as their productivity rises because of their investments. It would be inconsistent with my criteria if a company did not raise wages appropriately of some employees when their tenure and productivity increased because the company realized that these employees did not have good opportunities at other companies. This behavior would violate my recommendation that a company maximize stockholder value, subject to obeying all laws and contracts, implicit as well as explicit.

To take an example of what I do not believe companies should do, a global company operating in a poor country should not pay higher wages for either adult or child labor, adjusted for the quality of the labor, than is the prevailing standard in the labor market of this country, as long as higher wages would lower the profits of the company. I am assuming the wages they pay do not violate any laws or contracts of the countries where they operate, and that they are not subject to such bad publicity that their profits actually would increase if they paid more. I should add that pressure to pay much higher wages in labor markets of developing nations reduces the number employed there by international companies, and would tend to worsen, not improve, the plight of the poor populations of these countries.

Even in cases where this does not contribute to profitability, top management may want to use company resources to promote environmental ends that are not required by law, give to local symphonies, promote fair trade coffee or other fair trade products, and engage in other acts that increase the managers' utility, prestige, and standing in their communities. In a competitive market for managers, management would have to take sufficiently lower earnings, bonuses, and options to in effect pay for the company assets and profits they use to boost their own welfare and community standing. So in such a competitive management market, management essentially engages in "socially responsible" behavior out of their own earnings. This would not lower stockholder value, and is consistent with my criteria.

If the management is entrenched, they might be able to give away resources to environmental and other groups without lowering their own earnings, but by lowering instead dividends and other payments to stockholders. Even this, however, would not affect stockholder returns if instead management could have taken higher earnings, bonuses, or stock options for themselves. Depending on what they would have done with their higher earnings, the use of company profits for particular social causes may or may not lead to better overall outcomes. But surely an important goal of any reform in corporate management is to reduce the entrenchment of management, and inject more competition into the market for CEOs and other top corporate leaders.

Whatever the degree of competition in the market for top management, the market for stock ownership is highly competitive. Those stockholders that want companies to use potential profits for environmental or other social causes might be willing to buy the stocks of companies that do this, even if that means lower monetary rate of return on their investments. If there are enough of these stockholders, then companies that engage in these practices would be maximizing stockholder values, and their behavior would be consistent with the criteria for corporate behavior that I advocate.

But such socially conscious stockholders are a small fraction of all owners of stocks, especially of large institutional funds and investors. These funds would avoid companies that are "socially responsible" until prices of the stock of these companies fell sufficiently to give the same risk-adjusted monetary rate of return provided by companies that do not engage in social behavior. This implies that new companies that are expected to contribute to various social goals beyond making profits, and respecting laws and contracts, will have lower IPO prices if they issue stock than they otherwise would have. In that case, the founders of socially minded companies will bear the cost of their social responsibility. That is appropriate and is not objectionable. I am bothered only when managers, founders, or others in control of corporations that behave in a "socially responsible" manner try to pass the cost of behaving in this way on to others rather than bearing the costs themselves.

THE SOCIAL RESPONSIBILITY OF CORPORATIONS—POSNER'S COMMENT

I agree with almost everything that Becker says, but will suggest a few qualifications. I can think of one situation in which "pure" charitable donations by corporations, i.e., donations that do not increase profitability, could benefit shareholders. Assuming that most shareholders make some charitable donations, they might want the corporations they invest in to make modest charitable donations on the theory that a corporation will have more information about what are worthwhile charitable enterprises than an individual does. For example, charities differ greatly in the amount of money that they spend on their own administration, including salaries and perquisites for the employees of the charity, relative to the amount they give to the actual objects of charity. Presumably corporations are in a better position to determine which charities are efficient than individuals are; if so, then shareholders may impliedly consent to some amount of charitable giving by their corporations. But not much. The reason is that one person's charity is another person's deviltry: a shareholder who is opposed to abortion on religious grounds would be offended if his corporation contributed to Planned Parenthood. The practical significance of this point is that corporations avoid controversial charities, so that the issue of implied consent becomes whether the shareholder would like his corporation to make a modest contribution to some set of uncontroversial charities.

For the reason suggested above, the answer may be "yes"—and for the additional reason that there is a tax angle. If the shareholder receives a dividend, the corporation will have paid corporate income tax on the income from which the dividend is paid. Suppose the corporation and the shareholder are both in the 20 percent bracket. The corporation earns $10, pays $2 in tax, and gives the shareholder $8. The shareholder gives the $8 to charity, which costs him $6.40, since he gets a 20 percent tax deduction. If the shareholder wants the charity to have $10, it has to dig into his pockets for another $2, which costs him $1.60 (because of the 20 percent deduction), and so the total cost to him of giving the charity $10 is $8. Now suppose that, instead, the corporation gives the $10 to charity, a deductible expense, at a cost to it therefore of $8. Then the charity receives $10 rather than, as before, only $8. The shareholder loses his $2 deduction, which means that the total cost to him of the transfer is, as before, $8. But the corporation is better off to the tune of $2, since it avoids the corporate income tax on the $10 in income that it gave the charity. And anything that benefits the corporation benefits the shareholder.

Given product market as well as capital market competitive pressures, charitable spending that is not profit maximizing because the cost exceeds the private benefits that Becker lists (public relations, advertising, government relations, and so forth) is unlikely to be significant. Even if corporate managers are not effectively constrained to profit maximization by their shareholders, expenditures that do not reduce the cost or increase the quality of the corporation's products will place it a competitive disadvantage with firms that do not make such expenditures.

A more difficult question has to do with a corporation's policy on obeying laws. From a strict shareholder standpoint, it might seem that corporate managers should obey the law only when the expected costs of violating it would exceed the expected benefits, so that managers would have a duty to their shareholders to disobey the law, perhaps especially in countries in which law enforcement is very weak, a country, for example, that had a law against child labor but was unable to enforce the law. This would be a case of a pure clash between ethical and profit-maximization duties. My view is that, given external (i.e., social as distinct from private) benefits of compliance with law, the ethical argument should prevail, so that a shareholder would be precluded from complaining that corporate management, by failing to violate the law even when it could get away with it, was violating its fiduciary duty to shareholders.

Another argument based on an externality, an argument that lies behind the law that forbids U.S. firms to engage in bribery abroad, even in countries where bribery is extremely common, is that reducing the amount of bribery in those countries will benefit U.S. firms in the long run by making the markets in these countries more open, to the advantage of efficient firms.

The fact that it will sometimes be in the shareholder interest for management to violate the law provides, moreover, a ground for punishing corporate managers sufficiently severely for corporate crimes that the punishment is not offset by shareholder gains for which the managers could be expected to be rewarded.

AFTERTHOUGHTS TO PART V

BECKER AFTERTHOUGHTS

The opposition to very high incomes for top executives has exploded during the past year as the financial crisis evolved. Many heads of investments banks and other financial companies received enormous levels of compensation, even when they ran their companies into the ground. This led to provisions in the bailout bills that Congress passed to limit severance pay and other compensation of executives who were helped by federal assistance. More generally, the mood in Congress is to enact further controls over the compensation of top executives, including how generous their severance pay could be if their companies are sold or merged with other companies. While I support strong punishments to executives who lied or behaved in other forms of illegal behavior, I firmly believe controls over their compensation would be a bad mistake. In a recent posting (October 5, 2008) I said, "Controls over wages and salaries have never worked well, and only encourage myriad ways to get around them, including generous housing allowances, vacation homes, easy access to private planes, large pensions, and other fringe benefits. There develops a war between the government's closing of loopholes, and the ingenuity of accountants and lawyers in finding new ones."

The issue of corporate responsibility has resurfaced during the last couple of years due to Bill Gates's promotion of "creative capitalism." We discussed this on February 10, 2008, and I will quote a passage from my comments there:

> Companies that combine the profit motive with environmental and other concerns can thrive in a competitive environment only if they are able to attract employees and customers that also value these other corporate goals. Then the added cost of pursuing nonprofit goals would be partially, if not entirely offset, by having customers who pay more for their products, such as fair trade coffees. Or these companies may be able to attract high-level employees relatively cheaply perhaps because the employees are excited by the prospects of spending some of their working time developing vaccines that can treat diseases common in poor countries. These appear to be the types of companies that Bill Gates wants at the forefront of his "creative capitalism" since he is encouraging companies to pursue recognition as well as profits.

I added, "Nevertheless, unlike the well-known negative position on corporate responsibility taken by my great teacher and close friend, the late Milton Friedman, and apparently also by Posner, I do not see anything counterproductive with Gates and others giving encouragement to corporations to be more concerned with goals like distinction along with an interest in making profits. The real test is how viable such motives are in a competitive market environment where the competition also includes companies motivated only by profits." My conclusion is that such goals and motives are likely to work for only a small fraction of corporations because most employees and executives are not willing to pay a lot to reduce poverty in Africa, and similar broad goals.

POSNER AFTERTHOUGHTS

The related issues of overcompensation of CEOs and other senior business executives, and of the growing inequality of income and wealth, both addressed in this part of the book, have achieved new salience as a result of the financial crisis that hit the nation and the world in the fall of 2008; the response to the crisis has included bailouts conditioned on capping executive compensation.

Even before the crisis, in a post on December 10, 2006 (reprinted in Part VIII of this book), I had noted the "phenomenal returns to hedge-fund operators, private-equity investors, and other finance specialists, astronomical CEO salaries," etc., and had pointed out some potential problems with the surge in wealth, including deflecting high-IQ people from entering careers in which the social returns may greatly exceed the private returns (government service, basic science, and teaching) and interfering, by massive philanthropy, with a coherent foreign policy. Major philanthropies such as the Gates Foundation do not coordinate their spending decisions with U.S. national goals, and distort political competition. But a more serious downside to the explosion of wealth in the upper reaches of the business community is the contribution of executive overcompensation to the financial crisis, specifically to the reluctance of executives to recognize and get off a bubble, such as the housing bubble that precipitated the crisis. A firm that drops out of a bubble before it bursts will be leaving a lot of money on the table, at least in the short run. And the decision to drop out is a hard sell to a firm's investors. Suppose a bank's management tells its investors that it's worried that the bubble will burst and so it is going to wind down its leverage, with the result that its investors' short-run return will fall. They will see that investors in the bank's competitors are continuing to make a lot of money, and they are apt to think that management is simply offering an excuse for failure. And the investors can lower their risk by diversifying their portfolio; they thus may *want* the bank to take risk that they can diversify away, because risk and return are positively correlated.

The tendency to hang in and hope for the best is strengthened if executive compensation is both very generous and truncated on the downside but not the upside. For then every day the firm continues to ride the bubble it generates a lot of money for the CEO and other senior executives, who know moreover that they will be OK if the bubble bursts because they have negotiated a generous severance package with the board of directors.

Overcompensation, with or without asymmetric treatment of gains and losses, has another effect in inducing excessive risk taking. The more generous a senior executive's compensation is, the greater his incentive to maximize profits in the short run, especially in a bubble, where the short run is highly profitable. This incentive can be checked by backloading compensation, for example, by giving the executive, instead of cash, stock in his company that he cannot sell for a significant period of time. And companies do that, but in many cases insufficiently to deflect executives from excessive focus on the short run.

Further comments by Becker and me on "creative capitalism" can be found in the book of that title edited by Michael Kinsley (2008).

VI

ENVIRONMENT AND DISASTERS

27

TSUNAMI

January 5, 2005

THE TSUNAMI AND THE ECONOMICS OF CATASTROPHIC RISK—POSNER

The Indian Ocean tsunami illustrates a type of disaster to which policymakers pay too little attention—a disaster that has a very low or unknown probability of occurring, but that if it does occur creates enormous losses. Great as the death toll, physical and emotional suffering of survivors, and property damage caused by the recent tsunami are, even greater losses could be inflicted by other disasters of low (but not negligible) or unknown probability. The asteroid that exploded above Siberia in 1908 with the force of a hydrogen bomb might have killed millions of people had it exploded above a major city. Yet that asteroid was only about two hundred feet in diameter, and a much larger one (among the thousands of dangerously large asteroids in orbits that intersect the earth's orbit) could strike the earth and cause the total extinction of the human race through a combination of shock waves, fires, tsunamis, and blockage of sunlight—wherever it struck. Other catastrophic risks include, besides earthquakes such as the one that caused the recent tsunami, natural epidemics (the 1918–19 Spanish influenza epidemic killed between 20 and 40 million people), nuclear or biological attacks by terrorists, certain types of lab accident, and abrupt global warming. The probability of catastrophes resulting, intentionally or not, from human activity appears to be increasing because of the rapidity and direction of technological advances.

The fact that a catastrophe is very unlikely to occur is not a rational justification for ignoring the risk of its occurrence. Suppose that a tsunami as destructive as the Indian Ocean one occurs on average once a century and kills 150,000 people. That is an average of 1,500 deaths per year. Even without attempting a sophisticated estimate of the value of life to the people exposed to the risk, one can say with some confidence that if an annual death toll of 1,500 could be substantially reduced at moderate cost, the investment would be worthwhile. A combination of educating the residents of low-lying coastal areas about the warning signs of a tsunami (tremors and a sudden recession in the ocean), establishing a warning system involving emergency broadcasts, telephoned warnings, and air-raid-type sirens, and improving emergency response systems would have saved many of the people killed by the Indian Ocean tsunami, probably at a total cost below any reasonable estimate of the average losses that can be expected from tsunamis. Relocating people away from coasts would be even more efficacious, but except in the most vulnerable areas or in areas in which residential or commercial uses have only marginal value, the costs would probably exceed the benefits. For annual costs of protection must be matched with annual, not total, expected costs of tsunamis.

In my book *Catastrophe: Risk and Response* (Oxford University Press, 2004), I try to be more precise about how one might determine the costs of catastrophes. There is now a substantial economic literature inferring the value of life from the costs people are willing to incur to avoid small risks of death; if from behavior toward risk one infers that a person would pay $70 to avoid a one in one hundred thousand risk of death, his value of life would be estimated at $7 million ($70/.00001), which is in fact the median estimate of the value of life of an American. Because value of life is positively correlated with income, this figure cannot be used to estimate the value of life of most of the people killed by the Indian Ocean tsunami. A further complication is that the studies may not be robust with respect to risks of death much smaller than the one in ten thousand to one in one hundred thousand range of most of the studies; we do not know what the risk of death from a tsunami was to the people killed. Additional complications come from the fact that undoubtedly more than 150,000 people have died or will die—and the total may never be known—and that there is vast suffering and property damage that must also be quantified, as well as estimates needed of just how effective precautionary measures of various scope and expense would have been. The risks of smaller but also still destructive tsunamis that such measures might protect against must also be factored in; nor am I confident about my "once-in-a-century" risk estimate. Nevertheless, it seems apparent that the total cost figure of the recent tsunami will come in at an amount great enough to indicate that there were indeed precautionary measures to take that would have been cost justified.

Why, then, weren't such measures taken in anticipation of a tsunami on the scale that occurred? Tsunamis are a common consequence of earthquakes, which themselves are common; and tsunamis can have other causes besides earthquakes—a major asteroid strike in an ocean would create a tsunami that would dwarf the Indian Ocean one.

There are a number of reasons for such neglect. First, although a once-in-a-century event is as likely to occur at the beginning of the century as at any other time, it is much less likely to occur in the first decade of the century than later. Politicians with limited terms of office and thus foreshortened political horizons are likely to discount low-risk disaster possibilities, since the risk of damage to their careers from failing to take precautionary measures is truncated. Second, to the extent that effective precautions require governmental action, the fact that government is a centralized system of control makes it difficult for officials to respond to the full spectrum of possible risks against which cost-justified measures might be taken. The officials, given the variety of matters to which they must attend, are likely to have a high threshold of attention below which risks are simply ignored. Third, where risks are regional or global rather than local, many national governments, especially in the poorer and smaller countries, may drag their heels in the hope of taking a free ride on the larger and richer countries. Knowing this, the latter countries may be reluctant to take precautionary measures and by doing so reward and thus encourage free riding. Fourth, countries are poor often because of weak, inefficient, or corrupt government, characteristics that may disable poor nations from taking cost-justified precautions. Fifth, people have difficulty thinking in terms of probabilities, especially very low probabilities, which they tend therefore to write off. This weakens political support for incurring the costs of taking precautionary measures against low-probability disasters.

The operation of some of these factors is illustrated by the refusal of the Pacific nations, which do have a tsunami warning system, to extend their system to the Indian Ocean prior to the recent catastrophe. Tsunamis are more common in the Pacific, and most of the Pacific nations do not abut on the Indian Ocean, but even if the risk of an Indian Ocean tsunami was only a tenth of that of a Pacific Ocean tsunami (a figure I have seen in a newspaper article), it was still worth taking precautions against; but there is a tendency to write down slight risks to zero.

An even more dramatic example of neglect of low-probability/high-cost risks concerns the asteroid menace, which is analytically similar to the menace of tsunamis. NASA, with an annual budget of more than $10 billion, spends only $4 million a year on mapping dangerously close large asteroids, and at that rate may not complete the task for another decade, even though such mapping is the key to an asteroid defense because it may give us years of warning. Deflecting an asteroid from its orbit when it is still millions of miles from the earth is a feasible undertaking. In both cases, slight risks of terrible disasters are largely ignored essentially for political reasons.

In part because tsunamis are one of the risks of an asteroid collision, the Indian Ocean disaster has stimulated new interest in asteroid defense. This is welcome. The fact that a disaster of a particular type has not occurred recently or even within human memory (or even ever) is a bad reason to ignore it. The risk may be slight, but if the consequences should it materialize are great enough, the expected cost of disaster may be sufficient to warrant defensive measures.

ECONOMIC EFFECTS OF TSUNAMIS AND OTHER CATASTROPHES—BECKER

John Stuart Mill, the great nineteenth-century English economist and philosopher, optimistically, but

I believe accurately, remarked on "...the great rapidity with which countries recover from a state of devastation, the disappearance in a short time, of all traces of mischief done by earthquakes, floods, hurricanes, and the ravages of war." The history of both natural and man-made disasters during the subsequent century and a half generally supports Mill.

The 9/11 terrorist attacks were quickly recognized as the beginning of a series of possibly more destructive attacks on U.S. citizens and property, and many commentators then believed it would cause a major economic depression. Yet it had a slight overall impact on the course of GDP and employment in the United States, although some industries and New York City were affected for several years. The Kobe earthquake of 1995 killed over six thousand persons, and destroyed more than one hundred thousand homes, still the economic recovery not only of Japan but also of the Kobe economy was rapid. The flu pandemic of 1918–19 killed about 30 million persons worldwide without having a major impact on the world's economy. The lasting economic effects are similarly small for most other natural disasters that have occurred during the past couple of centuries.

Many natural catastrophes have very low probabilities of occurring, but cause considerable destruction of both life and property when they do happen. The recent tsunami in the Indian Ocean is one horrible example: it killed many more people than either 9/11 or the Kobe earthquake. But bad as it is, the loss of life is much smaller relative to the populations of the nations affected than some previous disasters. For example, the Lisbon earthquake of 1755 may have killed sixty thousand people, other earthquakes in the past are alleged to have killed in the hundreds of thousands, and I mentioned the flu epidemic of 1918–19 that killed tens of millions worldwide.

History and analysis both indicate that the economic recovery of the nations most adversely affected by this tsunami will be rapid, although it will take longer in the resorts and coastal regions hit the hardest. The expectation of rapid recovery explains why Asian stock markets did not change much after the tsunami struck: Indonesia's and Malaysia's actually rose a little during the last week of December, while Thailand's declined a little, and Sri Lanka's declined by a few percent.

I fully agree with Posner that it is worth spending considerably more to provide better early warning systems about the future occurrence of earthquakes and tsunamis, asteroids that might strike the earth, and other catastrophes. But no matter how much is spent and how much planning takes place, natural catastrophes will continue and will sometimes be unexpected.

There are two ways to protect against natural and other disasters: one is through insurance that helps compensate persons badly hurt by loss of family member or property. The other is through self-protection, which means actions to reduce the probability of the disasters from happening—as when a person drives more carefully to reduce the likelihood of getting into an accident, or when countries agree to reduce emissions of greenhouse gases in the hope of reducing the probability of severe global warming.

As more is learned about various natural disasters, more self-protective actions would become available. But for many of the very infrequent ones, even given generous estimates of the value of life of the type discussed by Posner, it does not pay to take expensive self-protection actions. The best response in these cases is to have an effective insurance system for those badly harmed. So I concentrate most of my comments about protection against disasters on insurance.

Survivors of disasters that strike rich nations usually have medical coverage to pay for their treatment and rehabilitation, and insurance to cover much of their property destroyed, while those who perish usually leave life insurance for their families, and the opportunity to obtain decent education for their children. By contrast, most individuals in poor nations of Asia and elsewhere mainly rely on help from their families and neighbors when disasters strike. Unfortunately, such help is not available when disasters attack many members of the same family and whole neighborhoods, as in major tsunamis and earthquakes.

An effective way for poorer nations to respond in the longer run would be to encourage greater investment in education. Since education raises the earnings of individuals and the per capita incomes of countries, education clearly makes it easier to cope with disasters—as Mill had already recognized when he emphasizes the importance of knowledge in hastening the recovery from disasters. Beyond that, however, my colleague at the University of Chicago Casey Mulligan and I have shown that educated persons take a much longer time perspective in their personal decisions. This means that they are much more likely to anticipate the incidence and location of natural catastrophes when they decide where to live and how their houses are built, and they better self-protect and self-insure themselves in other ways as well.

But in the short run, greater access to private market insurance, even if subsidized by governments, is important. Regrettably, such insurance is not likely to be available to, or chosen by, the type of very poor families disproportionately affected by this tsunami. The large outpouring of aid from rich nations will help only temporarily in the very near term. The next best alternative to private insurance would be government disaster programs in poor countries that designate areas hit by major earthquakes, hurricanes, and other catastrophes, man-made or natural, as eligible for disaster assistance. Such programs could make sufficient payments to poor families of husbands and fathers who died, and to families that lost most of their property, to help put them on their economic feet, without causing much of a drain on the government budgets of even poorer developing nations like Indonesia and Sri Lanka.

The moral hazard effects of such programs are always worrisome—families might continue to build homes on earthquake fault lines if they expect government compensation when their homes are destroyed, or continue to build close to the shore in potential waterborne disaster areas. There is no perfect offset against such rational responses to government coverage of losses, but incomplete protection ("copayments"), and regulatory exclusion of certain types of construction and other vulnerable activities in potential disaster regions would encourage individuals to consider the risks involved in their actions.

28

MAJOR DISASTERS

September 4, 2005

MAJOR DISASTERS AND THE GOOD SAMARITAN PROBLEM—BECKER

Although the death toll from Hurricane Katrina is not yet known, the loss in life and property makes this one of the worst natural disasters in American history. Coming less than a year after the Great Tsunami that killed about three hundred thousand people in Asia, this experience has many wondering whether the world is facing much more erratic and violent weather, possibly due to global warming.

I do not know the answer to this question, but important public policy issues are raised by major disasters, even if they will not increase in severity over time. One major question is whether individuals, companies, and local governments have the right incentives when they determine where to locate plants, oil drilling rigs, refineries, factories, homes, roads, levees, and bridges.

Location decisions would be optimal if those making these decisions had to bear the full social cost of any damages to their property and person from a disaster. Under these conditions, greater insurance premiums in areas that are prone to hurricanes, earthquakes, tsunamis, and other disasters would reflect the greater risk to life and property in these areas. The expected loss for those not insuring would rise in proportion to the greater risk. People, companies, and governments would then build homes, roads, businesses, and the like in disaster-prone regions only if the benefits exceeded the full risk of damages.

However, generous private and public help to victims of terrible disasters, while highly desirable, distort such rational calculations. Congress just voted over $10 billion of relief help to victims of Katrina, the Red Cross and other private groups have already had pledges of over $200 million of private help, other nations have offered generous assistance, and the United States has the Federal Emergency Management Agency that provides substantial assistance to people and businesses in areas that are declared to be disasters. Presidents are making greater and greater use of this agency to declare regions in need of emergency assistance.

Such public and private assistance in the event of disasters make it more likely for persons, companies, and public activities to locate in high-risk areas because they will often be spared much of the losses. They also may not take out insurance against risks that would inflict large losses; for example, rather few New Orleans homeowners had flood insurance. Studies have shown a small propensity to insure against low-probability natural disasters that cause great damage. See Howard Kunreuther and Richard J. Roth, *Paying the Price: The Status and Role of Insurance against Natural Disasters in the United States* (1998). So private and public generosity to victims of disasters help distort many predisaster decisions.

This distortion goes under the name of the "Good Samaritan" paradox in philosophy and economics. To illustrate this problem, consider the behavior of loving parents toward their children. Such parents would come to the assistance of their children if they get into financial trouble, have serious medical problems, or experience other difficulties. At the same time, they want their children to use their money wisely, work and study hard, prepare for future contingencies, and lead a healthy life, so that they can avoid personal disasters.

Unfortunately for the parents, children can distinguish reality from lectures, and threats that will not be backed up by parental behavior. If they anticipate that their parents will help them out if they get into trouble, and if they are not so altruistic to their parents, they would consume and possibly gamble excessively, and they might quit good jobs to "find themselves." Parents might then be indirectly encouraging the very behavior by their children that they want them to avoid.

The federal government and private philanthropy are in a similar Good Samaritan situation with respect to families, businesses, and local governments that build where there is likely to be flooding, landslides, hurricanes, earthquakes, and other major natural disasters. The federal government and others may wish they did not build so much in these areas, and the government may hope for diversification elsewhere. Yet if the government's advice is ignored, and if there is terrible suffering from a disaster, all humane and politically sensitive governments and philanthropic organizations would help, even though they wish the victims had made more socially efficient decisions before disaster struck.

A particularly important location decision facing the United States is whether it should encourage a greater decentralization of its oil, refinery, and natural gas facilities. Katrina shut down about 1.5 million barrels of oil production, 16 percent of American natural gas production, and about 10 percent of U.S. refining capacity at a time when there is little slack in worldwide refining capacity, and the region's electric and natural gas distribution system has also been knocked out. "Altogether, about 800 manned platforms, plus several thousand smaller unmanned platforms, feed their water and gas into 33,000 miles of underwater pipelines." Daniel Yergin, "The Katrina Crisis," *Wall Street Journal,* September 2, 2005, p.A14.

Much of the cost of this shutdown will be borne by the country as a whole, partly already reflected in the decision to release some of the 700 million barrels of oil in the Strategic Oil Reserve—the U.S. government has no gasoline reserves, although some other countries do have such reserves. The Gulf energy complex seems especially vulnerable not only to a future natural disaster, but also to well-planned terrorist attacks.

The ability to decentralize natural gas and to some extent also oil production is limited by the federal moratorium on natural gas and oil production in the Outer Continental Shelf. The recent energy bill includes a requirement to prepare an inventory of these reserves, and some effort is being made in Congress to relax the moratorium. The damage from Katrina indicates that such steps are more urgent than they appeared even a few weeks earlier.

Can anything generally be done to weaken before disasters strike the inefficient incentives caused by the natural and laudable tendency of governments to help the victims of terrible disasters? To start, it would help to have tougher zoning restrictions in disaster-prone areas to reduce construction and raise their capacity to withstand major shocks. These restrictions would apply, for example, to areas subject to bad flooding, perhaps because buildings and roads would be below sea level, as in New Orleans, and to buildings on large faults that are particularly subject to earthquake damage. After the great destruction caused by the 1989 California earthquake, that state toughened its building code to make it more likely that buildings could survive major earthquakes. Perhaps they did not toughen them enough since California can expect a large amount of federal assistance once again in the event of a future serious earthquake. Asian nations have restricted rebuilding in some areas devastated by the Great Tsunami.

In addition, anyone who does build in designated high-risk areas should be required to carry insurance that covers most of their losses, the way many states mandate liability car insurance. This requirement would place the bulk of the cost of damages on the individuals and businesses that locate in risky areas, and the companies that insure them. Provisions have to be made for persons considered too poor to have adequate insurance, and insurance companies would need to have sufficient resources in the event a major disaster strikes. Many states already require insurance companies to have minimum levels of liquid capital.

Given the need to help victims of disasters, there is no perfect way to induce individuals, businesses, and local governments to incorporate more fully into their decisions the risks of living and building in disaster-prone areas. But more can be done, and Katrina proved that despite 9/11, the United States is still terribly ill prepared to handle a major disaster. It is scary to contemplate how well the country would respond to even greater disasters, such as one induced by a future and even more deadly terrorist attack.

KATRINA, COST-BENEFIT ANALYSIS, AND TERRORISM—POSNER

The Speaker of the House of Representatives, Dennis Hastert, got into trouble, and had to apologize, for suggesting that maybe New Orleans should be abandoned rather than rebuilt. He raised a valid issue; that he got into trouble for doing so just proves the adage that, in politics, the phrase "to tell the truth" is synonymous with "to blunder."

Not that it can yet be said that New Orleans should be abandoned; that conclusion could emerge only from a complex analysis. The point is rather that the analysis should be undertaken. The broader issue is the role of cost-benefit analysis in the analysis of disaster risk. In addition, the disaster in New Orleans is a timely reminder of the risk of terrorism.

Because New Orleans is both below sea level and adjacent to a sea (Lake Pontchartrain is connected via another lake and a strait to the Gulf of Mexico), the city is extraordinarily vulnerable to just the sort of flooding that occurred when the levees broke as a result of Hurricane Katrina. To decide whether to rebuild or abandon the city, the cost of reconstruction, plus the expected cost of a future such disaster, should be compared to the cost of either building a new city or, what would be cheaper and faster, simply relocating the present inhabitants to existing cities, towns, etc., a solution that would require merely the construction of some additional commercial and residential facilities, plus some additional infrastructure. Of course New Orleans has great historic and sentimental value, and this should be factored into the analysis, but it should not be given conclusive weight. Perhaps it should be given little weight, since the historic portions of the city (the French Quarter and the Garden District) might be rebuilt and preserved as a tourist site, much like Colonial Williamsburg, without having to be part of a city.

The decision to abandon or not cannot be left to the market. It could be if federal, state, and local government could credibly commit not to provide any financial assistance to the city's residents, businesses, and other institutions in the event of another disaster—but government could not make such a commitment. Or if government could require the residents, businesses, etc., to buy insurance that would cover the complete costs of such a disaster. But again it could not; insurance in such an amount, to cover so uncertain a set of contingencies, could not be bought in the private market.

So the decision would have to be made by government, and, ideally, it would be based on cost-benefit analysis. In such an analysis, the expected cost (that is, the cost discounted by the probability that it will actually be incurred) of a future disastrous flood would probably weigh very heavily and could easily tip the balance in favor of abandonment. The reason is only partly that constructing levees and making other improvements that would provide greater protection against the danger of flooding would be very costly (such a program was proposed in 1998 that would have cost $14 billion, according to Mark Frischetti, "They Saw It Coming," *New York Times,* September 2, 2005, p. A23); it is also that the levees, sea gates, etc., would remain highly vulnerable to terrorism. Breaches similar to those that caused the recent flood, but created without warning by terrorist bombs, would cause much greater loss of life because there would be no time to evacuate the population, whereas with the warning of the approaching hurricane 80 percent of the New Orleans population left the city before the flood. The expected cost of a terrorist attack on rebuilt levees cannot actually be calculated because the probability of such an attack cannot be estimated. But it should probably be reckoned nontrivial given the wide publicity that the vulnerability of the city to flooding has received and the fact that a port city is more vulnerable to terrorism than an inland one because terrorists approaching from the sea are less likely to be detected before they attack, since they would be spending little time on U.S. territory. (Analytical techniques for adapting cost-benefit analysis to situations in which risks cannot be estimated with any precision are discussed in chapter 3 of my book *Catastrophe: Risk and Response* [2004].) Of course, massive amounts of money could be devoted to protecting the vulnerable rebuilt city from a terrorist attack, but that would be just another substantial cost that abandonment would avert.

New Orleans is becoming more vulnerable not only because of the terrorist threat, but for three other reasons as well. The city is sinking because (paradoxically) flood control has prevented the Mississippi River from depositing sediment to renew the subsiding silt that the city is built on. The wetlands and barrier islands that provide some protection against the effects of hurricanes are disappearing. And global warming is expected to increase sea levels and also to increase the severity and frequency of storms—all factors that will make New Orleans more vulnerable to future floods.

It might seem that if, as current estimates have it, the cost of the damage inflicted by Hurricane Katrina will prove to be "only" $100 billion, the expected cost could not have been too great, since the probability of such a flood as occurred presumably was low. But while the annual probability was low, the cumulative probability over a relatively short period, such as one or two decades, was probably quite high. Moreover, $100 billion is almost certainly a gross underestimate, because it ignores the loss of life (economists are currently using a figure of $7 million to estimate the value of life of an average American), the tremendous physical and emotional suffering of the hundreds of thousands of refugees from the flood, and the lost output of the businesses and individuals displaced by the flood. These are real social costs, as an economist reckons cost. What is not a social cost is certain purely pecuniary losses that will be made up for elsewhere in the economy; for example, the loss of convention business by New Orleans will be a gain to other cities.

Another hidden cost of rebuilding rather than abandoning the city is the uncertainty concerning how much time it will take to rebuild and what the former residents will do in the meantime. If they expect to return to the city in several months, they will find it difficult to obtain remunerative employment in the meantime.

For simplicity, I have assumed that the choice is between rebuilding New Orleans and abandoning it. Realistically, given politics and the typical (and on the whole commendable) American reflex refusal to accept defeat, the choice is the scale of the rebuilding. I urge that careful consideration be given to rebuilding on a considerably reduced scale from what the city was before the flood.

Speaking, as I did earlier, of terrorism, an article in the *Washington Post* this morning (Susan B. Glasser and Josh White, "Storm Exposed Disarray: What Went Wrong," p. A1) provides support for those who claim that the slow response to the New Orleans flooding shows that the nation has not made adequate preparations for responding to a terrorist attack by means of weapons of mass destruction—a significant (though again unquantifiable) and growing danger. An attack with nuclear, radioactive, or biological weaponry could easily require the evacuation of an entire city without warning and with much greater loss of life.

It seems that, four years after the 9/11 attacks, we are still not taking the threat of terrorism seriously. There are four basic counterterrorist tools: (1) Threat assessment, which means conducting cost-benefit analyses designed to identify the targets that are most vulnerable to terrorist attack, having in mind the goals of the terrorists (so far as we can determine them), the value of the target, and the cost of hardening (defending) it. (2) Hardening at least the most vulnerable targets. (3) Warning intelligence (which of course failed us on 9/11), designed to detect impending attacks. (4) Emergency response measures if an attack occurs, designed to minimize human and property damage.

(1) has made little progress, in part because of political obstacles; all elected officials except the president and vice president have geographically circumscribed constituencies and naturally resist efforts to devote proportionately more resources to defensive measures that would benefit only outsiders. (2) has made very little progress, because of cost. (3) has improved, though not as much as it should have. (See my book *Preventing Surprise Attacks: Intelligence Reform in the Wake of 9/11* [2005], and my just-published monograph *Remaking Domestic Intelligence* [August 2005].) And judging from the New Orleans disaster, (4)

remains completely inadequate. One possible response would have been for the president to declare martial law and place a general who had combat experience (i.e., someone who knows how to coordinate a large number of people in circumstances of urgency and uncertainty) in command of all federal, state, local, public, private, military, and civilian response agencies and personnel. The article in the *Washington Post* this morning that I mentioned notes the bureaucratic logjams that delayed the response; martial law would have overcome them. My idea about how to respond to such a disaster may be excessively dramatic and quite unsound; I am no expert. But ever since 9/11 it has been known that there could well be a terrorist attack utilizing weapons of mass destruction and that, if so, the correct emergency response might involve the evacuation of a city. It is disheartening to think that after four years there are still no plans, preparations, or command systems for dealing with such an eventuality.

29

FEDERALISM, ECONOMICS, AND KATRINA

October 9, 2005

FEDERALISM, ECONOMICS, AND KATRINA—POSNER

Much of the debate over the response to Hurricane Katrina has centered on the question of the division of responsibilities among the different levels of government—federal, state, and local. Concern has been expressed that for the federal government to have played a more aggressive role, for example by taking command of all response efforts and perhaps placing them in the hands of the regular army (as distinct from the National Guard, which is state rather than federal, although the president is authorized to "federalize" it in situations of war, insurrection, or civil disturbance and thereby place it under federal military command), would have violated the tenets of federalism and perhaps specific provisions of the Constitution allocating powers between federal and state (including local) government, and specific statutes such as the Posse Comitatus Act of 1878, which limits military participation in law enforcement.

Issues of federalism cannot be resolved solely by reference to economic criteria. The reason is that, the Revolution having been waged by states (the former British colonies) linked in a loose confederation, the Constitution, while tightening the federation, recognizes the states as quasi-sovereign entities. Even if it would be efficient to do without states and have as centralized a government as France has, this could not be done without amending the Constitution, and indeed perhaps without replacing it with a completely new Constitution adopted in a constitutional convention.

Nevertheless, it is of course possible to analyze the economizing principles of federalism, and that is what I shall try to do in this posting.

From an economic standpoint, federalism is a scheme of decentralized governance, designed to optimize the provision of government services. In the governmental as in the private business setting, there are disadvantages to a strictly hierarchical ("U-form"—unified or unitary), as distinct from a more loosely coupled or "horizontal," method of organization ("M-form"—multidivisional). With strict hierarchy, information flows from the bottom of the enterprise up to the top echelon of management, and commands flow back down based on decisions made at the top. Inevitably, information will be filtered and otherwise lost or garbled on its way up, and as a result the top managers will perforce base their decisions on information that is frequently incomplete or inaccurate;

and likewise commands will tend to be misunderstood on their way down the successive links in the chain of command. The centralizing of decision-making power will reduce competition, diversity, and flexibility; mistaken decisions will be more costly because they will bind the entire enterprise; and mistakes will be frequent because the top managers will not be given a full array of alternatives to choose among because their subordinates will filter out most of the alternatives on the way up in order to spare the top managers from being overwhelmed by information.

The other side of this coin, which is illustrated by the regime that preceded the Constitution—namely the Articles of Confederation, which created a very loose-knit federation of the states to conduct the Revolutionary War, and the inadequacies of which led directly to the Constitution—is that the lack of a central authority can result in suboptimal performance. Each division of the firm (or state or other regional or local government in a federal system) will tend to ignore the effects of its actions on the other divisions; each will be reluctant both to incur costs that benefit the other divisions (external benefits) or to avoid imposing costs on the others (external costs). Centralization is a way of internalizing costs and benefits throughout the enterprise by coordinating the divisions and making sure they are pulling together.

Since there are both costs and benefits to centralization, we can expect that usually the best organization will be one that has elements of both central control and divisional autonomy—one that has some hierarchy but not too much, and divisions that are only semi-autonomous. And so we observe in our federal system as a result of the provisions of the Constitution and, in particular, their (loose) interpretation by the Supreme Court. The states are allowed a considerable degree of autonomy in matters of taxation and regulation (including licensure), administration of schools and prisons, highways and other infrastructure, criminal law enforcement, etc., but Congress, the Supreme Court, and the president have a considerable override power. Congress is empowered to regulate interstate and foreign commerce; and the Supreme Court, by interpretation of the commerce power, has forbidden the states to impose tariffs and other impediments to interstate trade and travel, even if Congress fails to act. Because the states have a degree of autonomy, they function, much as the divisions of a software or pharmaceutical firm would, as laboratories for (social) experimentation. Policies invented in one state, if successful, can be copied by others. Also, people can sort themselves between states in accordance with their preferences; the right to move to a different state supplements voting power in controlling the action of government officials.

In the case of response to emergencies, one of the factors I discussed earlier—the effect of hierarchy on information flows and command responses—figures prominently, along with (depending on the scale of the emergency) externalities. The officials closest to a problem have the best information and also can act most quickly on it. We wouldn't be well served by having (only) a federal fire department, so that in the event of a local two-alarm blaze the local fire chief would have to inform Washington and get permission to fight the fire. This is the point made by those who believe that the Federal Emergency Management Agency, even under competent leadership, should not be in charge of emergency responses to catastrophes.

But not all catastrophes are local. What is more, given mobility of responders, it does not make sense for every locality to invest in achieving self-sufficiency in responding to an emergency, regardless of the scale of the emergency. Suppose, as in the case of Hurricane Katrina, that the catastrophe simultaneously engulfs a large number of cities and towns in several states. Insofar as a coordinated response is optimal, and given transaction costs, which are especially high in an emergency situation, it doesn't make much sense to leave the response to state and local governments. Each state will seek to optimize its response to the damage caused it, and each locality to the damage caused that locality, disregarding the costs and benefits of its actions to the other states and localities. Moreover, as in a military situation in which one doesn't know where the enemy will attack, an effective response to an emergency requires the maintenance of reserves that can be deployed to the threatened spot, and those reserves have to be held and controlled centrally.

I conclude that while state and local government can and should be given exclusive responsibility for responding to run-of-the-mill local emergencies, the federal government should have standby responsibility for regional and (of course) national emergencies, as well as for emergencies that, as in the case of the flooding of New Orleans as a result of Katrina, wreak destruction on such a scale that would not have been efficient for the local government to prepare to meet. If you tell a city that it will receive no assistance in the event of a disaster, however great, it will overinvest in preparing to respond to disaster. Suppose for the sake of simplicity that the country has only two cities, that the cost of responding to an average disaster is 1 and to a cataclysm is 20, but that the probability that there would be two cataclysms at the same time is close to zero. Then if the federal government refuses to assist in local disasters, no matter how destructive, the two cities may incur a total cost of prevention of 40, whereas if the government invests in providing the necessary backup capability, the total cost of prevention will fall to 22 (1+1+20).

If this analysis is correct, then it was the federal government's responsibility to prepare to assist in an emergency of the scale of Hurricane Katrina. Such preparations would have been consistent with an optimal allocation of responsibilities between central and local government.

COMMENT ON FEDERALISM, ECONOMICS, AND KATRINA—BECKER

Posner gives good arguments why the federal government has important advantages in fighting emergencies, like the recent devastating hurricanes, that wreak havoc over a broad area that involves several cities and states. But bigger and centralized governments are also more bureaucratic, and respond slowly and erratically. Surely, the local government of New York City responded faster to the 9/11 terrorist attack than did the federal government, even though New York's response could also be criticized.

None of the governments responded quickly or effectively during the Katrina emergency, even ignoring the lack of preparation for the overwhelming of the New Orleans levee system by a powerful hurricane. Fortunately, since there was advance notice of Katrina's destructive path, most of the vulnerable population evacuated their homes and businesses, and took other protective measures.

While I agree with Posner's general discussion of the different advantages and disadvantages of local and centralized authority, I still have a strong preference toward decentralized authority whenever that is possible. One reason is that local governments have a better feel for the special needs of its own population than a distant central authority can ever have.

A second important consideration is that individuals can move from one locality or state to another in search of better schools and other public services. This is an enormous advantage that can never be duplicated when power and decision making are centralized. Competition among states and cities within a country puts considerable pressure on lagging state and local governments because people vote with their feet. They move where there are education and other services that better meet their needs.

Unfortunately, this type of competition works well only for individuals and families that are reasonably well informed about alternatives elsewhere, and who have the resources and inner energy to take the large and risky step of moving to a possibly better and often distant location. Most richer and better-educated persons can do this, but many studies demonstrate that poorly educated persons are far less likely to move across cities and states than are the more highly educated.

The population that remained in New Orleans during Katrina and who suffered the most had low incomes and education. This is not surprising since the low educated, as I just indicated, are usually less likely to move to take advantage of better opportunities elsewhere. Many do not own cars, and have to take public transportation, and they must find places to go. But without minimizing the importance of these considerations I want to emphasize another factor at work in the Katrina episode that contributed to the particularly heavy suffering of persons at the bottom end of the income and education distribution.

Governments at all levels—federal, state, and local—simply failed to take decisive and appropriate actions to meet the emergency brought on by Katrina. So families were mainly left to their own devices, and most of them had enough initiative to take as effective action as was possible. Of course, they could not do everything since their homes and shops were in place and often had to be abandoned.

The poor were hurt most by the government's failure partly for the reasons just indicated, and partly because they have become heavily dependent on governments to take care of them. This "dependency culture" created and nurtured perhaps unintentionally by welfare, Medicaid, and other government programs saps initiative and energy, and greatly weakens the habit of making one's own decisions. Dependency on government is especially devastating in serious emergencies, such as that caused by Katrina, when governments fail to take quick and appropriate actions.

It may be best to give the federal government responsibility for meeting emergencies that cast a wide net over a large area encompassing many localities and states. But each emergency is somewhat different, and it is hard to believe that even after large and numerous investigations of each failure, a large bureaucracy like the federal government is likely to take fast, effective, and decisive actions.

This is one important and usually overlooked reason to reform transfer programs and legislation to help the poor so that they have much greater responsibility in organizing and managing their lives. They need to be induced to look for private housing as well as jobs, and to be held responsible for bad decisions rather than being excused because they are "victims." Such changes in these programs for the poor will probably not make governmental responses to emergencies any better. Yet they could significantly reduce the enormous damage done from catastrophic events to families who can least afford further losses. These families will respond quicker and more successfully to catastrophes if they are more accustomed to taking care of themselves.

30

POST-CATASTROPHE PRICE GOUGING

October 23, 2005

SHOULD PRICE GOUGING IN THE AFTERMATH OF CATASTROPHES BE PUNISHED?—POSNER

Hurricane Katrina has produced a mass of interesting revelations. One is that more than half the states have laws forbidding "price gouging," often defined with unpardonable vagueness as charging "unconscionably" high prices. These laws are rarely enforced. But the sharp run-up in gasoline prices as a result of Katrina (and also Hurricane Rita, which followed almost immediately), impeding imports of crude oil and causing a number of refineries in the path of the hurricanes to shut down temporarily, prompted a flurry of enforcement threats and even a few fines. It also prompted denunciation by politicians of greedy refiners and gasoline dealers, and proposals for federal legislation prohibiting "unconscionably excessive" gasoline price increases.

What prompts such reactions besides sheer ignorance of basic economics (a failure of our educational system) and demagogic appeals by politicians to that ignorance is the fact that an unanticipated curtailment of supply is likely to produce abnormal profits. The curtailment reduces output, which results in an increase in price as consumers bid against each other for the reduced output. In addition, the reduction in output is likely to reduce the sellers' unit costs; the reason is that sellers normally sell in a region in which their costs are increasing—if they were decreasing, the sellers would have an incentive to expand output further. With both price rising and cost falling, profits are likely to zoom upward. (Some gas stations are reported to have seen their profits increase by 400 percent shortly after Hurricane Katrina struck.) In times of catastrophe, with consumers hurting, the spectacle of sellers benefiting from consumers' distress, while (it seems) deepening that distress by charging them high prices, is a source of profound resentment, and in a democratic society profound resentments trigger government intervention.

Such intervention is nevertheless a profound mistake, and not only from some narrow "economic" perspective that disregards human suffering and distributive justice. If "price gouging" laws or even merely public opinion deters refiners and dealers from charging the high prices necessary to equilibrate demand and (reduced) supply, there will be shortages. Consumers will still be paying a higher price than before the shortage, but they will be paying the higher "price" in the cost of time spent waiting in line at gasoline stations, or (if they drive less because of the shortage) in the form of restricted mobility. And those who need the gasoline the most, not being able to express their need by outbidding other consumers for the limited supply, will suffer the most from the shortages. The only beneficiaries will be people with low costs of time and nonurgent demand.

But here is an interesting wrinkle. Admiralty law and common law (both are systems of judge-made law, but they are classified separately by lawyers because they used to be administered by separate courts) alike forbid certain practices that might be described as "price gouging." Suppose a ship is sinking, and another ship comes along in time to save the cargo and passengers of the first. The second ship demands, as its price for saving the cargo and passengers of the first ship, that the owner of the ship give it the ship and two-thirds of the rescued cargo, and the captain of the first ship, on behalf of the owner, being desperate agrees. The contract would not be legally enforceable; under the admiralty doctrine of "salvage," the second ship would be entitled to a "fair" price for rescuing the first, but to no more.

In a parallel case, also maritime but governed by common law rather than admiralty law (the *Alaska Packers* case, well known to law students), seamen on board a ship that was fishing for salmon in Alaska waters went on strike, demanding higher wages. The captain of the ship agreed because, the fishing season in these waters being very short, he could not have hired a replacement crew in time to make his quota. Again, however, the court refused to enforce the contract, in essence because it had been obtained under duress.

These cases, it turns out, are subtly but critically different from the "price gouging" alleged in the wake of Katrina and Rita. The refiners and dealers who raised prices after the hurricanes disrupted gasoline refining had not created the situation that resulted in a reduction in supply. If they had, say by agreeing to increase price above the existing level, they would have been punishable for violating the antitrust laws. (There were some accusations of price fixing, but as far as I know they have not been substantiated.) Similarly, in the salvage case, the rescue ship is not being asked to ration a limited supply by raising price; there is no one else competing for the rescue service—there is just the one ship in distress. And in *Alaska Packers,* there was no labor shortage, which would have justified seamen in demanding higher wages; the seamen created the shortage by refusing to work. From an economic standpoint, their workers' cartel was symmetrical with my hypothetical refiners' or dealers' cartel. Both are examples of opportunistic behavior—behavior designed to take advantage of an unforeseen opportunity to charge a monopoly price by threatening to withhold output. The hurricane-induced scarcity of gasoline that pushed up prices was not an artificial scarcity, but a natural one. The price increases generated by a natural scarcity (or indeed any scarcity not created by the person or firm imposing the increase), while they may generate "windfall profits," are unavoidable in a way that price increases due to a shortage created by a cartel are not.

A further exception to taking a hard line against responding to a natural scarcity by imposing price controls, some would argue, is the rare situation in which the consequence would be an intolerable gap between wealth and welfare. Suppose there is a highly limited supply of human growth hormone, so that if price is allowed to ration demand, all the hormone will be purchased by rich people who would want their sons and daughters of average height to be taller, and no hormone will be purchasable by poor people, or even people of average income, who have children who will be dwarfs unless they get the hormone; they simply are outbid by the rich. In such a case, there may well be a compelling moral argument for allocation of the limited supply on a basis other than price, presumably some utilitarian concept of welfare: aggregate happiness would be promoted by allocating the hormone on the basis of need rather than ability to pay. This was not a factor in the market's response to the incipient gasoline shortage caused by the hurricane.

Not only are the duress and welfare objections to price allocation inapplicable to the run-up in gasoline prices, but higher prices for gasoline are a source of substantial external benefits (that is, benefits not conferred on the parties to the transaction, so that the parties do not have an incentive to consider them in deciding on the price and other terms of the contract). By reducing the amount of driving and (if the higher prices persist) a switch to more fuel-efficient cars, higher gasoline prices cause a reduction in the amount of carbon dioxide emitted into the atmosphere—a major cause of global warming—while also reducing more conventional forms of automobile air pollution. A reduction in driving also reduces traffic congestion, which imposes costs in the form of delay on all drivers in congested areas. Finally, a reduction in the amount of oil consumed in the United States would make the nation more secure by reducing the wealth and economic leverage of the vulnerable, unstable, or hostile nations, such as Saudi Arabia, Iran, and Venezuela, that control so much of the world's oil supply.

In short, the social benefits of gasoline "price gouging" appear to exceed the social costs by a large margin.

COMMENT ON PRICE GOUGING—BECKER

Protests against "price gouging" in times of shortfalls in food supplies and other goods go back thousands of years. Alleged gougers and speculators have been hanged, assaulted, and ostracized. The recent energy bill passed by the House of Representatives has many good provisions, but also requires the Federal Trade Commission to set standards for "price gouging," and to punish offenders. Price controls emerged in virtually all countries, including the United States, during World War II and other wars, when many products were in reduced supply. It might seem "where there is smoke there is fire," but I fully agree that prices should be allowed to rise to their equilibrium levels when supply is reduced due to natural and other catastrophes.

As Posner indicates, attempts to suppress prices of gasoline or other goods that experience a great reduction in supply will require using less efficient ways to allocate the limited supply. The main alternative to higher prices is rationing in some form or another, such as selling on a first come first served basis, selling to persons willing to bribe the suppliers, and so forth. All these ways are inefficient, and discourage production instead of solving the problem of reduced availability of certain goods. Anyone who remembers the long lines and waits of an hour or more to get ten gallons of gasoline after President Carter imposed gasoline rationing can appreciate the wasteful costs created by nonprice methods of allocating a limited supply.

Another example is the rent controls that many nations imposed during and after World War II. Most have since removed their rent controls, but certain cities like New York have kept them, although in a modified form. Most serious studies of the effects of rent controls in New York and elsewhere show that they speed up the deterioration of housing quality, they cause an inefficient allocation of the limited housing stock, and usually they harm rather than benefit the poor and the young who more frequently have to find housing in the rental market. Rent controls generally benefit middle-class and older renters who often stay in large apartments at ridiculously low rents because it is too expensive to move to smaller apartments available on the open market.

The angry reaction of consumers to high prices caused by a major catastrophe usually is not directed at the persons or companies that profit. For example, customers are now very upset at owners of gasoline stations as they have posted continual increases in prices due to reduced supplies of gasoline resulting from Katrina, and the rising price of oil. But the profits of most gas station owners went down, not up, after Katrina. They have to pay more for the gas they buy, and the higher prices cut back on the demand for their gasoline. It should be pretty obvious that a rise in the price of a major input in production, such as gasoline is to retail gas stations, lowers rather than raises their profits since costs of production have risen.

On the other hand, profits have increased to operators of refineries that were not damaged by Katrina because the damage to Gulf oil refineries raised the wholesale price of gasoline, the main product of refineries. However, the higher prices and greater profits induced undamaged refineries to squeeze greater production out of their limited capacity, and companies hastened to repair the refineries that were damaged to cash in on the high prices. In fact, many were repaired in a remarkably short time. If price were not allowed to rise, profits of undamaged refineries would have been reduced, but the supply of gasoline would have increased at a slower, probably much slower, rate.

Faced with cutbacks in supply, companies often voluntarily sell at lower prices to their regular and best customers to increase the goodwill of these customers, and also because there may be an implicit long-term contract with these customers to keep prices relatively stable. They sometimes combine low prices to favored customers with rationing of the quantities they give them, while raising prices sharply to their customers who buy less, or more irregularly.

I have no problem with Posner's two examples of legitimate use of controls over prices. In the salvage at sea case, controls are warranted because there is not time during a rescue effort to work out what would be the appropriate sharing rule. The attempt of the Alaskan seamen to hold up the owners for higher wages while at sea presumably broke an implicit contract that wages are fixed for the duration of the fishing trip.

But shouldn't price controls also be used in poor countries when they experience a catastrophic shortfall in the supply of a food staple, such as rice or potatoes (the Irish potato famine is the best-known example)? The poorest families may be unable to pay the higher prices, and they could face starvation. Still, I do not believe price controls are a good solution, for they discourage greater production and imports of the scarce food, and they encourage farmers to hoard their food crops. Governments of these countries, and richer countries too through humanitarian aid, should instead become active in buying rice or whatever crop is involved, and reselling that to poor families at lower prices. Or these governments should increase income transfers to the poor that would enable them to pay the high market prices.

In the modern world, famines are caused not by high prices, but by bad governmental policies. Famines are virtually unknown in modern democratic societies. Yet famines and large-scale starvation are still sometimes found in dictatorships, such as in China during Mao's Great Leap Forward. The problem there was not high prices, but Mao's foolish policies. He first caused farm output to fall by his misguided attempt to leap forward. He then forcibly took much of the limited supply of food from farmers, so that many of them starved to death, in order to feed city populations. In addition, he sold some of the reduced crop of grains abroad for hard currencies rather than importing grains to ease the food crisis.

31

GLOBAL WARMING AND DISCOUNT RATES

February 4, 2007

GLOBAL WARMING AND DISCOUNT RATES—POSNER

The latest report of the Intergovernmental Panel on Climate Change, issued on Friday, confirms the scientific consensus that the emission of carbon dioxide and other greenhouse gases, as a result of the combustion of fossil fuels such as oil and gas, and other human activities (such as deforestation by burning), is having significant and on the whole negative effects by causing global temperatures and sea levels to rise. See *Climate Change 2007—The Physical Science Basis:* Contribution of Working Group I to the Fourth Assessment Report of the IPCC, http//ipcc-wg 1.ucar.edu/wg1/docs/WG1AR4_SPM_PlenaryApproved .pdf, visited December 8, 2008. When I discussed global warming in my book *Catastrophe: Risk and Response* (2004), I considered the evidence that global warming was a serious problem for which man-made emissions were the principal cause altogether convincing—and since then more evidence has accumulated and the voices of the dissenters are growing weaker. The global-warming skeptics are beginning to sound like the people who for so many years, in the face of compelling evidence, denied that cigarette smoking had serious adverse effects on health.

What has changed since I wrote my book is that not only is the evidence that our activities (primarily the production of energy) are causing serious harm even more convincing, but also that the scientists are increasingly pessimistic. It is now thought likely that by the end of the century global temperatures will have risen by an average of seven degrees Fahrenheit and that the sea level will have risen by almost two feet. Besides inundation of low-lying land areas, desertification of tropical farms, and migration of tropical diseases north, global warming is expected to produce ever more violent weather patterns—typhoons, cyclones, floods, and so forth.

There is much uncertainty in climate science, and climate scientists concede that their predictions may be off—but they may be off in either direction. Far worse consequences are possible than those thought highly likely by the authors of the report, including a temperature increase of twelve rather than seven degrees Fahrenheit, higher sea levels that could force the migration inland of tens of millions of people (or more), the deflection of the path of the Gulf Stream, causing Europe's climate to become Siberian, and abrupt, catastrophic sea-level rises due to the sliding of the Antarctic ice shelf into the ocean. Not only has the consensus among scientists concerning the harmful anthropogenic (human-caused) character of global warming grown, but the scientific consensus is increasingly pessimistic: recent evidence indicates that the global-warming problem is more serious than scientists thought just a few years ago.

My own view, argued in the book, is that the risk of *abrupt* global warming—a catastrophe that could strike us at any time, with unknown though presumably low probability—is sufficiently costly in expected-cost terms (that is, multiplying the cost of the catastrophe by its probability) to warrant taking costly measures today to reduce emissions of carbon dioxide and other greenhouse gases. Both the scientists and the policymakers, however, are mainly focused on the long-term costs of global warming—costs that will unfold over the remainder of this century. That focus makes the choice of the discount rate important, and potentially decisive.

A discount rate is an interest rate used to equate a future cost or value to a present cost or value. As a simple illustration (and ignoring complications such as risk aversion), if the interest rate is 5 percent, the present value of $1.05 to be received in a year is $1, because if you are given $1 today you can invest it and have $1.05 in a year. That is financial discounting. But discounting is important even when financial considerations are not the only ones involved in a choice. If you have a very strong preference for spending money now rather than a year from now, you might prefer $1 today to $1.50 a year from now.

These approaches don't work well when the question is how much we should spend today to avert costs that global warming will impose in the year 2107. Suppose we estimated that those costs would be $1 trillion. Then at a discount rate of 5 percent, the present-value equivalent of the costs is only $7.6 billion, for that is the amount that, invested at 5 percent, would grow to $1 trillion in one hundred years. At 10 percent, the present value shrinks to $73 million.

So it is possible to argue that, rather than spending a substantial amount of money today to try to prevent losses from global warming in the future, we should be setting aside a modest amount of money every year—$73 million this year to deal with global warming in 2007, the same amount next year to deal with global warming in 2008, and so on. Of course we would also want to spend money to prevent the lesser losses from global warming that we anticipate in earlier years. For example, suppose we estimate that the loss in the year 2057 will be $100 billion. Then at the same 10 percent interest rate, we would want to spend $852 million this year.

Thus two effects are being balanced in computing the present equivalent of future losses from global warming—the larger loss in the more distant future, and the greater shrinkage of the larger loss, because of its remoteness from today, by the operation of discounting. The latter effect will often dominate, as in the examples, but of course this depends critically on the choice of discount rate. At an interest rate of 3 percent, a $1 trillion loss in 2107 has a present value not of $73 million or $7.6 billion, but of $52 billion. However, when either of the latter two figures is added to figures representing the present value of losses in intermediate years, the sum will be formidable.

A very high discount rate, implying that optimal current expenditures to avert the future consequences of global warming are slight, could be defended on the ground that the march of science is likely to deliver us from the consequences of global warming long before the end of the century. Clean fuels for automobiles as well as for electrical plants (where already there is a clean substitute for oil or coal—nuclear power, though it is more expensive) will be developed, or carbon dioxide emissions from electrical plants will be piped underground, or artificial bacteria will be developed that "eat" atmospheric carbon dioxide. These are not certainties but they are likely, and so they provide a good argument for using a high discount rate, such as 10 percent—and perhaps for considering no losses after 2107, on the theory that the problem of global warming is almost certain to be completely solved by then.

Nevertheless there are at least three arguments for incurring hefty current expenditures on trying to reduce carbon dioxide emissions in the near term.

The first is that global warming is already imposing costs, and these will probably increase steadily in the years ahead. Discounting does not much affect those costs. They may well be great enough to warrant remedial action now.

The second argument for incurring heavy expenditures today to reduce global warming is that there is a small risk of abrupt, catastrophic global warming at any time, and a small risk of a huge catastrophe can compute as a very large expected cost. "Any time" could of course be well into the future, and so there is still a role for discounting, but it is minimized when the focus is on imminent dangers.

The third argument is that reducing our consumption of energy by a heavy energy tax would confer national security benefits by reducing our dependence on imported oil. Our costly involvement in the Middle East is due in significant part to our economic interest in maintaining the flow of oil from there. It is true that because our own oil is costly to extract, a heavy energy tax would not cause much if any substitution of domestic for foreign oil. But that is fine; our oil would remain in the ground, available for consumption if we decide to take measures abroad, such as withdrawing from Iraq, that might reduce our oil imports.

Heavy U.S. energy taxes would induce greater expenditures by industry on developing clean fuels and techniques for carbon sequestration, might persuade other big emitters like China and India to follow suit, and by reducing emissions of carbon dioxide would slow the increase in the atmospheric concentration of the gas. Drastic reductions might actually reduce that concentration, because carbon dioxide does eventually leach out of the atmosphere, though at a slower rate than it is built up by emissions.

DISCOUNTING GREENHOUSE GAS EFFECTS IN THE DISTANT FUTURE—BECKER

Under present scientific calculations, environmental damage from global warming at current rates of CO2 emissions will be large, especially during the latter half of this century and throughout the next few centuries. With such long-delayed effects, uncertainty about magnitudes of the damages is enormous. And it is obvious that the size of the rate at which future effects are discounted, if they are discounted at all, will make an enormous difference to estimates of the total value of the damages.

The main concern expressed about discounting of future utilities in evaluating public policies is that it would give the welfare of future generations much less weight than the welfare of present generations. Even with the "small" discount rate typically used in policy analysis of 3 percent, the effects of global warming on the utility of generations fifty years from now will be weighted only a bit more than one-quarter as much as the effects on the utility of the present generation. Generations one hundred years in the future would be weighted a mere one-sixteenth as much as the present generation. With a 3 percent rate, the weights are cut in half every twenty-four years, or approximately every generation.

Is this fair to future generations? The well-publicized Stern Review on the Economics of Climate Change for the British government thinks not, which is why the calculations in the report generally use a social discount rate close to zero. William Nordhaus of Yale University who has done substantial research on evaluating the costs of greenhouse warming uses about a 3 percent social discount rate. He shows that one should use a significant discount rate to match the discount rate to evidence on the long-term return on capital, the growth of consumption, and savings rates.

Suppose the utility damages from global warming to generations fifty years from now are equivalent to about $2 trillion of their welfare. At a 3 percent discount rate, this major damage would be valued today at about $500 billion, while any spending today that reduces the harm to future generations would be valued dollar for dollar. Then with a 3 percent discount rate it would not pay to eliminate these very harmful effects on future generations if the cost were $800 billion (or more generally at least $500 billion) to largely eliminate the future harm from greenhouse gas emissions through steep taxes on emission, carbon sequestration, and other methods. To be sure, benefits would exceed the present value of costs of greenhouse warming if damages were discounted only at 0 percent, 1 percent, or as high as almost 2 percent discount rate. When analyzing effects much further into the future, such as 150 years into the future, the discount rate used is even more crucial. The overwhelming reason why the Stern Review gets so much larger estimates of damages than work by Nordhaus and other is the use of a negligible discount rate in the review.

To illustrate the advantage of using a discount rate that reflects the return on capital, assume that the long-term return on investments in physical capital is 3 percent. If instead of spending $800 billion on eliminating greenhouse gases, suppose it were invested by the present generation in physical capital, and that all the income yielded by the investment were also invested with a 3 percent return. Then the value of this amount saved to generations fifty years from now would be $800 billion×(1.03) 50, or more than $3 trillion. Hence future generations would be better off if instead of the present generation investing the $800 billion in greenhouse gas–reducing technologies, they invested the same amount in capital that would be available to future generations.

One criticism of this argument is that if the resources were not invested in greenhouse gases, they would not be invested in other capital that would accrue to future generations. Perhaps not, but during the past 150 years, later generations in the United States and other developed and developing nations have been much better off than earlier generations when measured by income, health, education, and virtually all other important criteria. This rising standard of living across generations has been achieved mainly through advances in technology and generous savings and investments for children and grandchildren by parents and their elected representatives. Why should this fundamental aspect of family and public behavior be changed as a result of the accumulation of very harmful greenhouse gases in the atmosphere?

Put differently, later generations have benefited from large and continuing advances in technologies of all kinds during the past 150 years, including those related to the environment. The rate of technological advance has not slowed down, and may even have speeded up, during the past twenty years. Parents and governments have chosen not to offset the benefits to later generations of advances in technology by leaving descendants less education or capital than they have. Of course, just the opposite has occurred.

Parental behavior toward their children and grandchildren illustrates the importance of discounting future benefits and costs. Many parents like their children at least as much as they like themselves, and would be devastated if any serious harm came to their descendants. Yet in evaluating how much they want to give to their children in the form of education, bequests, or education, they recognize that savings and education have positive rates of return. If they invest say $40,000 in their children's education, the benefits to children would be much greater because of the high return on education—say it would be $80,000. By recognizing this, however, parents are in effect discounting the benefits they provide children since they would be costing the $80,000 benefit to children at $40,000.

Using a social discount rate of say 3 percent does not sweep away the greenhouse gas problem. The latest climate report cited by Posner strongly suggests that the problem is quite serious, perhaps even starting fifty or fewer years from now. However, it does imply that low weight be given to effects on the utility of generations 150 years from now, and even more so four hundred years from now. Common sense also dictates that technologies will be much improved in the future, including technologies related to improving health, income, and the environment. A positive and nonnegligible discount rate is the formal way to recognize the importance of these and related considerations.

32

EFFICIENT WATER CONSERVATION

February 27, 2007

HOW TO CONSERVE WATER EFFICIENTLY—BECKER

The sharp rise in world population and income during the past five decades has stimulated greatly increased demand for clean water, and concern about whether the supply of water would be adequate to meet these needs. Demand for usable water in the future will surely continue to grow at a significant pace unless steps are taken to reduce demand, while the supply of water could grow more slowly, especially if global warming reduced rainfall and increased evaporation of water. The best way to bring demand into balance with supply is to introduce much more sensible pricing of water consumption than is common in most countries.

Many discussions of water conservation create the impression that households are large and inefficient users of clean water for drinking, eating, bathing, and toilet flushing. That is a myth. About 40 percent of all the freshwater use in the United States is for irrigating land for agriculture, another 40 percent is used to produce power, and only 8 percent is used for domestic use; these percentages are similar in other countries. Moreover, about a third of all the water used by households in rich countries goes to water lawns and for other outdoor purposes, so probably no more than about 5 percent of the total demand for water is for personal use.

Water used is usually a poor measure of the net amount of water consumed since much water is returned either immediately, or after evaporation and condensation, to the source pool, where it can be used again. Thermoelectric plants use a lot of water for cooling purposes, but typically have a very high reutilization rate (about 98 percent). Household use is also efficient, with a reutilization rate of about 75 percent. As a result, neither power producers nor households are big net consumers of water. Irrigation of farmland absorbs much water since most irrigation systems have low reutilization rates. In California, the biggest water-using state, irrigation systems have a reutilization rate of only about 40 percent.

Governments usually try to close the gap between the supply and demand of usable water by command and control policies that regulate water use, usually starting with households. Many local governments have introduced requirements for low-flow toilet flushes, bans on lawn watering except during certain hours or days, requirements for more efficient household outdoor watering systems, and other water-conserving regulations. None of these regulations do anything to economize on the water used by farmers and industry, the main demanders of water.

Water is wasted in many ways by all sectors, and regulations do nothing to affect the main source of wasteful use of water: the inefficient pricing of water. Most irrigation systems in the world price water through annual flat fees, and not through charges that rise with the water consumed. Often domestic water use is not priced at all, and when priced, flat fees are far more common than fees that depend on use. As with any other scarce good, water is wasted when the cost of using more is negligible.

The obvious solution is to implement fees that rise with the amount of water demanded. Such fees are especially important in the agricultural sector since farming is a heavy consumer of water. Consumption ideally would be defined as net use after reutilization is accounted for. With this measure, the fee per gallon of water used would be low to power plants since they recover almost all the water they use. Farmers would tend to pay a lot both because they typically use much water, and also because most agriculture irrigation systems do a poor job of recovering the water used.

Fees that rise with consumption would reduce the demand for water partly by cutting demand. For example, households would water their lawns less frequently, and sometimes would replace natural grass with artificial grass, or with rock gardens and trees.

Farmers would cut their demand for water by switching away from crops that require much water, such as rice, toward crops that need less, such as wheat. They would also switch to more efficient irrigation systems, such as spraying and dripping rather than flooding (which is the cheapest), if the price of water took account of reutilization rates. With proper water pricing, California and other regions that need expensive irrigation system to grow rice and other water-intensive crops would switch to other crops, or to other uses of their land, so that water-intensive crops would become more concentrated in areas with abundant water supplies. More generally, with sensible water pricing in different countries, arid parts of the world would not grow food that absorbs much water, and would shift to other crops and activities that they would exchange for these foods.

Some opponents of effective metering of water demand claim that it would not reduce the use of water because of the mistaken belief that most of the water used goes to households for drinking and personal hygiene. The demand for water for personal use may not be very responsive to price, but households in developed countries use lots of water for lawns and swimming pools that would be sensitive to the price of water. Also public and private golf courses and some other recreational facilities require much water, and these uses too would respond to higher water costs. Clearly, the use of water in agriculture and industry would be sensitive to its price.

Effective water pricing is even more important to poor countries since they cannot afford expensive methods of increasing the supply of usable water, such as desalinization, and since a large fraction of their water is used in agriculture with inefficient irrigation systems. Yet most poor countries make little effort to price water sensibly.

Implementation of significant fees is not easy politically since households and farmers believe they have a right to as much water as they can get. In particular, farmers in richer countries are well organized politically, and often resist efforts to raise the cost of water they use to irrigate their land. Perhaps their opposition could be weakened if they received generous reductions in their water fees when they introduce irrigation systems with high reutilization rates.

THE SCIENCE AND ECONOMICS OF WATER SHORTAGE—POSNER

The scarcer the supply of a natural resource, the more important it is to have an institutional structure for allocating it efficiently among demanders, both present and future. In this respect usable fresh water is not fundamentally different from other scarce resources, such as oil and gas. The qualification in "usable" is important. Global warming does not diminish the world's supply of fresh water, but it reduces the supply of usable fresh water. Spring snowmelt is an important source of fresh water in many parts of the world, including California. That source will diminish as rising global temperatures cause more precipitation to take the form of rain rather than snow—and rain is much harder to collect and distribute than the spring runoff from melting snow. Higher global temperatures also increase the demand for water, as does an increasing, and increasingly prosperous, global population.

Of course, in principle, an increase in the demand for a good relative to its supply is not a problem. Price quickly rises, reducing demand and thus reestablishing equilibrium; so no more shortage. In the slightly longer run, moreover, the higher price leads to increased supply; in the case of water, one can anticipate greater use of desalination, that is, converting sea water into fresh water. Between water conservation by consumers trying to reduce their water bill, and increased supply of fresh water by the water industry, there should be no shortage, in the sense of an imbalance between demand and supply resulting in queuing, black markets, degraded quality, technological stagnation, politicking (Becker mentions discrimination in water pricing in favor of households and farmers), and corruption.

The problem is that the market in fresh water is inefficient. Becker focuses on the inefficient pricing of publicly owned water supplies—for example, charging a flat rate regardless of the quantity consumed, or failing to take account of reutilization (that is, the consumption of return flow). But a deeper problem is the institutional structure. One aspect is public ownership of water systems. There is no reason why a city should own the water company any more than it should own the cable television company. It is true that these are both networked services and therefore have aspects of natural monopoly; it would be wasteful to have multiple grids of water pipes in the same city. But through the contractual process a city can exploit "competition for the market"—that is, it can award a contract for the sale of water to whatever provider offers the best deal for the city's residents.

A still deeper institutional problem is the inefficient system (or systems) of property rights in water. In the western United States, where water is scarce, users obtain a property right by "appropriation," that is, by actually using water from a lake or stream. The amount they take is recorded and that is their property right. Any return flow can be appropriated by a downstream user. Now suppose an upstream user wants to sell his appropriation. He cannot do so without getting the consent of any downstream user who may be adversely affected by the sale because he had appropriated a portion of the upstream user's return flow. There may be many of those users, thus greatly increasing the transaction costs of reallocating water to a higher-valued use. In addition, because ownership of water rights is based on use, there is no incentive to hold water off the market, for future use; if one doesn't use the water one has appropriated, one loses one's property right.

The basic problem is that the same resource is jointly rather than singly owned, so that before it can be sold there must be a transaction among the owners, and the more owners, the higher that initial transaction cost. The problem is greatly exacerbated when an interbasin transfer is being contemplated, that is, a transfer of water from one watershed to another. For then all the users of return flow in the originating watershed will be deprived of their water.

Such problems are not unique to water, and are not insoluble. A parallel problem in oil is solved by unitization. Very often a number of separate oil companies will be drilling into the same underground oil field, and each has an incentive to take as much as it can as fast as it can (for example, by drilling more wells), for what it leaves in the ground will be taken by other companies. The oil-producing U.S. states authorize "compulsory unitization," whereby if two-thirds of the owners of the land above a common oil field vote to conduct their operations under common management, the rest are bound. (Requiring unanimity would create serious holdout problems.) A similar regime might be feasible for the users of a lake or stream. This would eliminate the inefficiency of a possession—or use—based system of property along with the inefficiencies associated with joint ownership.

In short, the solution to water shortages is likely to be privatization and intelligently designed property rights, using the institutional framework of natural resources such as oil, gas, coal, and other mineral resources as a model. This solution seems, moreover, as apt to African nations facing acute water shortages as it is to the milder problems of U.S. water supply.

AFTERTHOUGHTS TO PART VI

POSNER AFTERTHOUGHTS

The focus of this part of the book is on catastrophes, including the Indian Ocean tsunami of 2004 and Hurricane Katrina of the following year. Some of the discussion in our posts on catastrophes may be relevant to the near collapse of the world's financial system in the fall of 2008. For example, one of the concerns with bailing out failed banks is "moral hazard"—the incentive that insurance creates to take risks. In like vein, it has been argued that one of the factors in the high casualty rate and property loss in New Orleans as a result of Hurricane Katrina was a "culture of dependency" that sapped a sense of personal responsibility for one's behavior. I am dubious. Many of the casualties were to residents of hospitals and nursing homes; such casualties were not attributable to a culture of dependency. Nor were the casualties to people who did not own cars, unless one believes that there would be no poor people if there were no social safety net, which is highly unlikely.

A legitimate concern is the danger, if government undertakes to provide emergency assistance for catastrophic losses, of subsidizing risky behavior, such as building in flood plains. That danger could be minimized by requiring that all such assistance be repaid by the recipient, unless indigent. This would encourage nonpoor people to buy insurance, avoid building in flood plains, and take other measures to protect themselves from catastrophic risks. More broadly, I believe that government assistance should *always* be based on need; the fact that a rich person sustains damage to his home in a catastrophic flood rather than in a flood caused by a stopped-up toilet is no reason for the government to compensate him.

Notable in the aftermath of Hurricane Katrina was the decline of the population of New Orleans: between the hurricane and July 1, 2008, the city's population fell by 47 percent. This is some evidence that the moral hazard effect of assistance to the city's residents in the wake of the hurricane was not great. It seems that most residents who were adversely affected by the flood incurred substantial monetary and nonmonetary losses that government and insurance companies have not made good on, with the result that they have left the area rather than counting on insurance or public aid to compensate them for any future disaster. Incidentally, there is very little evidence of "price gouging" in the wake of Katrina, despite concerns that this would be a response by oil producers and gasoline dealers to the temporary reduction in refinery capacity caused by the hurricane.

Concern with global warming, another catastrophic phenomenon about which we blogged, has grown, as also have suggestions, and in some cases actual efforts, for responding to it. One response has been the carbon-offset movement. A number of firms, such as TerraPass, sell "carbon offsets" to consumers worried about global warming. You give TerraPass information about your driving, flying, and the size of your house, and TerraPass computes your annual carbon dioxide emissions and offers for a price to offset some or all of them by investing the proceeds from your purchase in projects (for example, wind farms) for reducing carbon emissions. In principle, if you purchase offsets for your entire carbon emissions, your net contribution to global warming is zero.

The carbon-offset movement is an echo of the "cap and trade" approach to pollution control, which is used for example to limit emissions of sulfur dioxide. In cap and trade, each polluter is given a permit to emit a certain quantity of a pollutant. The total amount permitted to all polluters will be less than the total pollution, because the aim is to reduce pollution, and polluters trade permits among themselves to minimize the cost of compliance. But the carbon offsets are voluntary. When you buy a carbon offset, you are making a charitable contribution to fighting global warming. Since charitable motivation is weak compared to self-interested motivation, carbon offsets are a poor substitute for a cap and trade system, quite apart from the doubts that have been raised about the efficacy of the projects in which the firms offering carbon offsets invest. The efficacy of the carbon-offset programs is limited because consumers are not the only emitters of carbon dioxide, because investments by the carbon-offset firms in reducing carbon emissions may to a great extent simply replace existing investments, and because the movement may create the false impression that modest reductions in the rate of annual increases in carbon emissions make a meaningful contribution to the fight against global warming. Because atmospheric carbon dioxide is absorbed by the oceans only very gradually (and the ability of the ocean to act as a "carbon sink" apparently is declining), a high annual level of carbon emissions tends to have a cumulative effect, so that even if that level were steady (rather than increasing, as it is), the atmospheric concentration would rise.

A related concern is that the movement encourages the belief that anyone who reduces his carbon footprint to zero has done his bit to combat global warming. Yet even if a million affluent American families did this, the resulting reduction in carbon dioxide emitted per year would be a microscopic fraction of total emissions. Combined with well-publicized projects by oil producers and other companies to reduce carbon emissions, the carbon-offset movement fools many people into thinking that global warming can be tamed by voluntary efforts. If people believe that voluntary efforts will suffice to solve the problem of global warming, there will be no political pressure to incur the heavy costs that will be necessary to avert the risk of catastrophic climate change.

BECKER AFTERTHOUGHTS

The discount rate is crucial in all problems of long-delayed effects, and global warming is a prime example of such delays. Kevin Murphy and I have been teaching on this issue for several years. Our general conclusion is that to a first approximation, the rate of return on capital is the right discount rate, regardless of the degree of weight placed on the welfare of future generations. A fuller analysis would also consider the impact of uncertainty about the severity of the future effects of global warming. The reason for using the return on capital is that this rate indicates how rapidly any saving by present generations accumulates to provide resources to future generations. Conflicts between present and future generations arise not over the discount rate to be used, but rather over how much present generations should save to provide for future generations. The historical evidence of the past couple of centuries is that present generations do not neglect future generations since later generations, especially in developing and developed countries, have been considerably richer than earlier generations.

VII

CRIME AND PUNISHMENT AND TERRORISM

33

CAPITAL PUNISHMENT

December 18 and 25, 2005

THE ECONOMICS OF CAPITAL PUNISHMENT—POSNER

The recent execution by the state of California of the multiple murderer Stanley "Tookie" Williams has brought renewed controversy to the practice of capital punishment, which has been abolished in about a third of the states and in most of the nations that the United States considers its peers; the European Union will not admit to membership a nation that retains capital punishment.

From an economic standpoint, the principal considerations in evaluating the issue of retaining capital punishment are the incremental deterrent effect of executing murderers, the rate of false positives (that is, execution of the innocent), the cost of capital punishment relative to life imprisonment without parole (the usual alternative nowadays), the utility that retributivists and the friends and family members of the murderer's victim (or in Williams's case victims) derive from execution, and the disutility that fervent opponents of capital punishment, along with relatives and friends of the defendant, experience. The utility comparison seems a standoff, and I will ignore it, although the fact that almost two-thirds of the U.S. population supports the death penalty is some, albeit weak (because it does not measure intensity of preference), evidence bearing on the comparison.

Early empirical analysis by Isaac Ehrlich found a substantial incremental deterrent effect of capital punishment, a finding that coincides with the common sense of the situation: it is exceedingly rare for a defendant who has a choice to prefer being executed to being imprisoned for life. Ehrlich's work was criticized by some economists, but more recent work by economists Hashem Dezhbakhsh, Paul Rubin, and Joanna Shepherd provides strong support for Ehrlich's thesis; these authors found, in a careful econometric analysis, that one execution deters eighteen murders. Although this ratio may seem implausible given that the probability of being executed for committing a murder is less than 1 percent (most executions are in southern states—fifty of the fifty-nine in 2004—which that year had a total of almost seven thousand murders), the probability is misleading because only a subset of murderers are eligible for execution. Moreover, even a 1 percent or one-half of 1 percent probability of death is hardly trivial; most people would pay a substantial amount of money to eliminate such a probability.

As for the risk of executing an innocent person, this is exceedingly slight, especially when a distinction is made between legal and factual innocence. Some murderers are executed by mistake in the sense that they might have a good legal defense to being sentenced to death, such as having been prevented from offering evidence in mitigation of their crime, such as evidence of having grown up in terrible circumstances that made it difficult for them to resist the temptations of a life of crime. But they are not innocent of murder. The number of people who are executed for a murder they did not commit appears to be vanishingly small.

It is so small, however, in part because of the enormous protraction of capital litigation. The average amount of time that a defendant spends on death row before being executed is about ten years. If the defendant is innocent, the error is highly likely to be discovered within that period. It would be different if execution followed the appeal of the defendant's sentence by a week. But the delay in execution not only reduces the deterrent effect of execution (though probably only slightly) but also makes capital punishment quite costly, since there is a substantial imprisonment cost on top of the heavy litigation costs of capital cases, with their endless rounds of appellate and postconviction proceedings.

Although it may seem heartless to say so, the concern with mistaken execution seems exaggerated. The number of people executed in all of 2004 was, as I noted, only fifty-nine. (The annual number has not exceeded ninety-eight since 1951.) Suppose that were it not for the enormous delays in execution, the number would have been sixty, and the additional person executed would have been factually innocent. The number of Americans who die each year in accidents exceeds one hundred thousand; many of these deaths are more painful than death by lethal injection, though they are not as humiliating and usually they are not anticipated, which adds a particular dread to execution. Moreover, for what appears to be a psychological reason (the "availability heuristic"), the death of a single, identified person tends to have greater salience than the death of a much larger number of anonymous persons. As Stalin is reported to have quipped, a single death is a tragedy, a million deaths is a statistic.

But that's psychology; there is an economic argument for speeding up the imposition of the death penalty on convicted murderers eligible for the penalty; the gain in deterrence and reduction in cost are likely to exceed the increase in the very slight probability of executing a factually innocent person. What is more, by allocating more resources to the litigation of capital cases, the error rate could be kept at its present very low level even though delay in execution was reduced.

However, even with the existing, excessive, delay, the recent evidence concerning the deterrent effect of capital punishment provides strong support for resisting the abolition movement.

A final consideration returns me to the case of "Tookie" Williams. The major argument made for clemency was that he had reformed in prison and, more important, had become an influential critic of the type of gang violence in which he had engaged. Should the argument have prevailed? On the one hand, if murderers know that by "reforming" on death row they will have a good shot at clemency, the deterrent effect of the death penalty will be reduced. On the other hand, the type of advocacy in which Williams engaged probably had some social value, and the more likely the advocacy is to earn clemency, the more such advocacy there will be; clemency is the currency in which such activities are compensated and therefore encouraged. Presumably grants of clemency on such a basis should be rare, since there probably are rapidly diminishing social returns to death-row advocacy, along with diminished deterrence as a result of fewer executions. For the more murderers under sentence of death there are who publicly denounce murder and other criminality, the less credibility the denunciations have.

MORE ON CAPITAL PUNISHMENT—BECKER

Posner has a good discussion of the various issue related to capital punishment. I will concentrate my comments on deterrence, which is really the crucial issue in the acrimonious debate over capital punishment. I support the use of capital punishment for persons convicted of murder because, and only because, I believe it deters murders. If I did not believe that, I would be opposed because revenge and the other possible motives that are mentioned and discussed by Posner, should not be a basis for public policy.

As Posner indicates, serious empirical research on capital punishment began with Isaac Ehrlich's pioneering paper. Subsequent studies have sometimes found much weaker effects than he found, while others, including a recent one cited by Posner, found a much larger effect than even that found by Ehrlich. The available data are quite limited, however, so one should not base any conclusions solely on the econometric evidence, although I believe that the preponderance of evidence does indicate that capital punishment deters.

Of course, public policy on punishments cannot wait until the evidence is perfect. Even with the limited quantitative evidence available, there are good reasons to believe that capital punishment deters murders. Most people, and murderers in particular, fear death, especially when it follows swiftly and with considerable certainty following the commission of a murder. As Posner indicates, the deterrent effect of capital punishment would be greater if the delays in its implementation were much shortened, and if this punishment was more certain to be used in the appropriate cases. But I agree with Posner that capital punishment has an important deterrent effect even with the way the present system actually operates.

Opponents of capital punishment frequently proclaim that the state has no moral right to take the life of anyone, even a most reprehensible murderer. Yet that is absolutely the wrong conclusion for anyone who believes that capital punishment deters. To show why, suppose that for each murderer executed (instead of say receiving life imprisonment), the number of murders is reduced by three—which is a much lower number than Ehrlich's estimate of the deterrent effect. This implies that for each murderer not given capital punishment, three generally innocent victims would die. This argument means that the government would indirectly be "taking" many lives if it did not use capital punishment. The lives so taken are usually much more worthwhile than those of the murderers who would be spared execution. For this reason, the state has a "moral" obligation to use capital punishment if such punishment significantly reduces the number of murders and saves lives of innocent victims.

Saving three other lives for every person executed seems like a very attractive trade-off. Even two lives saved per execution seem like a persuasive benefit-cost ratio for capital punishment. But let us go further and suppose only one life was saved for each murderer executed. Wouldn't the trade-off still be desirable if the life saved is much better than the life taken, which would usually be the case? As the deterrent effect of capital punishment is made smaller, at some point even I would shift to the anti- capital punishment camp. But given the difference between victims and murderers, the deterrent effect would have to be considerably less than one person saved per murderer executed before I would shift positions, although account should also be taken of the considerable expense involved in using capital punishment.

Of course, one wants to be sure that the number of persons wrongly executed for murder is a very small fraction of the total number executed. Posner argues convincingly that the safeguards built into the American system are considerable. They do not prevent any innocent persons from being executed, but they certainly make the risk very low. Capital punishment cannot be used if the goal is never to erroneously execute anyone, but then its deterrent effect is lost completely.

European governments are adamantly opposed to capital punishment, and some Europeans consider the American use of this punishment to be barbaric. But Europeans have generally been "soft" on most crimes during the past half-century. For a long time they could be smug because their crime rates were well below American rates. But during the past twenty years European crime has increased sharply while American rates have fallen—in part because American apprehension and conviction rates have increased considerably. Now some European countries have higher per capita property crime rates than the United States does, although violent crimes are still considerably more common in the United States. At the same time that America was reducing crime greatly in part by greater use of punishments, many European intellectuals continued to argue that not just capital punishments, but punishments in general, do not deter.

To repeat, the capital punishment debate comes down in essentials to a debate over deterrence. I can understand that some people are skeptical about the evidence, although I believe they are wrong both on the evidence and on the common sense of the issue. It is very unpleasant to take someone's life, even a murderer's life, but sometimes highly unpleasant actions are necessary to deter even worse behavior that takes the lives of innocent victims.

FURTHER COMMENTS ON CAPITAL PUNISHMENT—BECKER

Our discussion last week on capital punishment generated a lot of comments that are worth discussing in more detail. Since capital punishment is so controversial, we decided to continue the same subject this week.

First, let me correct a misunderstanding in some of the comments. I never claimed the evidence is anywhere near conclusive that capital punishment has an important deterrent effect. I stated that the evidence from quantitative studies is decidedly mixed, yet I concluded that "the preponderance of evidence does indicate that capital punishment deters."

Although the weight of the positive evidence should not be overstated, the frequently stated claim that some other studies prove that capital punishment does not deter is clearly false.

My belief in its deterrent effect is partly based on these limited quantitative studies, but also because I believe that most people have a powerful fear of death. David Hume said in discussing suicide that "no man ever threw away life, while it was worth living. For such is our natural horror of death..." Schopenhauer added also in discussing suicide "...as soon as the terrors of life reach a point at which they outweigh the terrors of death, a man will put an end to his life. But the terrors of death offer considerable resistance..."

Nevertheless, the main point of my comment last week was not to try to prove that capital punishment deters murders, but rather to argue against the view that it is "immoral" for the state to take lives through capital punishment even if we assume that the deterrent effect on murders is sizeable. Indeed, I believe that deterrence can be the only reasonable basis for capital punishment. Revenge, retribution, and other arguments sometimes made to justify capital punishment are too subject to government abuse, and have been abused.

Some readers interpreted my views as implying that a major goal of government policy should in general be to save lives. That is not my belief. I am against governments interfering, for example, with the rights of people to overeat even when that causes obesity, disease, and possibly early death because overeaters are primarily "harming" themselves. In my view, people should have the right to do that.

Murder, on the other hand, involves taking the lives of others, and any reasonable discussion has to distinguish such behavior from individuals taking actions that affect only their own lives. In economists' language, murder involves the most severe negative externalities. If we assume for the sake of this discussion that there are two fewer murders for each murderer executed, the state would reduce two of these severe externalities for each murderer that it executes. This issue of the effect of capital punishment on innocent victims has to be confronted by even those most opposed to its use. And I frankly do not see how any reasonable and relevant philosophy could oppose the use of capital punishment under the assumptions of this example.

Admittedly, the argument gets less clear-cut as the number of lives saved per execution falls from two to lower values, say, for example, to one life saved per execution. In this case, I compared the qualities of the life saved and the life taken, to the dismay of some readers. In particular, I wrote that "wouldn't the trade-off still be desirable if the life saved is much better than the life taken, which would usually be the case?" I do not see how to avoid making such a comparison. Consider a person with a long criminal record who holds up and kills a victim who led a decent life and left several children and a spouse behind.

Suppose it would be possible to save the life of an innocent victim by executing such a criminal. To me it is obvious that saving the lives of such a victim has to count for more than taking the life of such a criminal. To be sure, not all cases are so clear-cut, but I am just trying to establish the principle that a comparison of the qualities of individual lives has to be part of any reasonable social policy.

This argument helps explain why capital punishment should only be used for some murders, and not for theft, robbery, and other lesser crimes. For then the trade-off is between taking lives and reducing property theft, and the case in favor of milder punishments is strong. However, severe assaults, including some gruesome rapes, may approach in severity some murders, and might conceivably at times call for capital punishment, although I do not support its use in these cases.

A powerful argument for reserving capital punishment for murders is related to what is called marginal deterrence in the crime and punishment literature. If say perpetrators of assaults were punished with execution, an assaulter would have an incentive to kill the victims in order to reduce the likelihood that he would be discovered. That is a major reason more generally why the severity of punishments should be matched to the severity of crimes. One complication is that capital punishment may make a murderer fight harder to avoid being captured, which could lead to more deaths. That argument has to be weighed in judging the case for capital punishment. While marginal deterrence is important, I believe the resistance of murderers to being captured, possibly at the expense of their own lives, is really indirect evidence that criminals do fear capital punishment.

Some readers asked whether I also favor public executions of convicted murderers, mangling of their bodies, and other methods used in some countries still, and in most countries in the past? I do not because they seem unnecessarily abusive of convicted murderers without any compensating gains. However, I admit I would reconsider this position if it were demonstrated that such added punishments have a large effect in reducing the number of murders. For those who find such a position "barbaric," I would ask how many innocent victims are they willing to tolerate before they might take a more positive position on these additional punishments?

Of course I am worried about the risk of executing innocent persons for murders committed by others. In any policy toward crime, including capital punishment, one has to compare errors of wrongful conviction with errors of failing to convict guilty persons. My support for capital punishment would weaken greatly if the rate of killing innocent persons were as large as that claimed by many. However, I believe along with Posner that the appeal process offers enormous protection not against wrongful conviction but against wrongful execution. And this process has been strengthened enormously with the development of DNA identification. However, lengthy appeals delay the execution of guilty murderers, and that can only lower the deterrent effect of capital punishment.

So to summarize once again my position on this controversial question, I favor capital punishment because and only because I believe it has "sizeable" deterrent effects. I would join the anti–capital punishment side if this view turns out to be wrong, if it were proven that many innocent persons are wrongly executed, or if it is administered in such a racially biased manner as to wrongly convict many black persons, and to be little used against white murderers. But I do not believe that the available evidence strongly supports any of these arguments against the use of capital punishment.

FURTHER COMMENTS ON CAPITAL PUNISHMENT—POSNER

Becker has presented in his post today a compelling restatement of the economic case for capital punishment. I have a few minor disagreements and qualifications, and I will first mention them and then respond to some of the very large number of comments that my last week's posting elicited.

I do not consider revenge an impermissible ground for capital punishment. Revenge has very deep roots in the human psyche. As I have long argued, basing the argument on work by evolutionary psychologists such as Robert Trivers, the threat of revenge must have played an essential role in maintaining order in the "ancestral environment." That is a term that evolutionary biologists use to describe the prehistoric era in which human beings evolved to approximately their current biological state. In that era there were no laws, police, etc., so the indignation that would incite a person to revenge himself upon an aggressor must have had substantial survival value and become "hard wired" in our brains. The wiring remains, and explains some of the indignation that people feel, especially but not only the friends and family members of murder victims, toward the murderer. It seems plausible to me (here modifying what I said in my original posting) that the net increment in utility that they derive from the execution (versus life imprisonment) of the murderer exceeds the net increment in disutility that the murderer derives from being executed rather than imprisoned for life. The strong support for capital punishment in public opinion polls provides limited support for this conjecture.

I do not favor public executions; nor dismemberment or other horrific modes of execution. The incremental deterrent effect might well be nontrivial, but would be outweighed by public revulsion. There is also the danger of brutalization. As Friedrich Nietzsche pointed out, making people squeamish is one of the projects of modernity, and may explain the banning of blood sports as well as the movement away from public and gruesome executions. The idea is that if people become unaccustomed to bloody sights they will be less likely to employ violence in their relations with other people. Still another objection to public and gruesome executions is that they offer murderers an opportunity to die as heroes by showing fortitude.

I agree that marginal deterrence is important and that it generally argues for reserving the heaviest sentences for the most serious crimes. But there are two important qualifications. First, a very heavy sentence may be necessary to deter a minor crime because the likelihood of apprehension is very low. The expected punishment cost of crime is, as a first approximation (ignoring attitude toward risk), the punishment if imposed multiplied by the probability of imposition, so if the probability is very low a compensating increase in punishment is indicated. This does not impair marginal deterrence as long as the crimes are not close substitutes: a heavy fine for litterers will not increase the robbery rate, whereas capital punishment for robbers would increase the murder rate (of robbers' victims)—were it not for my second qualification. Even if murder and robbery were both capital crimes, there would be marginal deterrence because the police would search much harder for a robber who murdered his victim; the more extensive search would compensate, in part anyway, for the loss of the information that the victim could have given the police to identify the robber. Moreover, capital punishment is merely a ceiling; even if robbery were a capital crime, judges and juries would be much less likely to impose the death sentence on a robber who had not killed his victim than on one who had.

Marginal-deterrence theory provides, however, a compelling reason to execute prisoners sentenced to life without parole who murder in prison; the threat of a sentence of imprisonment can have no deterrent effect on them.

Becker mentions the possibility of racial discrimination in execution. Studies done some years ago—I do not know whether they would be descriptive of current practice—revealed the following pattern: murderers of black people were less likely to be executed than murderers of white people. Since blacks were more likely to murder other blacks than to murder whites, this meant that blacks were less rather than more likely to be executed than whites, relative to the respective murder rates of the two races. (Blacks commit murders at a much higher rate than whites.) The explanation offered was that judges and juries tended to set a lower value on black victims of murder than on white ones. From this some observers inferred that capital punishment discriminates against blacks. The inference is incorrect. The proper inference is that murderers of blacks are underpunished.

I turn now to the comments on my posting. A long comment by "ohwilleke" makes a number of interesting points, but they do not support his opposition to capital punishment. He notes first of all that many factors influence the murder rate besides the probability of execution. That is true, but it does not, as he suggests, make it "insanely difficult to make any econometric estimate" that is not "meaningless." Econometrics, which is to say the set of statistical methods used by economists to try to tease out causal factors, enables the particular factor of interest, in this case the probability of execution, to be isolated. The methods are not entirely reliable, which is why neither Becker nor I claim that economists have proved that capital punishment deters; we merely claim that there is significant evidence that it does. I note how many commenters remark correctly that murder rates are higher in the South, even though that is where most executions occur, than in other regions. But that is not an argument that executions do not deter. The higher the background rate of murder, the more severe one expects punishments to be. A high murder rate implies a high expected benefit from murder and so the expected cost of punishment has to be jacked up to offset that greater benefit.

Ohwilleke's comment claims that the "error rate" in capital punishment is 10 percent. This is incorrect. Not a single person among the 119 that he contends were erroneously sentenced to death was executed. That is a zero error rate.

One commenter asks whether capital punishment "really deter[s] the type of person who actually does the murdering?" Of course if someone in a state that has capital punishment commits the kind of murder that puts him at risk of such punishment, the threat of capital punishment has not deterred. This is the usual situation with criminal punishment. People who commit crimes are people for whom the expected cost of punishment, combined with the other costs of crime, is less than the expected benefit of the crime. The purpose of punishing these people is not to deter them—by committing the crime in the face of threatened punishment they have shown themselves to be undeterrable—but to deter people who, were it not for the expected punishment cost, would commit the crime because its other costs were lower than its expected benefit.

Finally, several comments usefully point out that capital punishment has a secondary deterrent effect: it induces murderers to plead guilty and receive a life sentence.

34

DOPING ATHLETES

August 27, 2006

DOPING IN SPORTS—BECKER

I watched on television Floyd Landis's stirring victory in the hard mountain-ascending stage 17 of the Tour de France after he stumbled badly in the difficult previous stage. Landis went on to win what seemed like a remarkable victory, but tests taken after stage 17 showed abnormally elevated levels of testosterone. The French then stripped him of his title as winner of the 2006 tour. Professional cycling is now in bad repute partly because of this latest scandal, and partly also because just prior to the tour several major riders were disqualified for testing positive for banned substances.

These cycling scandals came not long after scandals in American baseball, where Barry Bonds, Jason Giambi, Mark McGuire, Sammy Sosa, and other stars appear to have been guilty of using performance-enhancing steroids to push them to record-breaking performances, especially in home run hitting. World class track stars, such as Olympic one-hundred-meter champion Justin Gatlin, professional football players, weightlifters, swimmers, and outstanding athletes in other sports also have either failed drug tests or are suspected of using banned substances.

Why should various chemicals, like steroids, blood transfusions, and other forms of drug doping, and looming possible gene doping, be banned in competitive athletic contests if the athletes know the risks to their health from using banned substances to enhance their performance? The principle justification for banning doping when it harms persons using "dope" comes from the fundamental nature of athletic competition. The reward system is based not so much on absolute performance levels, although that does count, as on performance relative to competitors. For example, Lance Armstrong, who has successfully fought off continuing claims that he used dope, is remembered primarily for his six consecutive triumphs in the Tour de France, not for his winning times in any of the races, or on any of the stages. Victories are primarily what count also in World Cup soccer and American football, in weightlifting and boxing, in running, in tennis, and all other competitive sports.

Rewards are related to victories because live and television audiences and the media are mainly interested in outcomes from competition, not absolute performance levels. That is, they pay primary attention to who wins tennis match, a baseball, basketball, or football game, a marathon, or other contests. In essence, competitive sports are an example of the "superstar" phenomena analyzed by my late colleague Sherwin Rosen. Superstars, including superior teams, get large rewards even when they are only slightly better than competitors, while those who are only modestly inferior receive much lower incomes and prestige. As a result, professional baseball, basketball, soccer, golf, tennis, and many other sports have a few performers and teams that do very well, like Tiger Woods, Roger Federer, and the New York Yankees, while the vast majority of their competitors get much more modest benefits.

In this environment, certain types of doping are attractive to athletes because they give them a competitive edge. The problem arises because overall outcomes when many of the performers use dope is essentially zero sum in the sense that if all leading athletes take steroids, other chemicals, or different forms of dope, they all tend to increase their performances without often having much effect on who wins or scores high in a race, game, or contest. In other words, participants may engage in doping to improve their performance and hence chances of doing relatively well, but obviously not everyone can improve their relative position. In a contest where relative performance is what matters, what may be rational for the individual athlete makes little sense for the collection of athletes.

This becomes a matter of concern when the performance enhancers, like steroids and other forms of doping, have a negative effect on long-term health. For then users of these enhancers are hurting themselves in the long run without on the average improving their short-term rewards from athletic competition, as long as competitors also use harmful enhancers. This is the main rationale for trying to ban steroids and other forms of doping from athletic competitions. It sometimes also leads to bans of other costly enhancers that on balance do not affect overall outcomes. For this reason, golf limits the number and size of clubs that can be used in competition, baseball bats cannot be "corked," professional tennis limits the types of rackets permitted, and professional baseball, soccer, and other team sports limit the number of players that teams can have on their rosters.

The same argument applies but in much weaker form to performance enhancers that benefit athletes using them, such as training hard and keeping in very good shape, eating a balanced diet and keeping weight at healthy levels, or spending time studying opponents and videos of one's own past performance. Athletes would tend to use more of these enhancers than if they were not competing, which helps explains why many of them "go to pot" after they retire from active competition. But since the effect of these enhancers is on the whole beneficial to athletes using them, or at least not very harmful, there is little concern about such activities, and no effort to regulate them.

To be sure, absolute performance also counts to some extent, such as the number of home runs in baseball, scoring averages in basketball, pass completion rates in American football, the number of goals scored by a soccer player, and speed in running the mile and other races. But even here there is a crucial relative aspect. Roger Bannister's breaking of the four-minute-mile barrier was noteworthy not mainly because four minutes has some special significance, but because no one had done that before. Baseball fans are upset that Bonds, McGuire, and Sosa apparently took steroids because that enabled them to break the single season record for home runs established by Roger Maris, who did not take drugs, allowed Bonds to pass Babe Ruth in total home runs—Ruth did not use enhancers unless one counts constantly getting drunk—and helped Bonds close in on the all time home run leader Hank Aaron, who has a squeaky clean reputation.

While the case for banning various types of drugs and other enhancers is strong, the ability to control doping is limited. For there is a continuing battle between bans and the discovery of new enhancers that have not been banned. So steroid use in baseball was not banned until after several major players greatly improved their slugging performance through using them. Perhaps some sports would like to restrict excessive use of weights and other forms of training, but detection and control of these activities would be impossible.

The result is a fragile equilibrium between the banning of various substances, enforcement of bans, and the search for new substances and ways to evade bans on old substances. This is not a perfect outcome, but I believe it is on the whole better for competitive sports and for participants than a policy that allows all kinds of performance enhancers and stimulants.

DOPING ATHLETES—POSNER'S COMMENT

Becker rightly stresses relative as distinct from absolute performance norms. I would add that this is a well-nigh universal phenomenon rather than one confined to athletics. The reason is that there are very few absolute standards in nonempirical fields of human endeavor. We form a judgment about the quality of a musical or literary work, an artist, a musical performer, and so forth, by comparison with other works, other artists, performers, etc. So it is natural for the writer, the artist, etc., to do whatever he can to increase his performance relative to his peers. The reason empirical fields are different is that in them success can be measured in absolute terms; a contribution to knowledge can be deemed important on the basis of the value of the knowledge alone.

Why then the objection to permitting athletes to use steroids and other drugs to enhance their performance? (The objection to permitting some athletes to cheat by using these drugs *sub rosa* is too obvious for discussion: that really is unfair competition. The objection would disappear if the ban were lifted.) One valid objection, which seems however minor, is that it complicates comparison with earlier athletes, who didn't have access to performance-enhancing drugs. But in many sports, such as baseball, they had an advantage denied to current athletes: black and Hispanic athletes were excluded from the competition. Other changes that complicate comparison between baseball players of this generation with those of earlier generations include the advent of night baseball, natural gains in height and weight because of better nutrition, improved vision correction, longer seasons, better equipment, better orthopedic surgery, more sophisticated techniques for managing a team, and better health care generally.

As Becker points out, no objections are raised to athletes' improving their performance by better training, more exercise, more practice, or abstention from alcohol and cigarettes. So maybe the root of the objection to the performance-enhancing drugs is that they have long-term deleterious effects on the health of the user. This in turn gives rise to an externality, since use by some athletes depresses the relative performance of nonusers. Yet I do not think that serious objections would be raised to self-destructive behavior in pursuit of athletic distinction as long as the behavior did not involve drug use. A football lineman will not be criticized for blowing himself up into a four-hundred-pound freak if he does it without the aid of drugs, even though the long-term effects on his health of the added weight are very bad and even though his weight gain may place pressure on other linemen to match it.

Nor do we criticize poets and other artists who deliberately lead unhealthy lives, either in search of experiences that they can incorporate into their work or out of sheer irresponsibility or mental derangement, even though they might be thought to be competing unfairly with the normals. Some associates at large law firms work much too hard for the good of their health in order to steal a march on their competitors, but they are not criticized either.

So is the ban on doping athletes just a mindless reaction against novelty and science, a Luddite reaction? Or does it just reflect a confusion between cheating when drugs are banned and lifting the ban? I think not. There are two valid reasons for the ban. One is the pure "arms race" character of the doping; there is no improvement in the entertainment quality of football if four-hundred–pound linemen confront each other rather than two-hundred-pound linemen. In contrast, the overworking law firm associates increase their firm's output.

The other justification for the ban is that it is a rational means of protecting children. Because successful athletes earn high salaries, because success as an athlete does not require a high order of intelligence, and because an athletic career to be successful must begin in high school (in the case of tennis, perhaps even earlier), there is enormous competition by minors to achieve athletic success. If performance-enhancing drugs were legal, their use by teenagers would be pervasive, and teenagers lack sufficient maturity to trade off the benefits of an athletic career (discounted by the very low probability that any given teenage athlete will have a really successful athletic career) against the long-term damage to their health. Of course adult athletes could be permitted to use such drugs but minors forbidden to do so, but such a legal regime would be difficult to enforce, especially given the "role model" status of adult athletes in the eyes of minors. The lifting of the ban would remove all stigma from the use of such drugs. Their legal and widespread use by star athletes would validate the drugs in the eyes of impressionable youth.

35

DRUNK DRIVING

December 24, 2006

FATALITIES FROM DRUNKEN DRIVING—BECKER

One of the most disturbing aspects of the holiday season is the sharp rise in automobile fatalities, in part due to drunk driving from overdrinking at parties and other celebrations. The United States has almost forty thousand deaths per year from automobile accidents, and about 40 percent are due to drunk driving. This exceeds the annual number of deaths from major diseases like prostate and breast cancers, and drunk driving deaths are also concentrated among young persons, while deaths from most diseases come at much later ages.

That the number of deaths per mile driven is not fixed but varies greatly with different conditions is seen from the wide differences among countries in the number of deaths per passenger vehicle. The United States is at the high end, and in 2004 had about 1.8 road traffic deaths per 10,000 vehicles, compared to less than 1 per 10,000 vehicles in Sweden and Norway, 1.1 in Germany, and 1.0 in the United Kingdom. A few countries in the more economically advanced nations have higher death rates than the United States, including South Korea at 3.6, and Hungary at 3.9. A number of factors help explain these international differences, including the quality of the roads, speed limits, minimum driving ages, age distribution of the driving population, density of traffic, amount driven per vehicle (presumably higher in America), and other factors. I concentrate on accidents due to drinking.

The American approach to drunk drivers has been more laissez-faire than other nations, with relatively light punishment for drunk driving, often even when it caused serious accidents. In the last couple of decades, however, under pressure from groups like Mothers against Drunk Driving (MADD), states and the federal government have begun to crack down on drunk driving, and driving by youth. Largely in response to such pressure, the minimum drinking age in all states has been raised from what was typically age eighteen to age twenty-one. States also established more standardized criteria for what constitutes driving while drunk, and have lowered the minimum level of blood-alcohol concentration that is taken to indicate driving while drunk from 0.10 percent to 0.08 percent. More checkpoints and patrols have been put on the road to give sobriety tests to suspected drunk drivers.

As a result, alcohol-related fatalities fell dramatically from 1982 to 1994. But the trend has stalled since that year, and alcohol-related driving fatalities have bottomed out at about seventeen thousand per year. When adult drivers cause their own accidents or that of their passengers because they were drunk, one can reasonably assume they and their passengers are capable before they get drunk of determining what risks to take, such as whether to drive, speed, how much alcohol to absorb, and other factors that increase their risk of an accident. But drunk drivers often kill or injure persons in other cars, or pedestrians, and in this way they impose what are called negative externalities on these innocent victims. This is the main case for public policies to reduce drunk driving and other externality-causing driving behavior.

One approach is to tax gasoline and perhaps cars to cut down the amount of driving. Another way is to tax alcohol to cut down the amount of alcohol consumed. But these are very blunt policy instruments because they punish also people who drive without driving while drunk, or people who drink even in large quantities without driving or otherwise endangering others. By punishing only people who are discovered to be driving while drunk, or who get into accidents because they were drunk, or who are much more likely than others to drive while drunk, such as teenagers, one avoids much punishment of drinkers or drivers who do not risk the lives and property of others, and concentrates punishments on those who either are likely to, or actually did, impose external costs on others. At the same time, this would discourage, perhaps greatly, the tendency to drive after heavy drinking.

My colleague, Kevin M. Murphy, prepared estimates for the United States for the year 2000 of the total cost imposed by drunk drivers who get into accidents on drivers and passengers in other cars, and on innocent pedestrians. These costs include estimates of the statistical value of the lives lost (see my post on September 3, 2006, for a discussion of this concept), the value of medical expenses for those injured, and the value of the property lost. The total of all these external costs from drunk driving in the year 2000 is about $15 billion, with the great majority of this total coming from the $5 million value placed on each of the more than two thousand innocent persons who lost their lives in that year because of drunk driving.

About 1.4 million persons in that year were arrested for drunk driving. Given the calculations in the previous paragraph, this means the cost imposed on others from driving while drunk amounts to about $10,000 per person arrested for drunk driving. This is a large amount, and provides a first order guidance to the punishment that should be imposed in some form on the drunk drivers arrested: large fines, suspended licenses, and jail terms in some cases. Such large punishments would match the damages done from drunk driving, and at the same time would encourage many persons to avoid driving while legally drunk. To show this with a little algebra, suppose that g percent of all drunk drivers (=N) are arrested, and let that be the same for everyone—presumably it is higher for those who actually cause accidents. Let the punishment to those arrested be d per person, which is Murphy's $10,000 figure, where $d=D/gN$, and D is total damages from all accidents caused by drunk driving. Then the total punishment to those arrested $= gNd = D$, which is the right number in order to have drunk drivers pay for all the damages to others that they cause.

On incentives to drunk drivers, the expected damages per drunk driver $= gd = gD/gN = D/N =$ damages per drunk driver $= pD/pN$, which is what it should be, where p is the assumed common probability that a drunk driver gets into an accident. The assumption of a probability common to all drunk drivers of causing an accident is clearly not perfectly accurate, but far better than the assumption that all persons who drink are equally likely to harm others. Moreover, the size of the punishment might not be the same for all those arrested, but could depend on alcohol-blood levels, the recklessness of the driving behavior, and the severity of the accident if they had been in an accident, past offenses, and other factors that try to relate punishment to the magnitude of the "crime" committed and the degree of individual responsibility.

To my knowledge, no state in the United States imposes anything approaching such serious punishments on persons arrested for drunk driving. In fact, they are generally much too lenient, and do not treat this as the serious crime that it is. Countries like Sweden are much harsher in their punishment of persons arrested for drunk driving. Driving with a blood alcohol level exceeding only 0.2 parts per thousand may lead to prison terms of up to six months, and the driver's license is usually suspended. Driving with a blood alcohol level of over 1.5 may lead to one year of prison. My experience there and in Norway is that these deterrents work very well, and induce people who are planning on drinking any significant quantities to be careful not to drive afterward. Several econometric articles by H. L. Votey (for example, "The Deterrence of Drunken Driving in Norway and Sweden: An Econometric Analysis of Existing Policies," 6 *Scandinavian Studies in Criminology* 79 [1978]) indicate that punishments by fine, revoking of driving licenses, and imprisonment are important in explaining the lower tendency in Sweden to drive while drunk and the lower rates of accidents due to drunk driving, although some of the results are disputed by H. Lawrence Ross. (See, for example, "Scandinavia's Drinking-and-Driving Laws: Do They Work?" in *Scandinavian Studies in Criminology,* 1978.)

The American approach to drunk driving is surprisingly soft, often including the treatment of drunk drivers who seriously injure or kill innocent persons because of reckless driving. Given the sharp increase during the past twenty years in the severity of punishments for felonies, and the over 2 million persons in jails or prisons, this reluctance to try to cut down the disgraceful number of highway deaths due to driving while drunk is anomalous and disturbing.

DRUNK DRIVING—POSNER'S COMMENT

This topic could be thought a continuation of our last week's topic, the ban on trans fats in New York City. We are again dealing with safety regulation. The case for punishing drunk drivers may seem clearer than the case for banning trans fats in restaurant meals because the externality is more pronounced and consumer competence is not in issue, but the appearance is deceptive. Becker's proposal for heavier penalties for drunk driving could be criticized as paternalistic, because it regulates an input rather than an output. If there are 1.4 million annual arrests for drunk driving, and if we assume realistically that this is only a fraction of the actual incidents of drunk driving, yet only two thousand innocent people are killed by drunk drivers, then it follows that most drunk driving is harmless. Why then punish it with arrests and severe penalties? Why not just punish those drunk drivers who cause deaths or injuries to nonpassengers? In fact we do punish such drivers, under such rubrics as reckless homicide (if the victim dies) or reckless infliction of bodily injury. And the punishments are severe. Why punish the 99-plus percent of drunk driving that is harmless? Indeed, if the penalties for reckless homicide are optimal, the implication is that the number of deaths from drunk driving, seventeen thousand a year, is also optimal.

This is actually a plausible inference. If there are only two thousand nonpassenger deaths (other than that of the drunk driver himself) caused by drunk driving every year (and how many of the accidents in which a drunk driver is involved are actually *caused* by the drinking?), then the probability of being killed by a drunk driver is very small, and the value of life estimate that I used in my post on the ban on trans fats should be usable here as well to conduct a cost-benefit analysis of drunk driving. The probability of a drunk driver's killing someone must also be small, given the number of drunk drivers implied by the arrest statistics. Suppose the annual probability that a drunk driver will kill a nonpassenger is .001 (as it would be, given the two thousand victim figure, if there are 2 million drunk drivers, which is a very modest extrapolation from the arrest figure, since many drunk drivers are not caught). Then the expected injury cost from drunk driving is $7,000 (.001×$7 million). (This corresponds to Becker's $10,000 figure, which seems to me too high, as it disregards the drunk drivers who are not arrested. Notice that if only a third of drunk drivers are arrested each year, the expected-cost figure drops to $3,333.) This implies that a driver who derives at least $7,000 in utility per year from drinking while driving (more commonly, shortly before driving) is behaving optimally and should not be punished at all.

The larger issue that the drunk driving question raises is the choice between ex ante and ex post regulation. Health inspections of restaurants and, yes, a ban on trans fats are examples of ex ante regulation. Such regulation prevents dangerous activity rather than waiting for the danger to materialize and using the legal system to punish the injurer. The tort system is an example of ex post regulation. If you drive recklessly but don't injure anybody, you have not committed a tort. Tort law comes into play only when an injury occurs. The theory is that an optimal tort penalty for the injury deters tortious conduct, not perfectly—or there would be no tort cases—but well enough.

Criminal law is a mixed bag. Crimes that result in injury are punished, usually quite severely, but much preparatory conduct—attempts and conspiracies—is punished as well, even when no harm results (the failed attempt, the abandoned conspiracy). Arrests for speeding—and for drunk driving—are examples of ex ante regulation. The economic argument for ex ante regulation is that ex post regulation is often inadequate. This is obvious in the trans fats situation—it would be impossible to figure out which victims of heart disease owed the disease, and to what extent, to which restaurants. In the case of reckless homicide, the answer is less clear. Suppose drunk driving is inefficient—the drunk driver derives less utility than the expected accident cost—and so we want to deter it by punishing the drunk driver who kills or injures a nonpassenger. Suppose the value of life is $7 million and 10 percent of the drivers are not apprehended. Then the optimal penalty would be a fine of $7,780,000 ($7 million÷.9). Few drivers could pay that, so the trick would be to impose an equivalent disutility on them by nonpecuniary means, such as imprisonment.

This is not to suggest that punishing drunk drivers who are arrested, the method that Becker endorses, can't achieve the correct deterrence. But punishing just the ones who kill might be more efficient—there wouldn't be as much need for policemen, there would be fewer trials and prison terms, and probably many drunk drivers are quite harmless, for it is unlikely that everyone who drives while drunk has an equal probability of causing an accident. In general, heavy punishment of fewer people is cheaper than light punishment of more people.

Thus, only if ex post punishment failed to deter optimally would there be a strong case for punishing drunk drivers who are not involved in accidents with nonpassengers (assuming drunk driving is inefficient, the assumption questioned earlier in this comment)—or at least a strong case based on the simple model of rational choice that underlies my analysis. Maybe drunk drivers systematically underestimate the effect of drinking on the likelihood of an accident, or believe that they can fully compensate for the danger by driving more slowly, or exaggerate the degree to which they can hold their liquor, or exaggerate their driving skill. Maybe their drunk driving behavior is addictive, and they do not realize, before starting to drink, that they won't be able to avoid drinking before they drive. These might be grounds for ex ante regulation—even for regulations anterior to arrest, such as stiff alcohol taxes.

36

INTERNET GAMBLING

August 6, 2006

ON INTERNET GAMBLING—BECKER

Gambling through lotteries, stocks, casinos, and in other ways is common throughout the world. Economists explain this by both process and outcomes. By "process" I mean that many people enjoy the thrill of the risk involved in gambling—this is sometimes called "the utility from gambling." This enjoyment of gambling is the dominant factor behind the many small gambles that people take while playing poker, cards, slot machines, blackjack, craps, and other games. Gambling is also attractive when, as with lotteries, it offers a small probability of winning a lot, and thereby changing significantly one's economic situation, even when combined with a large probability of losing a little. Economists explain this by assuming the marginal utility of income in rising in some income intervals.

Put in this context, the popularity of online gambling is not at all surprising. It offers highly convenient access to gaming situations from one's home or office that includes also flexibility as to amount wagered, many different types of gambles, and relatively good odds. Nor is it surprising, however, that the American government and the governments of most other countries are unhappy about Internet gambling, and try to either prevent or tax it.

The approach to gambling by state and local governments of the United States is fairly typical of what happens elsewhere. Gambling was long officially banned in all states except Nevada, but it persisted illegally in the form of numbers, bookies, card games, and in other ways. The hit musical of several decades ago *Guys and Dolls,* based on a story by Damon Runyan, centers around a floating game of craps in New York hosted in different venues to avoid police. Eventually, state governments saw the tax revenue potential of state-run lotteries when combined with continued prohibitions on private lotteries. Lotteries then spread from state to state. Many states now also license casinos and tax them heavily, and the federal government got into the gambling picture by the strange method of giving Indian tribes special advantages in running casinos.

Governments are concerned about online gambling primarily, I believe, because it threatens the revenue and other political advantages they get from taxing and tightly regulating various forms of gambling. Internet gambling is very hard to regulate and tax because online companies can set up in remote places and make gambling available to practically anyone who has access to the Internet. In fact, many online gambling companies are located either in ships at sea or in very small countries that allow them to operate in return for a cut of the profits. For example, the big online betting company BetOnSports, currently being prosecuted in federal court, has its headquarters in Costa Rica, and has other offices on the island of Antigua.

The House of Representatives by a large majority passed a bill in July that attempts to curb online poker games, sports betting, and other Internet-based wagering. Among other things, the bill would bar the use of electronic payments, such as credit card transactions, in online wagering. This bill came six years after a similar measure was defeated. Many attribute the change in the House's vote to the Jack Abramoff scandal. That may have been the precipitating factor, but the main reason is the rapid growth in online gambling during the past six years to about $12 billion per year worldwide, with about half of that in the United States. Online gambling is fast becoming a major threat to government revenue from gambling, and to its control over how and where gambling takes place.

Supporters of this bill argue that easy access to online gambling is dangerous because it encourages and strengthens gambling addictions. The fact is, however, that gambling is even less addictive than drinking, and is not nearly as addictive as smoking. Moreover, gambling addicts can already find many ways to gamble. The vast majority of online gamblers bet modest sums for pleasure, such as the estimated 23 million Americans who now play online poker (the Pokers Players Alliance, which claims more than twenty-five thousand members, opposed the bill).

Other supporters of a ban on online gambling claim that it is used to launder money obtained from drugs and other illegal activities. The laundering argument against gambling is largely irrelevant, given the many other ways to launder money.

I favor allowing online gambling, given the weak arguments against it, the common human desire to gamble, and also that addictive aspects of gambling are greatly exaggerated. Indeed, I also believe it should remain tax free, along with purchases of other services through the Internet. For tax-free online gambling would put pressure on governments to reduce taxes and various restrictions on lotteries and other forms of gambling. Lower taxes and fewer regulations would give individuals cheaper access to ways to satisfy the mainly harmless desire to play games for money, and to bet on sporting and other events, including lotteries.

As with many other laws, restrictions on gambling mainly impact the poor and middle classes since wealthier individuals can and do gamble through equities, derivatives, housing, and in many other ways that are not readily available to families with modest incomes. There are many ways to spend money in ways that others do not approve. Why single out families with modest incomes who may enjoy the excitement of gambling, or the dreams gambling provide about striking it rich?

INTERNET GAMBLING—POSNER

An article in the *New York Times* of July 25 describes the efforts of the federal government to prevent Americans from gambling online in Internet casinos located outside the United States. The article reports that 8 million Americans engage in Internet gambling, spending a total of $6 billion a year.

Gambling outside specific, authorized venues, such as Nevada (the state that has the fewest restrictions on gambling), Indian casinos, riverboat casinos, pari-mutuel betting at racetracks, and state lotteries, is illegal. Illegal gambling is a standard example of a radically underenforced, "victimless" crime ("victimless" in the sense of being a voluntary transaction, as distinct from a coerced transaction such as theft). The gambling laws are underenforced largely because gambling is victimless, which makes detection difficult and also reduces the public's willingness to devote resources to preventing it. The argument for criminalization is that gambling is an unproductive and often an addictive activity that, by virtue of its addictive character, drives the gambling addicts to bankruptcy.

In fact gambling is productive in an economic sense because it increases the expected utility of the gamblers; otherwise there wouldn't be gambling. It is as productive as any other leisure-time activity that does not involve the acquisition of useful skills or knowledge. Granted, the attraction of gambling is a little mysterious from a rational choice perspective. Because of the need of the casino or other gambling establishment to cover its costs, the gambles that are offered are bad in the sense that the net expected monetary payoff is negative. The state lotteries derive significant revenues (an average of 2.3 percent in the forty states that have state lotteries) from the sale of lottery tickets precisely by offering particularly bad odds: on average, of every $1 in revenue from the sale of lottery tickets, only 50¢ is paid out in winnings.

So only risk preferrers should derive net expected utility from gambling. Yet most gamblers probably have health, homeowners, and other forms of insurance and thus demonstrate risk aversion. For just as only a risk preferrer will accept bad gambles, so only a risk averter would buy insurance, since the insurance company's loading fee makes the net expected monetary payoff from insurance negative.

Some people believe irrationally that they are inherently "lucky," not realizing that "luck" is something observed ex post; no one has an asset called "luck" that enables him to beat the odds. Other people are so desperate or miserable that their marginal utility of money is very low, which truncates the downside risk of a gamble. Suppose, to take an extreme case, that you have only $1 left in the world. There isn't much you can do with $1, so, even if you were risk averse, your most sensible move might be to buy a lottery ticket, on the theory that it is really costless.

(Thus, welfare programs encourage gambling by reducing the cost of gambling away one's financial resources.) The principle that this example illustrates is that if marginal utility is increasing in income, the benefit of winning a bet and thus increasing one's income will confer more utility than an equal loss will confer disutility.

And finally, there is an inherent human fascination with uncertainty and randomness, and these features of our environment and experience can be observed with particular clarity in gambling. In this respect, gambling is a consumption good rather than an investment good.

It is true that some people become addicted to gambling and go broke. A 2000 study by the economists John Barron, Michael Staten, and Stephanie Wilshusen estimated that an abolition of casino gambling would reduce personal bankruptcies by 1.4 percent nationwide and by 8 percent in counties in which or near which casinos were located. However, given the enormous number of people who gamble, the percentage who go broke as a consequence of their gambling must be very small. This raises a serious question whether the harmless activity of a vast number of people should be curtailed to protect the small fraction who become addicted to it and as a result engage in self-destructive behavior.

If gambling addiction is considered a genuine mental disorder rather than a preference, it perhaps could be controlled by "suitability rules" (a weak "perhaps"—the costs of enforcement might well be prohibitive) that would limit the percentage of a person's income or assets that he could spend on gambling. This would be a counterpart to the suitability rules that forbid securities brokers to buy highly risky securities for people for whom such investments are "unsuitable" by virtue of their financial situation.

Addiction to gambling is more costly the more difficult it is to declare bankruptcy and thus wipe out one's debts. The Bankruptcy Abuse Prevention and Consumer Protection Act of 2005 did just that: made it more difficult to declare nonbusiness bankruptcies. It will be interesting to see whether the act reduces the amount of gambling and gambling-related bankruptcies.

The addiction argument is pressed in the legislative arena by the casinos and the other legal gambling establishments in support of restricting other gambling. The establishments argue that they try to prevent their customers from bankrupting themselves. But as far as I know, this is true only in the sense that they make sure that their customers can pay their losses.

Internet gambling poses a strong competitive threat to the conventional legal gambling establishments, including state lotteries. Those establishments have high overhead expenses—large staffs, expensive equipment (one-arm bandits, casino buildings, casino boats)—with the exception of the state lotteries, but the states, as I have noted, depend upon them as a revenue source, in lieu of taxes, which are unpopular. (The purchase of a state lottery ticket is a voluntary tax payment of one half the ticket price.) Moreover, except for the lotteries, legal gambling imposes substantial time costs on the gamblers, who have to travel to the casino or the racetrack to place a bet. It is because of the overhead expenses and the states' revenue hunger that the odds offered the gambler are so bad (they are even worse, when the time cost of the gambler is added). There may also be monopoly rents further worsening the odds, since competition in the gambling industry is so restricted in most states, a factor in the recent Abramoff scandal involving efforts to prevent competition with Indian casinos.

Internet gambling establishments have very low expenses, enabling them to offer an approximation to fair odds, and do not require any travel by the gambler. One would think fair odds an enormously attractive feature of Internet gambling to gamblers. At fair odds, which is to say with no loading expense (a gamblers' nirvana that Internet gambling, if allowed to operate without threat of criminal prosecution—which obviously drives up its costs—might approximate), the net utility of gambling soars because there is no longer a net expected financial loss.

So the legal casinos are correct that they offer a measure of control over gambling: by offering only bad odds, they reduce the demand for their product.

(The analogy is to the monopolistic provision of a product, which by reducing demand reduces the amount of pollution generated by the manufacture of the product.) It is doubtful, however, that this effect justifies the elaborate legal restrictions on the gambling industry.

37

PREVENTIVE WAR

December 5, 2004

PREVENTIVE WAR—BECKER

Combating crime mainly relies on deterrence through punishment of criminals who recognize that there is a chance of being apprehended and convicted—the chances are greater for more serious crimes. If convicted, they can expect imprisonment or other punishments—again, punishments are generally more severe for more serious crimes. Apprehension and punishment reduce the gain from crimes; in this way, it deters others from criminal activities.

Individuals can also be punished simply for planning or intending to commit crimes. The evidence required to punish intent has to be convincing, but the standard is weaker for violent crimes, like plotting murder, since punishment after the crime does not do anything for those murdered. In addition, individuals who cannot be deterred are sometimes punished simply because it is considered likely that they will commit crimes in the future. This is a major justification for forced hospitalization and psychological treatment of potentially violent and mentally unstable persons.

These arguments about intent apply much more strongly to preventive actions against terrorist organizations and rogue nations. The conventional approach to war in democratic states favors retaliation after attacks. This was the rationale for the Mutually Assured Destruction (MAD) doctrine during the height of the Cold War: the United States was prepared to unleash devastating nuclear destruction against the Soviet Union if attacked with nuclear weapons, and visa versa for the Soviets. That worked, although there were several close calls, as during the Cuban crisis.

But this approach is no longer adequate to fight terrorist organizations, states that sponsor terrorism, and dictatorial states that want to destroy their enemies. For it is becoming increasingly possible for terrorist organizations and governments to unleash biological, chemical, or nuclear weapons that will cause massive destruction. Retaliation may be slow and difficult if terrorists are widely dispersed so that it is hard to generate sufficiently severe reprisals to discourage their attacks. Rogue governments also are more capable of using these weapons surreptitiously, so that it might be many obstacles to determining who was responsible if they chose not to admit their responsibility. It is already difficult to know which groups are responsible for terrorist acts except when they brag about them.

In addition, many state sponsors of terrorism often prey on the zeal of individuals who are willing to kill themselves in promoting what they consider a higher cause. These suicide bombers clearly cannot be punished after they commit their acts (although their families could be) because they forfeit their lives while attempting to kill and injure others. One can try to raise the probability that they will fail—through barriers, walls, and other protective activities—but free societies are so vulnerable that these can never be strong enough deterrents.

The only really effective approach is to stop them before they engage in their attacks. This is accomplished by tracking them down and imprisoning or killing them based on evidence that they intend to engage in suicidal attacks. Those planning such acts can also be punished on the basis of intent.

The same argument applies to dictators who are willing to use weapons of mass destruction to attack their enemies when they do not care if many of their populations are killed and maimed by retaliation from other countries. Dictators, like Saddam Hussein, may also greatly underestimate the likelihood of massive responses because sycophants feed them bad information, or they believe that democratic victimized states will be reluctant to make swift and decisive responses.

Admittedly, the evidence is usually more imperfect when trying to prevent attacks than when responding to attacks. Mistakes will be made, and the evidence of intent must be analyzed carefully. But criminals are convicted too on less than 100 percent certain evidence. As Posner says in his commentary, it is necessary to consider probabilities, not certainties.

Moreover, the degree of certainty required before preventive actions are justified has been considerably reduced below what it was in the past because the destructive power of weaponry has enormously increased. Perhaps most worrisome, the power of weapons continues to grow, and to become more easily accessible. Critics of preventive wars and other preventive actions against rogue states and terrorist groups ignore these major changes in weaponry and their availability. Democratic governments have to recognize that they no longer have the luxury of waiting to respond until they are attacked.

PREVENTIVE WAR—POSNER

The U.S. invasion of Iraq, the U.S. decision not to invade Afghanistan before the 9/11 attacks, and concern with the apparent efforts of Iran and North Korea to obtain nuclear weapons raise acutely the question of when if ever a preemptive or preventive war is justified. If "preemptive war" is defined narrowly enough, it merges into defensive war, which is uncontroversial; if you know with certainty that you are about to be attacked, you are justified in trying to get in the first blow. Indeed, the essence of self-defense is striking the first blow against your assailant.

But what if the danger of attack is remote rather than imminent? Should imminence be an absolute condition of going to war, and preventive war thus be deemed always and everywhere wrong? Analytically, the answer is no. A rational decision to go to war should be based on a comparison of the costs and benefits (in the largest sense of these terms) to the nation. The benefits are the costs that the enemy's attack, the attack that going to war now will thwart, will impose on the nation. The fact that the attack is not imminent is certainly relevant to those costs. It is relevant in two respects. First, future costs may not have the same weight in our decisions as present costs. This is obvious when the costs are purely financial; if given a choice between $100 today and $100 in ten years, any rational person will take $100 now, if only because the money can be invested and through interest compounding grow to a much larger amount in ten years. But the appropriateness of thus discounting future costs is less clear when the issue is averting future costs that are largely nonpecuniary and have national or global impact.

Second, and more important, and well illustrated by the failure to find weapons of mass destruction in Iraq, if the threat of attack lies in the future it is difficult to gauge either its actual likelihood or its probable magnitude. But this is not a compelling argument against preventive war. What is true is that a defensive war is by definition waged only when the probability of an attack has become one; the attack has occurred. The probability of attack is always less than one if the putative victim wages a preventive war, because the attacker might have changed his mind before attacking.

But while the probability of a future attack is always less than one, the expected cost of the future attack—the cost that the attack will impose multiplied by the probability of the attack—may be very high, perhaps because the adversary is growing stronger and so will be able to deliver a heavier blow in the future than he could do today. It may be possible to neutralize his greater strength, but that will require a greater investment in defense. Suppose there is a probability of .5 that the adversary will attack at some future time, when he has completed a military buildup, that the attack will, if resisted with only the victim's current strength, inflict a cost on the victim of 100, so that the expected cost of the attack is 50 (100×.5), but that the expected cost can be reduced to 20 if the victim incurs additional defense costs of 15. Suppose further that at an additional cost of only 5, the victim can by a preventive strike today eliminate all possibility of the future attack. Since 5 is less than 35 (the sum of injury and defensive costs if the future enemy attack is not prevented), the preventive war is cost justified.

A historical example that illustrates this analysis is the Nazi reoccupation of the Rhineland area of Germany in 1936, an area that had been demilitarized by the Treaty of Versailles. Had France and Great Britain responded to this treaty violation by invading Germany, in all likelihood Hitler would have been overthrown and World War II averted. (It is unlikely that Japan would have attacked the United States and Great Britain in 1941 had it not thought that Germany would be victorious.) The benefits of preventive war would in that instance have greatly exceeded the costs.

38

ETHNIC PROFILING

January 23, 2005

IS ETHNIC AND OTHER PROFILING DISCRIMINATION?—BECKER

The value of using group membership in judging unobserved characteristics is uncontroversial most of the time, and so is hardly noticed. For example, automobile insurance companies consider young unmarried males as a relevant group in determining driver insurance premiums because they tend to have more car accidents than older males or young women. These higher insurance rates also help cut down the number of auto accidents by reducing driving by accident-prone young males. Yet given that group membership is almost always an imperfect predictor of unobserved characteristics, some individuals will be treated much worse (or better) than their true characteristics justifies. In the driving case, young unmarried males who are careful and responsible drivers will pay more for insurance than they would in a world with better information. They might be discouraged from driving because they suffer from the bad driving of other young unmarried males.

Still, limited information about individuals means that group identities is often useful in gaining information about them. However, the use of religious, racial, or ethnic characteristics for national security protection and in fighting crime has been a political hot potato, and has led to accusations of discrimination on the basis of race and other characteristics. For the use of group identities in order to treat different groups differently may be the result of a desire to discriminate against various minority groups instead of a desire to act effectively to prevent some undesirable actions.

On top of the current agenda is the effort by organizations fighting terrorism to treat Muslims with greater suspicion. Is it justified to single out young Muslim males from the Middle East for much more careful searches at airports, or for tougher requirements to gain tourist visas and green cards? Or are employees at stores that are trying to prevent theft of their goods justified in watching minority customers more carefully than they watch others? Macy's was recently fined for allegedly watching blacks and Hispanics more carefully, although the company denies that such profiling of customers is their policy.

Efficient actions would say minimize the amount of terrorist activities in the United States, given a limited amount to be spent on preventing terrorism, or would minimize store theft, given a budget for security personnel. Then security checks at airports would try to both catch terrorists before they board a plane, and to discourage future airport terrorism by raising the chances that they are caught at the airport. Similarly, store security both tries to apprehend thieves, and to discourage future store theft.

If young Muslim Middle Eastern males were in fact much more likely to commit terrorism against the United States than were other groups, putting them through tighter security clearance would reduce current airport terrorism. Whether such religious and ethnic profiling furthers the second goal, of deterring future terrorism, depends on the degree of responsiveness of different potential terrorists to a greater likelihood of being caught. If the degree of response by different groups were proportional to their average propensity to engage in terrorism, then checking young Muslim Middle Eastern males more carefully would also help deter future terrorism at airports.

On the other hand, profiling by average propensities might be inefficient if the marginal propensity to reduce terrorism with more careful checks were smaller for groups like Muslims that might have higher average propensities. That could well be true if these groups were more fanatical and less easily deterred by the prospects of being caught. Then the "deterrent" effect on future terrorism would be opposite to and might be stronger than the "apprehension" effect on current terrorism.

The deterrent effect is less likely to dominate the apprehension effect when the difference in average behavior is greater. This is why it is efficient to profile young male Middle Eastern Muslims for terrorist attacks at airports, and perhaps it is efficient also to watch minority shoppers more carefully at stores. To be sure, such profiling is "unfair" to the many young male Muslims who are not terrorists, and to the many minority shoppers who are honest. That could be made up in part by compensating groups who are forced to go through more careful airport screening through putting them in shorter security lines, or in other ways. Similarly, innocent shoppers who are stopped and searched could be compensated for their embarrassment and time.

To be sure, some profiling by governments and the private sector has been due to prejudice against various groups, not as a way of achieving efficiency. So it is crucial to be able to distinguish whether a profiling is efficient from whether it is evidence of discrimination. This distinction can be made in the terrorist field (similar considerations apply to fighting crime) by keeping records on the fractions of young Muslim males and others who were searched and found with weapons or other evidence of intent to commit a terrorist act. If the fraction were much greater among Muslims searched than among others, this would at least be consistent with an emphasis on efficiency rather than discrimination.

A further test would be to determine what happens to apprehension rates as the amount spent on airport security increased or decreased. The profiling policy would again be consistent with efficiency if greater spending on airport security reduced the apprehension rates of young male Muslims who were searched about as much as the apprehension rates of others.

So it is possible to provide analytical criteria and guidelines to determine when particular types of profiling are explained by efficiency considerations rather than discrimination. By using these guidelines to analyze data on apprehension rates, one can determine in an objective manner whether discrimination rather than efficiency is responsible for different treatment of members of ethnic, religious, or racial groups.

COMMENT ON PROFILING—POSNER

At one level, "profiling" is unexceptionable. If witnesses report a theft by a young black male, it would be absurd for the police to look for suspects among other groups in the population. Profiling becomes interesting only when the differential probability of "guilt" is much smaller. Even then, it is unproblematic, as Becker notes, when the disfavored group is not a sensitive minority. No one objects when smokers are charged a higher price for life insurance than nonsmokers, even though many smokers outlive many nonsmokers. Even when the condition that puts one in the disfavored class is involuntary, such as having a family history of cancer or heart disease, "discrimination" on this basis (what economists call "statistical discrimination") is generally considered permissible because it is not exploitive or based on hostility or contempt and it does promote a more efficient allocation of resources.

Profiling based on race, sex, or national origin, however, is intensely controversial. It is helpful in discussing it to make two distinctions: between ordinary crimes and Islamist terrorism (for example, al Qaeda), and in the terrorist case between profiling U.S. citizens and profiling foreigners. I will be discussing these issues purely as issues of policy rather than of law.

In the case of ordinary crimes, where for example profiling might take the form of disproportionately frequent searches of vehicles driven by Hispanics because Hispanics are disproportionately represented in illegal drug trafficking, I would expect profiling to have little effect on the crime rate. The reason is the positive elasticity of supply of persons who commit victimless crimes, which is to say crimes resulting from the outlawing of products or services for which there is a demand. If one class of suppliers is driven out of business, this makes room for others. Given the fixed budget for law enforcement assumed by Becker, the increased apprehension of Hispanic drug couriers would be offset by a reduced risk to non-Hispanics of being apprehended for transporting drugs, and so the non-Hispanics would flock to replace the Hispanics as couriers. The ethnic composition of the illegal work force would be altered by profiling, but the crime rate would be affected only to the extent that Hispanics are more efficient drug couriers because of language and other ties to major drug supply countries; the net effect on the crime rate would probably be small.

In the case of terrorism, a similar replacement effect can be anticipated, although it would probably be smaller. Assume a fixed budget for screening airline passengers and a reallocation of funds within the budget limit to enable more young male airline passengers who appear to be Muslim (or of Middle Eastern origin, but for simplicity I'll assume that Muslim appearance is the screening criterion) to be subjected to intensive screening, as distinguished from the limited screening to which all passengers are subjected. Then fewer passengers who do not fit the profile will be screened (this is implied by the fixed budget), which will induce terrorist groups to make greater use of female Muslims (as happened in suicide attacks in Israel), older Muslims, and young Muslims who do not appear to be Muslim, for members of these groups will now be less likely to be apprehended than before the adoption of profiling. The elasticity of supply of terrorists is probably not as great as that of drug couriers, but it is positive and will reduce the effect of profiling. A parallel analysis recommends against concentrating too many of our antiterrorist resources on the protection of New York and Washington, since terrorists can substitute other targets.

The benefits of airline passenger profiling are thus likely to be modest, and the costs may be great in the case of Muslims who are U.S. citizens. Being singled out on the basis of race, religion, or ethnic origin is intensely resented by the people who are discriminated against and could undermine their loyalty to the United States if they have strong ethnic and religious ties with the nation's enemies. A paramount goal of U.S. antiterrorist policy should be to prevent the disaffection of U.S. citizens of the Muslim faith and Middle Eastern ethnicity. That goal would be undermined by profiling. I do not think compensating them financially for the additional inconvenience would rectify the problem; indeed, it would underscore their differentness from their fellow citizens. (This is also an argument against reparations for blacks and American Indians.)

The argument for the efficiency of profiling is further undermined by relaxing Becker's assumption of a fixed security budget. By increasing the budget for airline security, it would become possible to screen everybody carefully. I suspect that the optimal policy is to subject more U.S. citizens of apparent Middle Eastern origin or Muslim religious identity to intensive screening than other citizens, but to subject enough of the other citizens to the same intensive screening so that the (lightly) profiled group does not feel markedly discriminated against—and so that substitution of terrorists who do not fit the profile is held in check.

My view with regard to profiling noncitizens is different. Noncitizens are not expected to be loyal to the United States and so the concern with alienating them by profiling is less acute. No foreigner expects to be treated identically to a citizen.

39

PRIVATIZING SECURITY

May 28, 2006

PRIVATIZING SECURITY IN IRAQ AND ELSEWHERE—POSNER

There are reportedly twenty-five thousand employees of private security firms in Iraq. Some 80 percent are employed by U.S. firms. It appears that most though not all of these employees are Americans, although I have not been able to locate a statistical breakdown. These employees provide armed guards for U.S. diplomats, journalists, and businessmen that ordinarily would be provided by the military, as well as providing military services (guarding convoys, training Iraqi troops, supplying food, and interrogation) under contract to the Pentagon. There is controversy over both the cost and discipline of these private security personnel.

Privatization is a perennial issue in economics, and it was part of the deregulation movement that began in the late 1970s. The issue reflects the fact that there is no hard-and-fast line between the provision of services by government and by the private sector, and that private provision of services is generally more efficient than public because political interference is less. Conventionally it is thought that only government can provide services that cannot be denied to people who refuse to pay for them, so that efficiency in a broader sense requires public provision of such services. The classic example is national defense. If I install an antimissile defense in my backyard, it will of necessity protect my neighbor as well even if he refuses to contribute to its cost. Because of such free riding, the argument goes, national defense will be underprovided if it is left to the free market.

That is correct, but it does not entail the actual *provision* of the service by government. The government must tax my neighbor to make him contribute to the national defense, but it can turn the tax revenues over to private companies to provide the actual service. The government already contracts out the manufacture of military weaponry. It could in principle contract out the operation of that weaponry as well. Education is a source of nonexcludable external benefits (everyone benefits from an educated population), so it is properly supported by taxes, but it doesn't follow that we need public schools, and indeed there is a great deal of private education indirectly financed by taxes; maybe all of it could be.

And likewise there is a long history of mercenaries, including the Hessians whom the British employed against us in the Revolutionary War and the "soldiers of fortune" heavily employed in Africa's incessant civil wars. The pope's Swiss Guards are a mercenary force. Swiss have been mercenaries since the Middle

Ages. The French Foreign Legion is a quasi-mercenary force. Part of it rebelled against the de Gaulle government in the early 1960s over his decision to withdraw from Algeria, and disloyalty is a traditional concern about mercenaries, though surely not a concern about American private security personnel in Iraq. Indeed, the term "mercenary" is usually reserved for foreigners; that is why members of the U.S. armed forces today are not referred to as mercenaries even though they are employed voluntarily rather than conscripted. By the same token, however, non-Americans employed by private security companies in Iraq are mercenaries.

Since we have a volunteer army, why should there be any concern about contracting out some or even many of its tasks? Many employees of the Defense Department are civilian; soldiers in a voluntary army are employees rather than slaves; and, as I mentioned, the manufacture of the weaponry is contracted out. Instead of just providing weapons and recruits, why not let the private market provide entire military formations? So Blackwater, one of the leading U.S. security contractors operating in Iraq, might be paid to furnish a tank battalion, complete with tanks and other equipment, officers, and enlisted personnel, to fight under U.S. command alongside army, marine, and national guard battalions.

But that would probably be inefficient, because military units that fight together have to be very closely coordinated, and that is difficult when they have different organizational cultures. (The enlisted personnel of the French Foreign Legion are subject to full military discipline, and the officers are members of the regular French army; that is why I called the Legion only "quasi-mercenary.") The contract security personnel in Iraq do not fight alongside the U.S. military but instead operate in a service or supporting rather than combat role, though not without risk—hundreds of them have been killed and many others wounded.

At first glance it might seem redundant for the military to hire contractors who in turn hire, say, armed guards, rather than to hire the guards directly, as soldiers. Soldiers are paid only between one-half and one-tenth as much as the security personnel furnished by contractors for service in Iraq, although the comparison is misleading because the soldiers tend to be less experienced (most of the private security personnel are veterans) and because pension, medical, housing, and other fringe benefits of soldiers are much more generous. This in itself is odd because if the two classes of worker—soldiers and contract security personnel—are doing the same work, why isn't the structure of their compensation the same? One reason is that for many soldiers the military is their career, while most of the contract security personnel in Iraq are temporary workers. Another is that there are nonpecuniary benefits to military service that are absent from its private substitute, including patriotic pride and the prestige that membership in our armed forces confers.

The difference between temporary and permanent workers is the basis for the principal economic rationale for the heavy use of contract security personnel in Iraq. The military needs "temps." The need is not unique to the military, of course. The private sector has many companies that provide temporary workers on a contract basis to firms that could hire permanent employees to do the work, thus cutting out the middleman. But if the firm's demand for workers fluctuates, it may be cheaper to match supply to demand by contracting with companies that have arrangements with workers available for temporary jobs than to hire additional permanent employees but then lay them off when demand is slack, or to go hunting in the labor market, whenever there is a surge in demand, for qualified individuals who want to do temporary work. In the past, the end of a war or other national emergency that had caused a surge in the number of military personnel has led to large reductions in those personnel, which made a military career economically insecure. In order to place twenty thousand additional soldiers on duty in Iraq, the military would probably have to hire a total of sixty thousand, since soldiers are rotated in and out of Iraq about every three years, and these soldiers might be surplus if the war ended or there was a large withdrawal of U.S. troops. Such fluctuations can be avoided by the use of temps.

But of course we have temps built into the existing, pre-contracting-out system. They are the members of the National Guard and other reserve units. They are part-time soldiers available for temporary duty in Iraq and other war zones. So a proper cost-benefit analysis of the contracting-out program in Iraq (which has not to my knowledge been conducted) would compare the costs of the contracts with the cost of enlarging National Guard or other reserve formations to a point at which fewer or perhaps no contract security personnel would be needed. The comparison might favor the contractors simply because the private provision of services tends as I said to be more efficient than the public.

There are, however, two residual concerns with the contract approach that should be considered. Both are political. The first is a suspicion that the use of the contractors is motivated not by cost considerations but rather by a political objective of concealing from the American public the extent of the U.S. commitment of troops to Iraq. The U.S. has about 130,000 troops in Iraq at present. The number would be about 150,000 if contract security personnel were replaced by U.S. soldiers; the number of casualties would also be higher. Increases in either number would reduce political support for the war.

The second is that contract personnel are less restrained in their use of force than our soldiers because the U.S. military command is less concerned about misbehavior of contract personnel than misbehavior of soldiers. The contract personnel are not in the chain of command; apparently they are also immune from prosecution by Iraqi authorities. According to one U.S. general, "These guys run loose in this country and do stupid stuff. There's no authority over them, so you can't come down on them hard when they escalate force ... They shoot people, and someone else has to deal with the aftermath. It happens all over the place." Yet the military is concerned with maintaining the goodwill of the Iraqi population, and that goodwill is impaired by excessive use of force by any foreign personnel. One might think, therefore, that the contracts would subject the employees to full military discipline—but if this were done, it would be difficult to maintain the fiction that they are not really soldiers and so shouldn't be counted in the total of U.S. military personnel in Iraq. Competition for these contracts should induce the contractors to screen the people they hire, but the screening is likely to be imperfect, and as a result the absence of a credible threat of criminal punishment, whether military or civilian, may indeed create a situation in which contract security personnel are less restrained in their use of force than our soldiers are.

ON PRIVATIZING SECURITY—BECKER

Posner has a fine discussion that covers lots of interesting issues. I will try to extend the analysis in a few directions.

Private security personnel are used throughout the American economy. There are more than 750,000 employees of security companies, which exceed the number of state and local police. Private guards regulate admission to important buildings, such as financial centers, patrol neighborhoods, transport money and guard banks, watch customers in shops to discourage shoplifters and robbery, and offer other kinds of protections services. Their numbers more than doubled since 1990, and grew even more rapidly after 9/11, especially in cities like New York. Posner suggests there are about twenty-five thousand private security employees in Iraq, which is only a drop in the bucket compared to the total number of private security personnel operating within the United States. Since private security companies are often hired for dangerous domestic activities, their role in Iraq is in many respects an extension of their domestic activities.

Israel's use of private security protection in dangerous situations is informative about the kind of responsibilities guards can have. Many suicide bombings by terrorist groups in Israel did succeed in terrorizing many Israelis. They became reluctant to use buses, go to restaurants and movie theatres—food take-outs and videos increased a lot, and bus travel declined—and they reduced their congregation in other public places. To alleviate these fears, restaurants, theatres, buses, and other private businesses spontaneously greatly increased their use of private guards to search individuals who entered an establishment or bus, and to watch out for potential terrorists. Evidence compiled for a study of terrorism by Yona Rubenstein and myself indicates that private guards remained cheap despite the large increase in their numbers. They also helped thwart a number of suicide attacks, sometimes at the cost of their lives.

Although private security guards are relatively cheap in Israel, it is not difficult to understand why American security personnel in Iraq are much better compensated than soldiers who serve there. Most of these soldiers signed up when the threat of actually being sent to a dangerous combat zone was pretty small. So their pay was largely determined by other factors, such as training they would receive by serving in the military, their young age, the attractions of military life, patriotism, and so forth. After the Iraq war started they had no choice over whether they went there—if ordered to go they went. By contrast, employees of private companies are older and more experienced, and they have to be induced to go; financial inducements are an important part of the inducement package. Enlistments in fact fell after the war started, so the military then had to offer larger bonuses and other inducements to stimulate enlistments and reenlistments. These higher military personnel costs are part of the estimates of the cost of the Iraq war by Bilmes and Stiglitz that we discussed in our posting on

March 19 on the cost of this war to the United States.

To my knowledge there is no compelling evidence that American private guards in Iraq have been likely to behave irresponsibly, cowardly, or use excessive force. The relevant comparison would be with the behavior of soldiers in Iraq, and I do not know of such comparisons. Posner quotes a U.S. general on the bad behavior of private security personnel in Iraq, but I would not put a lot of weight on the general's assertions. Most military officers prefer to have security forces under their command, so they are tempted to overstate the performance of their troops relative to that of private security personnel.

To be sure, the military has some advantages over private security forces since the military can impose discipline that is unavailable to private companies, such as military trials, imprisonment, court-martials, and other punishments. On the other hand, private companies are forced to compete against each other for the Iraq and other security business. Competition induces companies to screen their employees and fire the bad apples since the Pentagon will stop using companies that supply ineffective personnel, or personnel that brings bad publicity because of an excessive use of force and other misbehavior.

Incidentally, since I believe private security usually performs very well, I never was convinced by the arguments to federalize employees who search baggage at airports. Private companies would do the job better than a single (monopoly) government employer if the standards of performance were clearly set by the government agency in charge of airport security. As in other sectors, a considerable advantage of private employees over federal government employees would result from the competition of different security companies for the business of providing airport security. I would expect competition among companies to have produced more innovation and greater efficiency in airport security checks than we have received, or will get, with federal employees.

40

ANTITERRORISM ALLOCATIONS

June 11, 2006

THE CUT IN ANTITERRORISM GRANTS TO NEW YORK AND WASHINGTON, D.C.—POSNER

The Department of Homeland Security will be distributing some $700 million this coming year to American cities for antiterrorism measures. The amounts allocated to New York and Washington, which are generally regarded as the prime U.S. targets for a terrorist attack, are about 40 percent lower than the current year's allocations, and this has engendered indignation on the part of officials of those cities. Other large cities have seen their allocations cut sharply as well. In part the change in allocations is due to the fact that Congress cut the overall amount of money for this program, but in larger part it is because of a deliberate decision to shift money to smaller cities. Michael Chertoff, the secretary of Homeland Security, defends the shift on two grounds: that the money should be used to build physical capacity to respond to terrorism rather than to fund recurring expenses such as salaries of emergency response personnel, and that New York, Washington, and a few other major cities have received the lion's share of the grants since the beginning of the program because they are the prime targets but their urgent needs have been attended to and it is now time to attend to the needs of the lesser targets.

The interesting policy questions are, first, should the federal government be making such grants to cities, and, second, what should be the basis for deciding how large a grant to make to each city? Taking the first question first, there is no doubt that the federal government and not just states and municipalities should spend money to protect the nation from terrorist attacks, since, as we know from the 9/11 attacks, an attack on a city (or on any other major target) has consequences far beyond the state in which the city is located. But should the government finance defensive measures by the cities or should it spend the money itself? The argument usually heard for the grant approach is that the locals know better their vulnerabilities and how best to reduce them. But the argument is weak because while the locals do know a great deal about the competence of their response personnel, they know little about terrorist threats—terrorist plans, methods, preferred targets, and so forth.

Moreover, when a pot of federal money has to be divided up among state or local governments, pork-barrel politics are bound to distort the allocation. Concern with this problem led DHS to employ anonymous committees of local security and emergency response officials to vet the grants, but partly because of their anonymity and partly because such officials are only quasi-professional, this version of peer review was not highly credible.

Furthermore, the locals may use the federal money simply to replace the expenditures they would otherwise have made on antiterror measures. Suppose a city wants to spend $10 million on such measures and would spend it out of its own funds, but it gets a grant of $10 million from DHS. Then it may simply reallocate the $10 million in its own funds that it would have spent on such measures to some unrelated program. To the extent that such reallocations occur, the $700 million DHS program, with all its entailed paperwork, peer reviews, and political controversy, is not a security measure at all but just a general federal subsidy of local government. Notice, moreover, that the less of its own money the city spends, the less secure it is against terrorist attacks, and it can use the lack of security to argue for an increased federal grant next year!

All this said, probably some sort of grant program makes sense simply because optimal antiterrorism measures require enlisting local facilities and personnel, and cities may underspend on these because the benefits will accrue in part, maybe major part, to other, perhaps far distant, cities; that is the externality point with which I began. I am puzzled why the program should favor communications equipment, computers, emergency vehicles, pathogen detectors, containment shields, and other capital goods over salaries; effective antiterrorism measures tend in fact to be labor intensive. Becker, however, suggests an explanation in his comment.

Moving to the second question, how should the amount received by each city be determined, one encounters baffling problems of measurement. Ideally, one would like the grant moneys to be allocated in such a way as to maximize the excess of benefits over costs. The costs are relatively straightforward, but the benefits are not. The benefits of an antiterrorism measure, for each potential target, depend on (1) the value of the target (not just in terms of financial loss, of course) to the United States, (2) the likelihood of its being attacked, (3) the likely damage to the target if it is attacked (which requires consideration of the range of possible attacks), and (4) the efficacy of a given measure to prevent the attack or reduce the damage caused by it. (2) and (3) are probably the most difficult to estimate accurately, because to do so would require extensive knowledge of the plans, resources, number, location, and motivations of potential terrorists. But (4) is very difficult too, because the effectiveness of increasing the number of policemen, or of installing surveillance cameras on every block, or of increasing the number of SWAT teams, or of taking other measures of prevention or response is extremely difficult to assess in advance.

About all that can be said with any confidence is that cities and other targets that are near the nation's borders (including coastlines) are probably more likely to be attacked than cities and other targets that are well inland, that larger cities are more likely to be attacked than smaller ones because the larger the city the easier it is for a terrorist to hide and move about in it without being noticed, that attacks on large cities are likely to kill more people and do more property damage than attacks on small ones, that among coastal cities New York and Washington probably are the prime targets because of their symbolic significance, but that to neglect the defense of the small inland cities would simply make them the prime targets, and that an attack on such a city might sow even greater fear nationwide than another attack on a large coastal city by making people feel that nowhere is safe. But no numbers can be attached to these probabilities. They belong to the realm of uncertainty rather than of risk, to borrow a useful distinction made by statisticians: risk can be quantified, uncertainty cannot be.

This analysis suggests that more antiterrorism resources should indeed be allocated to the large coastal cities than to other potential targets, but that is the pattern even after the recent cuts. What seems indeterminate is the precise amount of money that should go to each city. That makes one wonder why DHS was willing to incur the political pain of drastically altering the existing grant pattern.

ANTITERRORISM ALLOCATIONS—BECKER

Posner discusses many of the thorny issues involved in the allocation of funds by the Department of Homeland Security to American cities to combat terrorism. I will concentrate my comment on how to align the incentives of cities to those of the country as a whole.

Posner points out that there is a conflict between the incentives of cities and those of the federal government. When cities do more to prevent terrorism against their residents and buildings, they also help the country fight terrorism against other cities and towns without getting compensated for that help. He also indicates that if the federal government simply gives money to cities, the cities may reduce the amounts they would otherwise spend fighting terrorism. Both problems arise in many infrastructure and entitlement programs, such as road building, Medicare for the poor, and the fight against contagious diseases.

These sources of the tendency for cities to underspend on antiterrorist activities can be at least partially overcome if Homeland Security did not outright give various amounts to different cities, but instead relied on the method used to combat similar issues that arise with other grant programs. The Department of Homeland Security should offer to give cities a certain number of dollars for each dollar they spend on antiterrorist activities. For example, if a city spent $30 million, they might get an additional $60 million from the federal government. In this example, a city would get to spend $3 for each dollar they used from their own funds to fight terrorism.

Federal matching of this type discourages cities from cutting back on their spending to fight terrorism since they lose say $3 for each dollar they cut back. Matching grants also induce cities to give de facto recognition to the fact that each dollar they spend helps residents of other cities as well by improving the overall American fight against terrorism. The ratio of federal spending to city spending should be a measure of the ratio of the benefits to other cities compared to the benefits to the city spending their own money to fight terrorism.

The matching need not be independent of how cities spent their own monies. Cities are more likely on their own to spend on salaries than on capital goods that are produced elsewhere since spending on employees gives jobs to local residents. The matching grants should then be oriented toward capital spending rather than labor spending. In fact, the Homeland Security program is so oriented, and that seems to me to make some sense.

However, matching grants, particularly if the ratio of federal to local contributions is large, can create the opposite problem from that created by outright grants; namely, cities may spend too much since their spending is multiplied through the amounts available in matching funds. This is usually controlled by placing upper limits on the amounts that could be received in matching funds. Cities that are especially attractive to terrorist attacks—such as New York and Washington—would spend more fighting terrorism even without federal grants. Still, on their own they may not spend enough, so the upper limits they could receive in matching grants should exceed that available to say Kansas City.

One problem is that as coastal cities like Los Angeles, San Francisco, Boston, New York, and Washington became better prepared to fight terrorism, terrorists might shift inland, to places like Detroit, Chicago, Cleveland, Omaha, Topeka, and elsewhere. As the bombing in Oklahoma City showed, even attacks in smaller cities cause considerable fear and consternation. That is why a federal program has to be national, and target smaller places as well as larger ones. Matching grants encourage smaller cities also to contribute to the fight against terrorism, and they will spend more when they become more vulnerable after the more attractive terrorist targets became better prepared. So the system is partly self-correcting through the incentives that cities have to protect their own citizens. But matching grants do not solve all the problems of how to best allocate limited federal funds. So the federal government will still need some guidelines that determine which cities should be given more Homeland money, although in a matched way.

41

COLLECTIVE PUNISHMENT

July 23, 2006

COLLECTIVE PUNISHMENT—POSNER

Concern has been voiced in some quarters that Israel should not be punishing Lebanon for the acts of Hezbollah, because Lebanon's army has not attacked Israel and it is unclear whether Lebanon has the ability to disarm or otherwise restrain Hezbollah. (There is also, however, doubt whether Lebanon has the will to do so.) In other words, Israel's conduct is being criticized as an exercise of collective punishment (likewise its military measures in Gaza), which involves punishing a collective for the act of an individual member, even if some or all of the other members of the collective bear no responsibility for the act. Israel has responded that since Hezbollah is a part of the Lebanese government, its acts are the Lebanese government's acts. That may be, but is to one side of the issue of the appropriateness of collective punishment. Israel has also defended its actions as targeted exclusively on Hezbollah, with any harms to Lebanese who are not part of Hezbollah's armed wing being inevitable accidents of war.

Without taking sides, but assuming for the sake of argument that Israel is engaged, in part anyway, in the deliberate infliction of collective punishment, I want to discuss the economics of collective punishment, which is a conventional legal tool that is efficient in many of its applications. An important modern example is the employer's liability for injuries resulting from acts by its employees within the scope of their duties. The employer may have exercised due care in the selection, training, assigning, monitoring, and disciplining of the employee who caused the accident, but if the employee was at fault and therefore is liable to the victim, the employer is also liable no matter how faultless its behavior. And usually it is the employer that ends up paying the entire judgment in the suit by the victim because the employee is more often that not judgment-proof. The law allows the employer to seek indemnity from the employee for any judgment the employer is required to pay the victim of the employee's tort, because the employee is the primary wrongdoer. But the judgment-proof problem renders the employer's right of indemnity of little or no value in most cases.

Another important example of collective punishment in law is the rule that all members of a conspiracy are criminally liable for the crimes committed by any member within the scope of the conspiracy, provided it was foreseeable. So if one member of a drug gang beats up a defaulting customer, the other members are apt to be guilty of assault and battery as well even though they had nothing to do with the beating. A related rule, the felony-murder rule, makes a criminal guilty of first-degree murder if a killing occurs in the course of his crime, even if the killing is by someone else and he did not authorize or even expect it—as in the case where a policeman in the course of trying to thwart the crime accidentally kills a bystander.

The theory behind these rules—the theory behind collective punishment in general—is that someone other than the actual perpetrator of a wrongful act may have more information that he could, if motivated, use to prevent the act than the government has. The employer may have been faultless in the particular case, but knowing that it is liable anyway will give it a strong incentive to exert control over its employees to prevent accidents—even by such indirect measures as reducing its work force by substituting robots or other mechanical devices for fallible human workers. Similarly, conspirators have an incentive to police their members to avoid getting themselves into unnecessary trouble; and the perpetrators of a bank robbery, for example, have an incentive to avoid being armed or provoking bank guards or police.

Collective punishment can properly be criticized when the cost of punishment to the innocent members of the collective is disproportionate to the benefits. This would be true if the government executed the family members of murderers. Such a measure would create powerful incentives for family members to monitor each other's behavior, and the murder rate would drop. Or would it? The law would deter the formation of families; and it might even induce families to murder members whom they thought likely to commit murders, since the family might be better able to conceal a murder within the family than the family member who was murdered would have been able to conceal his own murders. In addition, even if the family-responsibility law was effective in reducing the murder rate, the rate of killing might rise; for suppose there were 10 percent fewer murders but for every murder that did occur an average of two family members would be executed.

The example, while extreme, illustrates the essential point about collective punishment: that it is an extremely costly method of punishment, because several or many people are punished for the wrongful act of one. For example, if the cost of punishment to a person punished is X, then if he is a member of a group of ten, all of whom are punished collectively for his act, the punishment cost is 10X rather than X. So collective punishment is properly regarded as highly exceptional. It is most likely to be optimal if either the collective punishment is very mild or the cost to the punisher of failing to prevent the wrongful act is very great, and in either case if in addition the alternative of individual punishment is inadequate. The first case is illustrated by mild collective punishment of children. It includes things like a parent's punishing both his squabbling children because he cannot figure out which one was at fault, or a teacher's keeping the entire class after school because he cannot determine which child threw a spitball at him. These are easy cases because the innocent member or members of the collectively punished group have the necessary information, and ability to act effectively on it, for preventing the misbehavior; they can do so at much lower cost than the punisher because the punisher cannot readily obtain the information necessary to identify the actual wrongdoer; yet the costs to the group of the punishment are slight.

The second case—optimal collective punishment when the cost of failing to prevent the wrongful is great—may be illustrated by Israel's policy of demolishing the houses of the families of suicide bombers. The suicide bomber himself is not deterrable, the harm he does is great, and the punishment method, while severe, is mild relative to the harm that a successful suicide bomber can inflict.

Because warfare is inherently indiscriminate, innocent persons whose only connection to the fighting is that they live in the combat zone are unavoidably "punished," but this is not collective punishment as a deliberate policy. For one thing, those persons will usually have no ability to restrain the combatants on their side. As for the conflict in Lebanon, however, a nation is undoubtedly responsible for predatory acts committed against another nation by groups operating openly on the nation's territory. That responsibility is an example of the kind of collective responsibility that warrants collective punishment for its breach, as in the somewhat parallel case of the employer's liability for the torts of its employees when they are committed within the scope of employment. But how do you "punish" a nation? The nation is the collective of its citizens. Punishing the nation means punishing its citizens even if there is nothing they can do or could ever have done to prevent the actions for which they are being held responsible. Assessment of the reasonableness of the punisher's course of action would then depend on such factors as the alternatives open to the punisher, the amount of damage inflicted by the group that the collectively punished population failed to prevent, the amount of damage that collective punishment inflicts on that population, and the likelihood that the punishment will succeed in getting the punished nation to take effective steps to prevent similar attacks by the rogue group in the future. The last point is vital because it is extremely difficult for one nation to prevent an attack mounted by a terrorist group from the territory of a nation that has acted as the group's willing or unwilling host. That is why the host nation is responsible for restraining the group and why, therefore, it may be a proper candidate for collective punishment.

A final point. I said earlier that a law imposing capital punishment on family members who failed to prevent one of their members from committing a murder would discourage family formation. In other words, collective punishment tends to cause defection from the group. This may be in the punisher's interest: if Lebanese flee southern Lebanon so as not to be "collectively punished" for the acts of Hezbollah, Israel will have a freer hand in dealing with Hezbollah there.

ON COLLECTIVE PUNISHMENT—BECKER

Collective punishments are part of "negative" incentives that are used to reduce crime, military aggression, and other injurious acts. There is often a strong case for such collective punishment to deter harmful acts. Punishing the individuals or groups who commit these acts through police, armed forces, and the judiciary is the first line of defense against such socially harmful behavior. Sometimes, in addition, "positive" incentives are used to encourage the help of private enforcers. This is accomplished by offering payments to whistle-blowers who report white-collar crime, to spies who give information on the military intentions of potential enemies, and to individuals who provide information on wanted criminals or unsolved crimes.

In his discussion in favor of collective punishment, Posner uses the example of employers who may be held liable for injuries due to acts by their employees while performing their duties. Employer punishment is often appropriate for the reasons Posner gives. A less good example frequently discussed is the owners of bars who are penalized for automobile accidents or other injuries caused by persons who became drunk at their bars. Similarly, some states hold the hosts of parties partly responsible for any automobile accidents or other injuries caused by guests who had too much to drink at their parties.

I believe that collective responsibility in these drunk driving examples and in many other situations is inappropriate because those being punished have little ability to deter the injurious behavior that is being discouraged. Can party hosts be expected to keep track of how much each of their guests has drunk, especially at large cocktail parties? That seems to me to an unwise use of negative incentives unless the goal is to discourage cocktail parties themselves. Otherwise, it is best to only punish the individuals who get drunk at parties and afterward injure others. They are the ones who can best keep track of how much they drink.

It is easier for managers of bars than party hosts to keep track of the number of drinks ordered by different patrons. However, punishments to bar owners after serving more than say four drinks to patrons who later commit acts that injure others would give heavy drinkers an incentive to barhop, and have their quota of four drinks at each of several bars. That might cut down the amount of heavy drinking since barhopping is more costly than drinking at a single bar, but it also punishes heavy drinkers who take care not to drive afterward or engage in different actions that cause injury to others. It surely would not make much sense to collectively punish the set of bars where patrons accumulate their excessive amount of drinking. So my conclusion is that in this case too the preferable policy is to only punish intoxicated persons who cause injuries to others, and not attempt collective punishment of bar owners.

To take a different example, parents should often be held responsible for harms to others caused by their younger children. Parents can discourage crimes and other antisocial acts of these children by the upbringing they provide, and also by the punishments they administer to children who engage in such acts. Since after a certain age, perhaps sixteen or eighteen, parents have much less control over children, parental responsibility for children's acts should diminish, and children's responsibility should increase as the children age.

At one time, children were responsible after the death of parents for any debts their parents left. Children were also punished for other antisocial behavior of their parents. This type of collective punishment has been eliminated by developed nations, presumably because children do not have the power typically to deter their parents from contracting debts or committing crimes. The only justification for such collective punishment of children in these cases would be that parents care about the children, and that caring parents would be less likely to enter into debts they cannot pay, or engage in antisocial acts, if children were held responsible for parental behavior. But such collective punishment to children would have little effect on selfish parents, and it would increase the suffering of their children who already are harmed by having selfish parents.

To take a different political example than the Lebanese one that Posner uses, should the German people have been held collectively responsible for the atrocities committed by Hitler and other Nazis? It was inevitable that many German people suffered from World War II, although bombing of Dresden and some other cities by the Allies was probably unnecessary. Collective punishment of leading Nazis was appropriate, as was the requirement that Germany pay reparations for property taken, for some of the damages caused by German occupations of various countries, and for the murder of millions of Jews, Poles, Russians, and other groups.

However, it would be more far-fetched to hold the German people responsible for the election of Hitler since he took steps to prevent the German people from voting him out of office. Moreover, people who voted for Hitler in the first place could not have easily anticipated the full dimensions of the horrors he would inflict on the world.

AFTERTHOUGHTS TO PART VII

BECKER AFTERTHOUGHTS

The possible use of capital punishment brings out so much emotion that it is almost impossible to discuss this in a reasonable way. Not long after writing my comments on capital punishment included in this section, I was in Italy addressing a large general audience on investments in education. Apparently, Italian newspapers had discussed my views on the possible use of capital punishment. During the Q&A discussion after my lecture, one elderly gentleman got up to ask me a question. His voice filled with emotion, he said something like I should be ashamed of myself, and that I should not be allowed to speak because of my views on capital punishment.

Perhaps given the strength of the emotional opposition to capital punishment, and the limited quantitative evidence supporting the deterrent effect of capital punishment on murders, it is best not to use such punishment unless the evidence gets stronger. Still, this is a scientific issue of some importance, particularly if its use would save significant numbers of innocent lives. Emotional opponents should not be allowed to discourage further work on whether capital punishment does have a sizable deterrent effect on the murder rate since the issue is of such importance.

I am writing this only a few days before the voting on who will be the next president of the United States. Polls are watched daily, but so too are online betting markets like the ones run by Intrade. The odds in the Intrade prediction market were against an Obama victory until early in 2008, remained at about the 50 percent level for several months thereafter, and began to rise sharply after the worsening of the financial crisis. At this time, the odds are 85 percent in his favor.

Comment after the election: these betting odds were a good predictor of election outcomes.

Such online betting markets have also been good predictors of the outcomes of past elections. Their advantage over polls is that in these markets bettors put their money at risk, whereas in polls they only reply to questions. These markets respond to the old advice, "Put your money where your mouth is." This information aggregation role of these types of online betting markets is one additional reason, not stressed in my original discussion, for allowing online gambling to continue. To be sure, some gambling, such as online poker games, do not provide much direct socially valuable information, although scholars may use such betting to learn more about how people calculate probabilities, and their attitudes to risk.

POSNER AFTERTHOUGHTS

Since our posts on sports doping, attention has shifted to drugs that enhance cognitive performance—drugs like Adderall, Modafinil, and Provigil that are used to treat genuine disorders but that can also be used by healthy people to improve cognitive functioning by increasing concentration, memory, wakefulness, and mental energy generally. (Coffee has many of the same effects, but they are much weaker.)

I believe that the case for banning intelligence doping is even weaker than the case for banning sports doping. There is a strong positive externality from increased cognitive functioning, since smart people usually cannot capture the entire social product of their work in the form of a higher income. Like other producers, part of the benefit that their production occurs inures to consumers as consumer surplus. A possible source of concern, however, is that because there is competition based on intelligence—for example, to get into good schools or win academic prizes or achieve success in commercial fields such as finance that place a premium on intellectual acuity—the availability of intelligence-enhancing drugs places pressure on persons who would prefer not to use them, because of concerns over their possible negative health consequences, to use them anyway. There is also a danger that such drugs produce only very short-term effects, for example on exam performance, that may exaggerate a person's long-term ability. (This is one of the reasons for objecting to exam coaching.) But against this is the fact that it is even more difficult than in the case of sports doping to draw a line between permitted and forbidden uses of cognition-enhancing drugs. Should people with an IQ above 100, which is the average IQ, be forbidden to use such drugs, but people below that level permitted to use them until it brings them up to 100? That would be absurd. The person with an IQ of 120 would argue compellingly that he should be allowed to take intelligence-enhancing drugs in order to be able to compete for good school placements and jobs with people having an IQ of 130. And so on up.

An interesting legal doctrine that bridges two of the topics addressed in this part of the book—drunk driving and collective punishment—is "social host" tort liability. The term refers to laws (statutes or, less commonly, common-law—that is, judge-made—doctrines), now in force in a majority of states, that make an employer, a bar or restaurant or liquor store, or a purely social host, liable in tort for a guest's (employee's, customer's, etc.) injuring someone while driving under the influence of alcohol (or it might be drugs), if the host knew or should have known that the guest was drunk and would drive, yet served or continued serving him liquor. The liability of commercial establishments that sell liquor to obviously drunk patrons is actually nothing new; it has long been imposed by state "dram shop" laws. The extension to other hosts is novel.

One way to think about social host liability is to imagine that an off-duty policeman is at a bar and sees an obviously drunk person leave and get it into a car and start to drive off. The policeman could arrest him. In effect, social host liability makes bars and other hosts a kind of auxiliary police force, though conscripted, rather than hired, to prevent criminal activity. The analogy can help us to see that social host liability is an example of collective punishment—that is, of threatening to punish those who fail to prevent a harm that cannot be as efficiently prevented directly.

Incidentally, a recent study finds that only 2 percent of drunk drivers are arrested. This reinforces the suggestion in my original post that ex ante regulation probably has little deterrent effect, and that it might be more efficient to rely on ex post regulation—severe punishment for a drunk driver who actually injures someone other than himself and (possibly) his adult passengers.

Regarding the allocation of antiterrorist funds as between federal agencies and local police and other local emergency services, I now incline to the view that the only respect in which a city has a comparative advantage concerns measures for gathering information about residents who might be terrorist supporters and for patrolling local sites and facilities (like the New York subway system). These information-gathering and patrolman-on-the-beat activities, which incidentally are labor intensive, are ones for which grants to cities make sense. But when it comes to capital expenditures, such as for radiation and pathogen detectors, radiation shields, communications equipment, and decontamination facilities, the federal government has the comparative advantage. Apart from being able to extract price concessions by buying in bulk, the federal government can assure compatibility across cities where needed (for example, in communications equipment), exploit economies of scale, base expenditures on more sophisticated appreciation of threats and technology, and resist grantsmanship and local political pressures. Thus, on reflection, I am inclined to change my mind and conclude that the Department of Homeland Security has it backward in emphasizing grants to cities for capital rather than for personnel expenditures.

VIII

THE WORLD

42

ECONOMIC AND POLITICAL FREEDOM

March 6, 2005

ECONOMIC AND POLITICAL FREEDOM: DOES ONE LEAD TO THE OTHER?—BECKER

President Bush's January 2005 inaugural speech stressed the importance of improving political freedoms worldwide: "So it is the policy of the United States to seek and support the growth of democratic movements and institutions in every nation and culture, with the ultimate goal of ending tyranny in the world." The right to vote freely and other political freedoms are valued everywhere, clearly demonstrated by the happy faces of many Iraqis when they went to vote for the first time in free elections. Pressure to liberalize politically may be spreading throughout the Middle East, as shown by recent small steps toward greater democracy in Egypt, Lebanon, and Saudi Arabia.

Men and women "in every nation and culture" also place high value on economic freedoms. These include the ability to own property and have it protected by law and contracts, the opportunity to change jobs, including moving off farms and to different cities and regions, the right to become self-employed, and the freedom to choose among hundreds of varieties of goods and services at competing establishments.

The Chinese are so happy with the economic freedoms granted them during the past twenty-five years that for the moment they have accepted sharp limits on their political freedoms, including a one-party system, a controlled press, and attempts to limit access to many Web sites. Similarly, Indians were content enough with their extensive political freedoms acquired after independence from Great Britain in 1947, so they did not press for economic freedoms until four decades later.

Since both economic and political freedoms are highly valued, it is essential to understand how they interact as nations evolve. The history of different countries during the past century strongly indicates that economic freedoms over time typically push societies toward political freedoms. To take a few examples, South Korea, Taiwan, and Chile all started their economic development under military regimes. Korea and Taiwan both began freeing their economies around 1960 after centralized direction of their economies failed to produce economic growth. Chile began opening its economy under General Pinochet in 1981, also after his centralized approach to the Chilean economy failed. Within two decades, all three nations had achieved, or were moving rapidly toward, political democracies, with vibrant competition for elections among competing parties, and a mainly free press.

The path from political to economic freedom, by contrast, is slower and more uncertain. It took India over four decades to begin to loosen its extensive controls over private companies, labor markets, start-ups, imports from abroad, and numerous other activities. It still has a long way to go. Mexico has had a free press and considerable political freedom for a century or so, but economic freedoms did not begin to evolve until the latter part of the 1980s. Israel has fierce competition among political parties, but continues to have an overly controlled economy.

To be sure, a few case studies are not conclusive, partly because one may pick and choose to come up with favorable examples. So examples have to gain support from analyses of as many nations as possible. International comparisons of these questions were started by the sociologist, Seymour Martin Lipset, and continued by many others, especially more recently by the economist Robert Barro. The consensus among these studies is that countries are likely to become democratic if economic growth succeeds in raising their average incomes to high enough levels. And countries with greater economic freedom, that is with freer markets and more secure private property, produce faster growth and greater prosperity than countries that sharply limit economic freedoms.

Moreover, this strong positive relation between economic freedom and growth is largely independent of the degree of political freedom.

These studies also find that the effect of political freedom on subsequent economic growth is weak. There is probably greater variability in economic performance under dictators, but on the average, totalitarian regimes and democracies do not differ greatly in their rates of economic progress. I believe that democracies are not especially successful at generating economic prosperity because powerful interest groups develop under democracies (and other political systems too). These groups compete for economic favors that often are at the expense of economic efficiency. For example, democratic nations have difficulty shifting away from policies that say restrict foreign and domestic private investments, as India did for so long, because both government and private enterprises that benefit from these restrictions lobby to continue them.

By contrast, when economic freedoms lead to greater prosperity, that encourages a widespread desire for more political freedom. With freer markets, entrepreneurs and management travel abroad more often to meet customers and suppliers, and incidentally learn about the freedoms elsewhere. A growing middle class takes trips to other countries, and they send their children abroad to study at top schools. University students read the great works that show the advantages of political freedoms. More families become highly literate as education progresses, and families learn about the world from cable and satellite television, and from the Internet.

As a result of these activities, a steadily increasing fraction of the population become aware of the political freedoms enjoyed by the leading nations, the great satisfaction from having the right to speak openly, to read conflicting opinions on different issues, and to vote for candidates with competing agendas. They begin to agitate for greater political freedoms, and eventually they become too powerful a force to be ignored.

This analysis implies, in particular, that if China continues to grow rapidly, the Chinese people will become increasingly dissatisfied with censorship and their limited political freedom. Already they have much greater freedom than under Mao to voice different opinions, and to criticize the government—if not done too stridently and openly. These forces will gather steam, and I believe they will lead before long to a much more open political process.

To be absolutely clear, I am not claiming that people value economic freedoms more than political freedoms. Rather, the argument is that economic freedoms tend to lead before long to political freedoms, while the reverse causation is slower and less certain. Put differently, private property and open markets help economies grow, which gives the political process a strong shove toward democracy. For this reason, the president's inaugural speech should have paid more attention to economic freedoms, along with his stirring and convincing case for democracy.

DEMOCRACY AND FREE MARKETS—POSNER'S COMMENT

I agree with Becker that a high standard of living is likely to lead toward democracy. The intermediate stage is political liberty. As John F.O. Bilson explains in his article "Civil Liberty—An Econometric Investigation," 35 *Kyklos* 94, 103 (1982), "Almost any reasonable theory of freedom would predict a positive correlation between freedom and real income. On the demand side, freedom must be considered a luxury good so that the resources devoted to the attainment of individual freedom are likely to be greater when per capita income is high. On the supply side, it is undoubtedly more costly to repress a wealthy person than a poor person and the need to do so is probably less acute." Although we tend to associate political liberty with rights against government coercion, for example, the rights conferred by the U.S. Constitution, rather than with democracy as such, it would be difficult to be secure in those rights without electoral competition; rulers who are not required to stand for election at frequent intervals are too powerful to be constrained by courts.

Becker gives good examples of how authoritarian governments evolve toward democracy as the standard of living rises. I agree that under modern economic conditions rapid economic growth requires a commitment to free markets. The puzzle is why, knowing that such growth will undermine authoritarian government, a dictator or ruling clique would want to allow economic liberty. To safeguard his power, one might think, a dictator would keep his country poor. That has been, in fact, an effective strategy for many, probably most, dictators. It may be that dictators adopt a policy of economic liberalization only when their political power is already in decline, so that the optimal strategy is to slow the rate of decline by buying off the population (temporarily) with greater economic opportunities, siphoning the people's energy from political to economic activity.

I also agree with Becker that there is no necessary tendency for democracy to promote economic liberty. This is implicit in the fact that every modern democracy grants rights *against* the democratic majority, notably property rights, as in the requirement in the Fifth Amendment that the government pay just compensation for property that it takes for a public use. This is recognition that democracy can endanger economic liberty. When we speak of the desirability of "democratic" government, what we should mean by democracy is not popular rule in some literal sense (the sense the word "democracy" bore in ancient Greece), but a system in which the principal officials are subject to electoral checks and in which the entire government has only limited powers over the citizenry. In a wealthy society, the democratic structure as I have sketched it will usually suffice to preserve considerable economic freedom; but in a poor society, the preconditions for such a structure may not exist and as a result democracy may undermine economic liberty seriously. There may be elections, even honest elections, but there may not be judges competent and independent enough to protect property rights securely and enforce contracts reliably. A democratic government may be populist in the sense of adopting policies that produce equality at the expense of growth ("killing the goose that lays the golden egg"). That is why there is no necessary correlation between democracy and prosperity.

But I think President Bush had something else in mind when he called for greater democracy in the Middle East and other areas of the world where authoritarian government predominates. I don't think his principal objective was to promote economic liberty in those countries. I think the point rather is that democratic societies tend to be less aggressive militarily than authoritarian societies. The reason is that most people in any society have no taste for the risks and violence of war. Democracies may find themselves involved in defensive wars, of course, but there are very few examples of democratic societies warring with each other; that is, democracies are rarely aggressors (rarely, not never). It is therefore in the U.S. national interest to promote democracy throughout the world, because if all nations were democratic the military threat to the United States would be greatly reduced. It is true that democracy in the Middle East might bring to power in some nations radical Islamist movements. Nevertheless if they were genuinely democratic they would probably find it difficult to rally their people to support a militaristic foreign policy, or to support terrorist movements that might provoke a violent response from the United States.

43

SIZE OF COUNTRIES

April 17, 2005

WHY SMALL HAS BECOME BEAUTIFUL—BECKER

In the Federalist papers, Alexander Hamilton argued for the proposed U.S. Constitution that gave the federal government great powers because he claimed large countries with strong central governments have freer internal markets, can better deal with foreign aggression, and can raise taxes more easily to pay for needed government services. Yet since 1946, the number of countries has grown from about seventy-six to almost two hundred. Some of that growth has been due to countries gaining independence from colonial powers, such as India or Zaire. Others resulted from a subdivision of countries into smaller units, such as the breakups of Czechoslovakia into the Czech Republic and Slovakia, or of Yugoslavia into several independent nations. Agitation to form independent nations continues in all regions of the world.

Has this splintering into smaller nations, often due to nationalistic aspirations, lowered their economic efficiency? My conclusion is that developments in the global economy during the past fifty years have greatly reduced the economic disadvantages of small nations enumerated for his time by Hamilton. In fact, being small now may even have efficiency advantages. This would help explain the splintering of nations along ethnic, religious, linguistic, and geographic lines.

In the past, larger nations generally provided bigger domestic markets with relatively low barriers to movements of goods, services, capital, and labor. By contrast, tariffs, quotas, and capital and immigration constraints severely limited the movement of goods, capital, and people across national boundaries. But many of these barriers have come tumbling down as international trade has boomed for the past half century, propelled at first by GATT and then by the World Trade Organization (the WTO). Members of the WTO are forced to have low tariffs and quotas on import of most goods and services, and to some extent, on capital as well. As a result, world imports and exports have grown since 1950 at the remarkable rate of about 10 percent per year

In other words, small countries can now gain the advantages of large markets through trading with other nations. So it is no surprise that international trade generally constitutes a larger fraction of the GDP of small nations than of large ones. For example, exports in 2004 relative to GDP are about 10 percent for the United States compared to 37 percent for Iceland. Most poor nations that experienced rapid economic growth during the past four decades also were extensively involved in international trade. This is true not only of the Asian tigers—South Korea, Taiwan, Japan, Singapore, and Hong Kong—but also of Chile and Mauritius. These are all small except for Japan. In addition, much greater use of international trade helped rescue the two giants, China and India, from their long economic sleep.

Smaller nations even have some advantages in a world with much international trade. Their exports are too little to be considered a threat to other nations, so they are not subject to as many barriers as those from large nations, They often specialize in niche markets that are too insignificant, or not accessible, to large nations. For example, the tiny principality of Monte Carlo with about five thousand citizens has become a tax haven and gambling center for rich sports stars and other wealthy individuals. Singapore and Hong Kong have been mainly trading centers for shipments of goods to their much larger neighbors. Mauritius has succeeded by concentrating on textiles and tourism.

Apropos of Hamilton's other arguments, small nations can now free ride on the military umbrella provided by the United States, NATO, or the United Nations. Small nations may still be at a disadvantage in providing other government services, but powerful groups in large nations often use the economies of scale in raising taxes and dispensing subsidies to exploit weaker ethnic, national, or economic groups. Smaller nations are usually also more homogeneous, so the powerful interests there have fewer other groups to exploit.

Tariffs and quotas on foreign producers impose a relatively big economic cost on small countries since they have little influence over the international prices of imports and exports. This cost reduces the ability of domestic producers to get politicians and voters to go along with their efforts to weaken competition from producers in other countries.

The economic consequences of the reunification of East and West Germany demonstrate some of these advantages of being smaller. East German productivity was much below that in West Germany when the communist government was overthrown. Economists both inside and outside of West Germany warned against the consequences of both exchanging one East German mark for one West German mark, and preventing East German wages from falling much below those in West German. The result not surprisingly has been very high rates of East German unemployment—still around 20 percent—with the unemployed and others supported by massive financial transfers from West German taxpayers. These transfers more than a decade after reunification still amount to 4 percent of total German income.

Both Germanys would have been better off economically if East Germany remained independent, and had an agreement with West Germany for free movement of goods, people, and capital across their borders. Wages in the East would then settle at a fraction of those in the West to reflect the lower productivity of East German workers. These low wages would attract companies from Germany and elsewhere to outsource some activities to the East that would provide jobs and raise employment and wages. Unfortunately, the prospects of attracting investments in East German have worsened with the expansion of the EU to include central European nations, like the Czech Republic, Slovakia, and Poland, with much cheaper, and less unionized, labor.

The split into the Czech Republic and Slovakia about a decade ago is also instructive. There was concern then that Slovakia would have trouble going it alone because they received transfers from the richer Czech region, and because many powerful leaders in Slovakia were ex-communists. But economic pressures forced a much more realistic assessment of what they needed, so Slovakia threw the communists out of power, and prospered by reforming rapidly toward a freer market economy.

My conclusion is that economic consequences no longer discourage secessionist movements that are driven by hostility among different religious, ethnic, linguistic, and other groups. This explains the continued secessionist pressure in some countries, such as the recent call by the main leader in the Basque region of Spain for a referendum there on whether they should become more or less completely independent from the rest of Spain. They already have considerable autonomy, so this example shows that giving power to regions is an imperfect substitute for full independence. Political pressure remains strong among French Canadians for Quebec to become independent from the rest of Canada, although this sentiment is weaker than a decade ago as Canadian regions have received greater autonomy. Many Kurds in Iraq, Iran, and Turkey still dream of an independent Kurdistan. The Tamils in Sri Lanka, and different groups in Indonesia continue their fight for independence. And is it any surprise that most Taiwanese do not want to become part of a greater China, despite growing threats from China?

Mainly due to the growth of the global economy and globalized trading, the evidence is overwhelming that small nations can now do very well economically, perhaps better than larger ones. In light of this evidence, it is surprising how many people, including economists, continue to believe that their economies will be ruined if secessionist movements succeed.

THE SIZE OF COUNTRIES—POSNER'S COMMENT

I agree with Becker that the costs to nations of being small have declined and that this decline, along with the dismantling of the colonial empires (mainly of Great Britain and France), are factors in the growth in the number of nations since World War II. I am going to focus, however, on the benefits side of nation size. Even if the costs of being small decline, unless there are benefits to being small one would not expect the decline to affect the number of nations, especially if we assume as we should that there are significant transitional costs to splitting up a nation.

The question of what determines the size or scope of a nation has parallels concerning the size of business firms and other private and public organizations, and even the size of animals. In the case of a firm, size is determined mainly by the relation of size to average cost. When the firm is very small, an increase in its size, by permitting greater specialization of its workforce, is likely to reduce the average cost of the firm's output and thus make it more competitive. But beyond some point the gains from specialization will be exhausted and average costs will begin to rise because of increased costs of control. Effective control of a huge firm may require multiple layers of hierarchy, slowing and distorting information flows, although decentralization, as in a multidivisional firm like General Motors or General Electric, may enable the number of layers of supervision, and the associated costs, to be minimized.

Economies and diseconomies of scale (or scope—roughly, cost as a function of the number of products a firm produces as distinct from the quantity it produces of a single product) in the conventional economic sense also play a role in the determination of the size of countries. But other factors play a role as well, such as the advantage of size in defending against other nations. Here the analogy is to animals. Large animals are less vulnerable to predators than small ones are, and as a result tend to survive longer. (I am speaking of the individual animal, not the species.)

Historically, size has been enormously important to national survivorship. The nations that have disappeared completely, such as Prussia, Burgundy, the Republic of Texas, and the countless small kingdoms and principalities in Italy and Germany before the unification of those nations in the second half of the nineteenth century, have generally been small countries, though Becker is correct to note the continued survival of tiny "niche" countries, such as Monaco; this suggests that there is no minimum efficient size of a country, as there is of a steel producer. Large nations, however, have frequently fissured, such as Austria-Hungary and the Soviet Union, suggesting the existence of diseconomies of scale in the "market" for nations. Pakistan, a large but noncontiguous state, split in two. South Africa lost Namibia, Indonesia lost Papua New Guinea, Ethiopia gained and then lost Eritrea, and so on. What is new is that smallish nations, like Yugoslavia and Czechoslovakia, have also split; nevertheless, the splitting of small nations remains an infrequent phenomenon.

As Becker explains, with free trade the gains in specialization to a nation from having a large internal market diminish. And changes in military technology have reduced the military value of a large population, though not of a large GNP, which is a function in part of population. Nevertheless, if one glances over the entire history of nation formation and dissolution since the Middle Ages, one sees that the decisive factor has been the rise of nationalism. Nationalism is the belief that national boundaries should follow the contours of a "nation" in the sense of a population that has a common language, race or ethnicity, religion, historical origin, or culture, at least if that population lives in a contiguous area rather than being a diffuse minority in a larger polity, as some "nations" in the sense just defined, such as Jews and Armenians, are. The territorial nations of Israel and Armenia are limited to the areas in which the members of the ethnographic nation inhabit a compact, contiguous geographical area.

The greater the differences—in values, skills, language, and so forth—between two "nations" that inhabit adjacent territories, the fewer their common interests, and this complicates governance if they are made parts of a single territorial nation, in much the same way that corporate governance would be complicated in a firm that sold life insurance, diamonds, and hubcaps. The added costs may be offset, however, and in the nation case by defense considerations as well as by economic ones. If barriers to trade make large internal markets important for economic growth, then different "nations" in the ethnographic sense may share a single territorial "nation." As those barriers recede and the military value of a large population declines, we can expect the nationalist principle to prevail. But this need not necessarily result in smaller nations. The mergers of the two Vietnams and of the two Germanys, and the reincorporation of Goa into India and Hong Kong into China, are examples of post–World War II boundary changes that have increased the size of nations. (And in all likelihood someday the two Koreas will be united and Taiwan will be absorbed into China.) It may be an accident that the number of nations in the world has increased since World War II. The number could have declined if more ethnographic nations had been divided up among different territorial nations rather than being combined in single territorial nations.

The merger of the two Germanys may have been an economic mistake, as Becker persuasively argues. But the diseconomies of scale in a nationalistic state, that is, a state with a homogeneous population (despite its racial, religious, and cultural heterogeneity, the U.S. population is homogeneous compared, for example, to Belgium, with its sharp regional division between French-speaking and Dutch-speaking populations, or even Switzerland), are small within a broad range. For just as a business firm can minimize diseconomies of scale and scope by decentralization, so a nation can greatly reduce those diseconomies by federalism. As a result, a large nation like the United States is able to compete economically with much smaller nations. In addition, its population size and consequent aggregate wealth enable it to achieve great military power, which prosperous small nations cannot do.

The analysis is incomplete, however, because one observes that many adjacent nations having a common language and culture do not merge: the United States and Canada, for example; Mexico and the other nations of Central America; the Spanish-speaking South American countries; Germany and the German-speaking Swiss cantons; and the Arab nations of the Middle East and North Africa. The explanation offered by Adam Smith for the American Revolution may have general application: within each ethnographic nation there is a governing class that anticipates greater benefits from ruling its nation than from sharing power with other elites within a broader territorial union.

44

HAMAS, PALESTINE, AND DEMOCRACY

January 29, 2006

HAMAS, PALESTINE, AND THE ECONOMICS OF DEMOCRACY—POSNER

President Bush has suggested that spreading democracy is the surest antidote to Islamist terrorism. He can draw on a literature that finds that democracies very rarely go to war with each other, although a conspicuous exception is the U.S. Civil War, since both the Union and the Confederacy were democracies.

Hamas, which has just won a majority in the parliament of the Palestinian proto-state, is a political party that has an armed terrorist wing and is pledged to the destruction of Israel. Can that surprising outcome of what appears to have been a genuinely free election be squared with the belief that democracy is the best antidote to war and terrorism?

The first thing to note is that one democratic election is not the equivalent of democracy. When

Hitler in 1933 was asked by President Hindenburg to form a government, the processes of democracy appeared to be working. The Nazi Party was the largest party in the Reichstag; it was natural to invite its leader to form a government. Within months, Germany was a dictatorship. So the fact that Hamas has won power fairly and squarely does not necessarily portend the continuation of Palestinian democracy.

But suppose Palestine remains democratic. What can we look forward to? I don't think the question is answerable if democracy is analyzed realistically. The great economist Joseph Schumpeter sketched in his 1942 book *Capitalism, Socialism, and Democracy* what has come to be called the theory of "elite" or "procedural" or "competitive" democracy. In this concept, which I have elaborated in my book *Law, Pragmatism, and Democracy* (2003), and which seems to me descriptive of most modern democracies, including that of the United States, there is a governing class, consisting of people who compete for political office, and a citizen mass. The governing class corresponds to the selling side of an economic market, and the citizen mass to the consuming side. Instead of competing for sales, however, the members of the governing class compete for votes. The voters are largely ignorant of policy, just as consumers are ignorant of the inner workings of the products they buy. But the power of the electorate to turn elected officials out of office at the next election gives the officials an incentive to adopt policies that do not outrage public opinion and to administer the policies with some minimum of honesty and competence. It was Fatah's dramatic failure along these dimensions that opened the way to Hamas's surprisingly strong electoral showing. Hamas cleverly coupled armed resistance to Israel with the provision of social welfare services managed more efficiently and honestly than the services provided by the notoriously corrupt official Palestinian government, controlled by Fatah.

In troubled times, such as afflicted Germany in the early 1930s and Palestine today, democratic elections provide opportunities for radical parties that provide an alternative to discredited policies of incumbent officials. The worse the incumbent party, the better even an extremist challenger looks. The German example suggests that moderation of a radical party when it takes power is not inevitable. The party may continue its radical policies and even use its initial popularity to destroy democracy. Hitler and Mussolini took power in a more or less orderly democratic fashion and Lenin by a coup, but in all three cases the consequence of the seizure of power by a radical party was the opposite of moderation. Hitler and Mussolini remained popular until their policies failed dramatically; there is no theoretical or empirical basis for supposing that popular majorities in all societies are bound to favor more enlightened policies than a dictator or oligarchy would.

How then to explain the empirical regularity that democracies rarely war with each other, and the concomitant hope that if Palestine were democratic it would stop trying to destroy Israel? The answer lies in considering what is required for democracy to take root rather than to make a rapid transition to dictatorship. Democracy is unstable unless anchored by legally protected liberties, including freedom of speech, freedom from arbitrary arrest, and property rights. The liberties in turn tend to be unstable without a measure of democracy. When there are no liberties, a one-sided election can result in a quick extinction of democracy, because there is nothing to prevent the winner from calling an end to the electoral game in order to perpetuate his control. When there is no democracy, rulers are not effectively checked, and corruption and other abuses flourish. The combination of democracy and liberty, as in the U.S. Constitution, provides an auspicious framework for prosperity, resulting eventually in dominance of the society by a large middle class. Middle-class people don't have much taste for offensive wars or violence in general. They are not specialized to such activities, which benefit primarily monarchs and aristocrats (who internalize martial values), impoverished adventurers, and (closely related to the adventurers) political and religious fanatics. (This is in general, not in every case; the Germany that Hitler took over was a middle-class republic, democratic though imperfectly so.) As Samuel Johnson said, people are rarely so innocently engaged as when trying to make money, since in a well-ordered society they can do that only through trade, which wars disrupt.

So democracy itself is not a panacea for the world's political ills and dangers. But if the Palestinians are able to develop a genuinely republican government and move rapidly toward embourgeoisement, there is some hope for the eventual emergence of a peaceful Palestinian state.

There is another point, special to the Palestinian situation, that provides a further ray of hope. With Hamas in power, its members are paradoxically much more vulnerable to Israeli military power than they were when Fatah was in power. The Hamas leaders then were scattered and hidden and efforts to fight them risked killing innocent civilians and discrediting the Palestinian government, with which Israel was trying to make peace. Given Fatah's inability to suppress Hamas, Israel could not crush Hamas by bombing the government buildings occupied by Fatah. Once Hamas is the government, however, further violence toward Israel by Hamas members can be met appropriately by massive military force directed against the organs and leaders of the government. This threat may cause Hamas to avoid attacks on Israel. Hamas's victory may be the best thing that has happened to Israel in years.

A COMMENT ON THE POLITICAL VICTORY OF HAMAS—BECKER

The election victory of Hamas sent a bombshell throughout the Middle East and the rest of the world. I will comment briefly on its implications for democracy among the Palestinians, economic development, and relations with Israel. I agree with Posner that it is hard to tell whether free elections will continue among the Palestinians. One free election means very little in forecasting the future—even the Weimar Republic had several elections before Hitler destroyed Germany's young democracy. Contested government, a free press, and other free institutions are far more likely to persist when they have been practiced for a long time. James Madison argued against Thomas Jefferson's proposal to continually change the American Constitution, and in favor of a stable constitution because of "that veneration, which time bestows on everything, and without which perhaps the wisest and freest governments would not possess the requisite stability" (Federalist Paper no.49).

Economically, the Palestinian Authority is a basket case: no foreign investment, little foreign trade, and emigration of the more talented, educated, and ambitious Palestinians to elsewhere in the Middle East, or to America. The Authority is barely kept afloat by aid from Europe, other Arab nations, and the United States that amounts to about $1.5 billion per year.

Hamas now has to choose between two radically different paths. In many respects the easiest one would be to maintain its charter that calls for the "obliteration" of Israel. Surely, however, that would further discourage foreign investment, and is likely to speed up the out-migration of talented Palestinians. In addition, it will mean the end of aid to the Palestinian Authority from America, and possibly also from much of Europe as well. A sizable reduction in foreign aid may force Hamas to try to introduce economic reforms, but these cannot succeed as long as its goal is to eliminate Israel.

The wiser course would be for Hamas to become more flexible and greatly moderate its hostile actions and rhetoric toward Israel. After all, Ariel Sharon while in power shifted from a hard-line policy toward the Palestinian Authority to a more moderate position, and the Israel economy is in far better shape than is the Palestinian economy. Hamas showed that it could win an election by downplaying its hostility to Israel, and instead emphasizing its ability to run the government more efficiently and with less corruption than Fatah. However, unless the new government can significantly improve the dismal Palestinian economic situation, Hamas's popularity is likely to erode. Yet the only way to retain human capital, attract foreign direct investment, and widen foreign trade, all essential for significant economic progress, is to reach a stable settlement with Israel.

For these reasons, I am more optimistic than Posner and many others about the chances that Hamas's victory will improve rather than worsen relations with Israel. Perhaps, as Posner argues, it will become easier for Israel to retaliate against Hamas leaders when they are physically more concentrated either in the Palestinian Parliament or in executive offices. But I do not consider that a crucial consideration.

My cautious optimism is based on the economic pressures Hamas will face as it tries to govern the Palestinians. Yet the Middle East is the most unpredictable region of the world. So I would not bet a lot on my analysis, especially in the near term, but I do disagree with the pessimistic views among the media and politicians about what Hamas will do after its astonishing political victory.

45

GOOGLE IN CHINA

February 20, 2006

GOOGLE IN CHINA—POSNER

Last week a congressional committee questioned representatives of Google, Yahoo, Microsoft, and Cisco concerning Chinese censorship and surveillance of Internet services (and, in the case of Cisco, equipment) provided by these companies. Google, for example, has acknowledged that it does not offer e-mail, chat rooms, or blogs in China, but only Web search, image search, local search, and Google news and that it censors these programs so that Chinese customers cannot search for "democracy," "Falun Gong," and other topics that China wants to shield its people from. Yahoo apparently provided information about one of its Chinese customers that led to his arrest and a ten-year prison sentence for political activity that would be legal in the United States. Cisco is said to have sold equipment to the Chinese police that assists them in monitoring dissidents. Members of Congress are incensed and are threatening legislation that might forbid U.S. companies to knuckle under to political restrictions imposed by China as a condition of permitting our Internet companies to do business there.

In general, U.S. companies, including Internet companies, are required to comply with the laws of every country in which they operate. Thus, for example, they have agreed to block access, in France and Germany, to Nazi Web sites, pursuant to those countries' laws against Nazi advocacy. They have agreed in a number of countries including the United States to block access to sites that infringe copyright. Like other companies that possess information that is not considered the "property" of the people who furnished it (and this is generally the case with respect to information voluntarily provided to an online vendor), the Internet companies often respond to informal government requests for information, and they are also subject to having such information subpoenaed.

Of course there is a difference between foreign laws that we regard as defensible, including some laws, such as those forbidding Nazi advocacy, that would be unconstitutional in the United States (which has by international standards an extravagant conception of freedom of speech), and laws that we regard as contrary to fundamental human rights, which is an accurate description of Chinese laws designed to suppress political freedom and, in the case of persecution of the Falun Gong and of some Christian sects, of religion as well; there are also forced-labor camps in China, torture, and other human rights violations.

If China were a small, poor country, its violations of human rights might induce international sanctions, such as were imposed on Rhodesia and South Africa before the fall of their racist regimes. But because China is an enormous country, rapidly developing, soon to be—perhaps already—the second largest economy in the world, and very much open to investment by foreign, including U.S., companies, sanctions are out of the question as a practical matter.

A separate question is the effects of sanctions. The theory of cartels is useful in illuminating that issue. When competing firms get together and agree to raise price (and thus limit output, since increased price will cause some customers to switch to other products) in order to increase their profits above the competitive level, they face two problems. First, each member of the cartel will have an incentive to cheat because by charging a price slightly below the cartel price it will have proportionately greater sales and its net revenue will rise. Second, firms outside the cartel will have an incentive to increase their output by selling slightly below the cartel price, for the same reason that impels cheating. The harder it is to cheat, and the smaller the fringe of competing firms outside the cartel, the more effective the cartel will be.

A sanctions regime is similar. Each country that has agreed not to buy from or sell to the sanctions target will have an incentive to cheat, and countries that have not agreed to the imposition of sanctions will have an incentive to increase their trade in the embargoed goods. So our Internet companies, were they under political or public relations pressure, or were they compelled by U.S. law, not to agree to conditions imposed by China, would have an incentive to try to circumvent the ban; and Internet companies in countries that did not impose such a ban would have an incentive to enter the Chinese Internet market.

But it is not clear to me how effective such incentives would be. The U.S. Internet companies would be reluctant to violate, or perhaps even to circumvent, U.S. law, since they are taking a big public relations hit from the revelations of their complicity with Chinese repression. And in the short run at any rate it does not appear that foreign Internet companies can provide close substitutes for the services that our companies provide. Of course in the long run an exclusion of our Internet companies from the vast Chinese market would stimulate the growth of foreign companies offering close substitutes for our companies' products. This assumes that faced with abolishing censorship of the Internet or losing Google search and other Internet services that U.S. companies uniquely provide, China would choose to lose the services. This seems, however, by far the likelier outcome given the perceived threat to the regime that political and religious freedoms pose. If so, then the only effect of the sanctions regime would be to slow Chinese economic growth slightly by reducing the Chinese people's access to Internet services that promote economic efficiency. One reason to think the effect will be slight is that China does have its own Internet providers, such as Baidu, which provides a

Google-like search service, although not as good a one as Google.

The deeper question is whether it is in the U.S. national interest either to promote Chinese democracy, religious freedom, etc., or to impede Chinese economic growth by inducing it to curtail its people's access to the Internet beyond the current censorship. The answer probably is "no." Lifting the repression lid from Chinese society might, for all I know at any rate, have destabilizing effects that might result in a worse government (from our standpoint) than the present one. Slowing Chinese economic growth might also be destabilizing, and would harm the world economy as a whole, and probably the U.S. economy. Then too, although there are inherent tensions between the United States and China, owing in part to the American military and political presence on the periphery of China, China is not an enemy and we don't want to make one by imposing sanctions on it. Although the behavior of our companies may be offensive and their claim to be altruistically motivated is ludicrous, it is unlikely that efforts to prevent the companies from complying with ugly Chinese laws will help either the Chinese people or the American people.

A possible intermediate solution, however, would be to forbid U.S. companies (or for them to agree under pressure of American public opinion) to assist the Chinese government in surveillance of their customers. There is a difference between censorship and surveillance. Most governments engage in some censorship, including our own (child pornography, national security secrets, copyright violations, defamation, false advertising, criminal solicitations, etc.). But for our companies actively to assist a foreign, repressive regime to persecute its political and religious dissidents is a step beyond. It is unlikely that the Chinese government would bar our Internet companies merely because they did not provide active assistance to Chinese police.

GOOGLING IN CHINA—BECKER

Posner has a very good discussion of many aspects of the controversy over the concessions to the Chinese government by Google, Yahoo, and a few other high-tech companies. I generally will come to similar conclusions but from a little different perspective.

I do believe that it is reprehensible for Yahoo to disclose the names of Chinese citizens using its services, particularly when the information Yahoo gave about one of them led to his arrest and imprisonment. Whatever one's beliefs about other rules of corporate behavior in China, disclosure of names of "dissidents" who face arrest and punishment is unacceptable.

During the remainder of my comment I will pretend that I am the CEO of Google (alas, I am slightly less rich) to discuss whether Google should accede to the demands by the Chinese government to prevent access to Google users in China to Web sites on democracy, the Tiananmen Square uprising in 1989, the Falun Gong sect, and a few other subjects.

Presumably, it might be very profitable to make these concessions under the very likely assumption that the government would not agree to any significant compromise.

However, profits in the Chinese market are not the only consideration, even from the viewpoint of maximizing Google's (and mine as CEO) market value. Google has a deserved reputation as a very independent as well as innovative company that does not cave in to unreasonable government demands. From our vantage point the Chinese government's demands are not reasonable. For this reason we did indicate on our Web site in China that we were excluding certain enumerated subjects from our search engine.

That said, under present conditions we are still providing millions of people in China, we hope that will climb to hundreds of millions, access to an unbelievable array of information. The subjects covered are far too numerous to enumerate, but let me just mention information about DNA and its discovery, medical treatments for breast and prostate cancers, the determination of prices under different market conditions, riots in the United States and elsewhere, the Becker-Posner blog, and many more.

Chinese Google users also have access to information that is highly informative about democratic institutions and processes. This includes discussions of elections in Japan, Great Britain, the United States, the turnover of parties in power in democracies, histories of countries that were transformed slowly, like Great Britain, or rapidly, like Japan, from powerful monarchies to lively democracies. They also have some access to information on the overthrow of communism in East Germany, Poland, and the Soviet Union, although that information is not as openly available as I would like.

In this way Google is still exposing millions of Chinese to information and knowledge that even a decade ago was unavailable to anyone in the West. Isn't this a priceless contribution to the welfare of the Chinese people, despite the restrictions placed on their access to certain subjects from using Google?

Suppose we at Google had refused to go along with the Chinese demands and were excluded from the Chinese market. It is very possible that our place would have been taken either by European or Japanese companies, or indigenous Chinese companies, only too willing to comply with the government's demands. In this case, American stockholders, workers, and taxpayers would be (a little) worse off, and the Chinese people would also be also worse off since these other companies are not as good as Google. The only gainer, aside from the company taking our place, would be the Chinese government since they would have a more docile search engine company to deal with.

A different scenario is that the Chinese people would have been deprived of a search engine for years. Perhaps that would slightly weaken the government because of increased resentment among the population, but it would hurt the typical Chinese computer user much more. Why should we be the instrument of making the Chinese people suffer any more than they already have during the past many centuries from isolation from Western technology and knowledge?

Let us also not forget that not only has the Chinese economy been expanding for the past quarter century at a remarkable rate, but so too have freedom of expression, travel abroad, and some other freedoms that are important parts of the foundation of a true democracy. The Chinese government supports strongly the economic progress, yet bemoans the increased freedom that naturally accompanies this progress. Government controls over these freedoms cannot keep up with their pace of development as the economy charges forward.

Software is rapidly developing that would enable Chinese users of the Internet to bypass their censors, and gain access to the information that they prevent us, Yahoo, and other companies from directly providing them. Chinese censors and other Chinese restrictions on basic freedoms are engaged in a losing battle as long as the economy, including its human capital, continues to go global. Even somewhat limited access to the vast information made possible by Google further pushes the battle in favor of freedom and against government restrictions.

Given these considerations, and admitting our concern as a company with maximizing the wealth of our stockholders and employees, does not the entry of Google into China even under these restrictive terms contribute to the tidal wave of freedom that is overwhelming the Chinese government?

I (that is, GSB) agree with the CEO, for I would give an affirmative answer to that question.

46

ECONOMICS OF NATIONAL CULTURE

April 2, 2006

THE ECONOMICS OF NATIONAL CULTURES—POSNER

In our last week's postings on the French riots precipitated by the new employment law, now in force, that allows employers to fire, without cause, during the first two years of employment employees under the age of twenty-six, Gary Becker and I offered some possible explanations for the riots that did not depend on any notion of a distinctive French political or social culture. But it is difficult to resist attributing some causal efficacy to cultural factors. The new law permits, though within a very limited scope, employment at will, the dominant employment contract in the private sector in the United States—and public opinion polls indicate that the French are more hostile toward capitalism than virtually any other nation; a recent poll finds that only 36 percent of the French have a favorable opinion of capitalism, compared to 71 percent of Americans. The French are at once highly statist, which is related to the rejection of capitalism, and highly prone to riots and work stoppages, which may also be, as I will suggest. They are unusually xenophobic, as indicated by their efforts to prevent the incorporation of English words into the French language, their resistance to foreign acquisition of French companies, and their emphatically independent line (going back to de Gaulle) in foreign relations and military matters. The French are, in short, culturally distinct. Can an economic account of cultural difference be given? If so, the starting points would be habit, on which Becker has written, and the economics of organizations, networks, and language, on all of which I have done some work. Much behavior is habitual, and this can be given an economic meaning. Behavior is habitual when it is done without conscious thought, or more precisely with limited thought. (More technically, behavior is habitual when cost and benefit are time dependent and cost is negatively related to time and benefit positively related to it. (See Gary S. Becker, "Habits, Addictions, and Traditions," 45 *Kyklos* 327, 336 [1992], and notice that the obverse case—cost positively, benefit negatively, related to time—is that of boredom.) One is conscious that one is brushing one's teeth, but the amount of thinking that is involved is very slight; one doesn't think about which tooth to brush next, how long to brush, how much toothpaste to put on the brush, and so forth. So transforming behavior from deliberated to habitual, usually by repetition, economizes on cognitive effort, and is thus cost effective. The cost of making it habitual is a sunk cost, moreover, which means that once behavior is habitual it is cheap to continue with it. This discourages change, since new costs would have to be incurred.

Culture is similar. The way in which people speak (including pronunciation, grammar, syntax, and vocabulary), gesture, hold their bodies, grimace, use knife and fork, greet one another, behave toward members of the opposite sex, and otherwise conduct themselves in their basic social interactions is to a high degree habitual, most of that behavioral repertoire having been learned and mastered in early childhood—when learning costs (notably of language) are low. To change one's cultural identity as an adult requires incurring heavy time costs, often with limited results—a foreigner is unlikely ever to lose all traces of foreignness. This is one reason why there are many different languages, even though it would be more efficient (costs of change aside) if everybody in the world spoke the same language.

Beliefs also have an important habitual element. If one is brought up to believe that being American or French is very special and that foreign attitudes and behaviors should be held at bay, the adherence to those beliefs is cheap. Once you believe something, you will be reluctant to incur the cost of changing the belief unless assailed by some doubt that you cannot easily resist; and people do not like being in a state of doubt. Most people cannot give a good account or defense of their beliefs; they believe something because they have always believed it, not because they have a good, conscious reason to believe it. Once a belief system is entrenched, it is likely to persist indefinitely until a very rude reality check causes the costs of continued adherence to the system to exceed the costs of change. That has not yet happened in France, a rich country—surprisingly so, given its high unemployment rate and overregulation. GDP per capita is the twenty-first highest in the world, and though significantly lower than that of the United States, is comparable to that of Germany and the United Kingdom, and higher than Sweden's. In addition, France has the world's third-highest life expectancy and its workers have a great deal of leisure. The country can afford high unemployment and a short work week for those who are employed because it has the most productive workforce in the world, though in part this is an artifact of high unemployment—the unproductive workers aren't employed. The high standard of living of the French, which actually understates the quality of French life because of their leisure and life expectancy, discourages the French from reexamining their political beliefs, since such reexamination would be costly, whereas continued adherence to their beliefs is costless in the sense of requiring no mental energy and not preventing the enjoyment of a good life by most people. A weak work ethic weakens resistance to the inconvenience caused by riots and work stoppages.

There is an interesting literature on organizational culture—the beliefs, norms, customary practices, methods, etc., that are found in, and vary among, particular organizations—that bears on our subject. The literature emphasizes the difficulty of changing an organization's culture. A famous study of our failure in Vietnam, by Robert Komer *(Bureaucracy Does Its Thing: Institutional Constraints on U.S.-GVN Performance in Vietnam* [R–967–ARPA, August 1972]), and a similar recent study by John Nagl *(Learning to Eat Soup with a Knife: Counterinsurgency Lessons from Malaya and Vietnam* [paperback ed. 2005]), document the inability of our government to change the organizational culture of our armed forces, even though it was plain to many people in government that that culture was poorly suited to the conditions of the Vietnam War. Business failures frequently stem from the same cultural inertia, even though business receives from the market strong signals that its culture is maladapted.

The explanation is in part the sunk-costs problem that I have emphasized, but also the "network" character of an organization's culture, which makes it necessary, in order to change the culture in a constructive way, to change a great many things at once, and some of the things may be very difficult to change. For example, when the Detroit auto companies began losing market share to Japanese manufacturers, they studied Japanese methods and decided to adopt one of them, the "quality circle" approach whereby workers were encouraged to take an active role in suggesting productivity enhancements. Transposed to the United States, the approach failed because workers realized that improvements in productivity might endanger their jobs. This wasn't a problem in Japan because workers in the Japanese automobile industry had de facto lifetime tenure, which our workers did not.

In Vietnam the obstacles to our armed forces' changing their organizational culture was that the culture was optimized to a continuing threat, namely, that of a conventional war in Europe. Secretary of Defense Rumsfeld has had a somewhat easier job of altering the armed forces' culture to make it more responsive to what is being called "postmodern warfare," illustrated by the struggle against global terrorism and the insurgency in Iraq, because the threat of a conventional war has receded. In addition, in seeking to transform the armed forces, Rumsfeld is aided by the fact that technological innovation, the key to his concept of transformation, is an element of the traditional U.S. military culture.

So culture is habit writ large and is difficult to change because habits are difficult to change. And changing national cultures, like changing social norms and customs (themselves a part of culture), is particularly difficult, because of the lack of centralized direction. In principle, the culture of a nation's military can be changed by an order of the commander in chief, though in practice such an order is likely to be foiled by passive resistance within the organization.

But a national culture has no hierarchy, unless the nation is totalitarian. To change a nation's language or any other deep-seated feature of its culture requires coordinated action without a coordinator. Imagine a country whose leaders thought it would be more efficient for drivers to drive on the right-hand side of the road rather than the left but decided to leave the change to the spontaneous decision of the drivers.

The dramatic though not complete changes in the German and Japanese national cultures that occurred in the wake of World War II were facilitated by the fact that in each case the war had smashed much of the existing national culture as well as demonstrated its dysfunctional character. That has yet to happen in France.

ON THE ECONOMICS OF NATIONAL CULTURE—BECKER

Posner emphasizes two important reasons, habit and coordination costs, for why cultures, including those of nations and companies, often change very slowly. I agree with his arguments on why habitual behavior and coordination-network effects are important, and do not have much to add directly to his discussion. Instead, I will try to explain the seeming contradiction that many aspects of national cultures change drastically and often surprisingly quickly. In a nutshell what I claim is that major economic and technological changes frequently trump culture in the sense that they induce enormous changes not only in behavior but also in beliefs.

A clear illustration of this is the huge effects of technological change and economic development on behavior and beliefs regarding many aspects of the family. Attitudes and behavior regarding family size, marriage and divorce, care of elderly parents, premarital sex, men and women living together and having children without being married, and gays and lesbians have all undergone profound changes during the past fifty years. Invariably, when countries with very different cultures experienced significant economic growth, women's education increased greatly, and the number of children in a typical family plummeted from three or more to often much less than two. Divorce rates often exploded, men and women married later, and living together without marriage became more common.

Ireland is an excellent example since not long ago Irish family patterns were the object of study by demographers only because they were so different. These patterns involved late ages at marriage, high birth rates, no divorce, and married women who spent their time mainly caring for children and their husbands. Enshrined in the Irish Constitution of the 1930s is the hope that married women would not work but instead they would be home taking care of their families.

All aspects of Irish family behavior changed radically during the past two decades: the typical family now has only about two children, divorce was legalized and is growing rapidly despite the Catholic Church's opposition, and the labor force participation of married women is becoming like that in other parts of Western Europe. The rapid economic growth Ireland experienced during the past couple of decades had a revolutionary impact on the incentives of parents to have many children, on attitudes about whether married women should work, and on whether married couples were obligated to remain together throughout their lives. What is fascinating about the Irish example is that these and other changes in family patterns of behavior occurred while Ireland remained a highly devout nation, with the highest rates of church attendance and other measures of religious belief in the Western world.

Similar changes have also occurred in very different cultures. Japan, South Korea, Taiwan, Hong Kong, and other Asian countries had rapid declines in birth rates from very high to very low levels as they experienced extraordinary economic growth during the second half of the twentieth century. Married children are much less likely to live with parents than before their economic development, divorce rates are rising, and married women have become active in the labor force. Birth rates have declined and other aspects of family behavior have changed also in the primarily Muslim country of

Malaysia, although these changes are generally smaller than in neighboring countries that experienced economic development.

Even the "unique" culture of the French changed enormously as it experienced rapid development after World War II. French birth rates also fell below replacement levels, although they are higher than in other parts of Western Europe (partly due to generous child subsidies in France), married women work in large numbers, and divorce rates have risen a lot. Nor are the radical changes in France restricted to the family. A leading French businessman spoke in English before an international audience recently because he said English is the language of commerce. President Chirac walked out before he began to protest his speaking in English. The command of English has been growing rapidly among French youth, and many French companies conduct their board meetings and other internal discussions mainly, sometimes entirely, in English. French McDonald's restaurants have been attacked, but they are highly profitable because many French young people go there. English words are growing rapidly in spoken and even written French, despite continual protests.

Yet, I am not suggesting full economic determinism, a la Marx. While economic progress and technological change do have enormous effects on "culture," some important national institutions, attitudes, and behavior change much more slowly. Among other examples, Posner mentions language, attitudes toward globalization, whether one drives on the left or right sides of a street, and units of measurement. Even various dimensions of family life change much slower in some cultures than in others. For example, while divorce rates have risen at rapid rates in Japan and South Korea, they are still much lower than those in the West, and the labor force participation of married women is also much lower.

Change is easier in those parts of culture that are due mainly to habit. For habits respond as economic circumstances, technologies, and incentives change. At first, habitual behavior is usually slow to change since past behavior exercises enormous influences over current behavior that is "habitual." But the initially slow changes induce further and more rapid changes in later behavior, so that the cumulative change may eventually be quite big. Smoking is habitual, even addictive, but that did not prevent large declines in smoking rates in all developed countries since the early 1970s after the evidence on its connection with cancer and heart disease became evident. In the past it was expected that women would stay home after marriage and have large families. These expectations changed greatly and rather rapidly as women's education and their job opportunities improved, and as the economic advantages of investing more in the education of children became apparent.

Change is harder in behavior that requires detailed coordination among different citizens. This is why measurement systems, basic street driving rules, the official language, and some other aspects of a country's institutions change very slowly, although languages get infiltrated by foreign and new words, and greater emphasis is placed on languages that are more important for communication with other countries. Despite French protests, English has become not only the international language of commerce, but also of advanced education instruction, and of communication through the Internet.

To relate this to last week's topic, how much of the opposition in France to the proposed youth labor law can be attributed to a special French culture? The propensity to riot is higher in France than say Germany, but strong and effective opposition to making discharge of employees easier is found also in Germany, Italy, and Portugal. Nor is the opposition restricted to Western Europe. So far the free-market-oriented Indian prime minister, Dr. Manmohan Singh, has not been able to make much of a dent in India's similar employment system, and the same difficulties in discharging employees are found in most of Latin America.

No, the conflict over the proposed youth labor law is not particularly "French," but basically comes from the opposition of labor market insiders with good jobs who do not want to give up their privileges. This is the same source of opposition to labor market reforms in France, Germany, Italy, India, Argentina, and other countries with widely different cultures. It is more interesting to ask why Anglo-Saxon countries like Great Britain, Australia, and New Zealand have moved toward flexible labor markets in response to the effects of globalization, whereas these other nations have not? I do not have the answer, but before we attribute this to a unique Anglo-Saxon culture, let us recognize that China has also introduced flexible hiring and firing practices as it moved rapidly to a market economy. China obviously has a radically different history and "culture" than Anglo-Saxon nations.

47

MICROFINANCE AND DEVELOPMENT

October 29, 2006

COMMENT ON MICROFINANCE—BECKER

I applaud the granting of the 2006 Nobel Peace Prize to Muhammad Yunus and the Grameen Bank. Sure, reducing poverty has at most an indirect connection with peace by encouraging democracy. Still, the Peace Nobel Prize has often been so political—it is different from other Nobel Prizes since the Peace Prize is awarded by the Norwegian Parliament—and frequently of such dubious merit, that it is a welcome change to have the prize given to someone who has really helped the very poor of the world.

Yet, all economists who have studied microfinance agree that it will never be more than a minor factor in ending poverty in any country. Economic growth requires secure property rights, encouragement of private enterprise, openness to international trade, stimulation of education, limited and sensible regulations, and reasonably honest government. Microfinance makes only a small direct contribution to any of these variables.

However, microfinance does accomplish something useful, and that is how it should be evaluated. So far microfinance has been mainly oriented toward women, although that is not necessary. It started in the primarily Muslim rural areas of Bangladesh, where women had great difficult borrowing money in any way to earn income as tiny scale entrepreneurs. Study of several of these programs suggest that in fact payback rates have been high since borrowers have been subject to great social pressure to repay, they have few alternative ways to borrow, and because of other factors. These studies also suggest that women who borrow gain bargaining power within their families. This shows up as an increase in the education of daughters and also sons, greater spending on medicines, and on women's assets, like gold, in families that have women who borrowed under one of these programs.

These programs are usually quite flexible, and sometimes approach the equity type loans that Posner advocates. If someone is having trouble repaying debt due to no fault of her (or his) own, microfinance lenders, as well as other lenders in these communities, often wait until times get better, instead of demanding all payments be made on time. In effect, microfinance often works out to be loans with returns that are quite sensitive to how well borrowers do.

Microfinance has spread to rural parts of non-Muslim countries, and these loans too are primarily given to women. Evaluations of the effects of loans in non-Muslim countries also show high repayment rates, and that female borrowers repay at higher rates than, and generally outperform, male borrowers. So loans in other countries appear to have similar effects as in Muslim countries like Bangladesh.

I do not believe there is much of a puzzle about why commercial institutions have not made such micro loans. For one thing, enforcement of repayment by any particular borrower from the group of all borrowers in a local area was originated by the Grameen Bank, and would not be easily copied by for-profit banks and moneylenders. But even if commercial lenders could have the same high repayment rates, these loans have not typically earned the rates of return required by commercial lenders in poor countries. The Grameen Bank and other groups active in making micro loans have had some financing from NGOs that do not seek to make commercial returns on their spending. So my belief is that despite the seemingly "high" interest rates on these loans, they have earned returns, adjusted for servicing, risk, and other costs, that are below market interest rates in their respective countries,

If private groups want to make gifts to rural women in poor countries, making them through micro loans is a much better way than many alternatives. Loans at considerable interest rates help donors select among a huge number of persons who believe they deserve help. For by requiring recipients to engage in productive activities that yield enough returns to pay interest and repay principal, micro loans in effect choose to help those with ideas and a willingness to work hard. What is a better way to choose among too many people who are really poor? In my judgment, it is always better as far as possible to reward people who try to help themselves.

The focus on women may be a good starting point in many countries since they have entrepreneurial ideas, and yet often have great difficulty in borrowing commercially, or even from their families. Still, one risk here is that the apparent borrower is a woman, but the real borrower is her husband, brother, or father, and she is simply a front for them. Moreover, many men in poor rural areas also have great difficulty getting access to funds, so these programs should include many more male borrowers as they grow in scope.

Individuals like Pierre Omidyar, one of the founders of eBay, has made a $100 million contribution to Tufts University for that university to invest in profit-making microfinance programs. I share his apparent belief in the principle that competition among for-profit firms is the best way to organize and allocate resources in an economy. It may be possible to get a fully for-profit sector that has large resources, and makes the small micro loans pioneered by the Grameen Bank. I hope so, but the many for-profit moneylenders and banks in poor countries in the past did not manage to make such small loans at rates that were both profitable and appealing to borrowers. So I am not convinced that his vision and that of some other American entrepreneurs will be successful. But their vision of harnessing incentives from the for-profit sector is the right way to try to improve microfinance.

MICROFINANCE AND THIRD WORLD POVERTY AND DEVELOPMENT—POSNER

The award earlier this month of the Nobel Peace Prize to Muhammad Yunus and his Grameen Bank of Bangladesh has directed attention to the phenomenon of microfinance, which Yunus and his bank have pioneered. The term refers to the making of tiny loans to poor people in underdeveloped countries, like Bangladesh. The amounts are sometimes only tens of dollars, the borrowers are small farmers, shopkeepers, artisans, and other minute commercial enterprises—overwhelmingly female (97 percent)—and the interest rates, which are designed to compensate the lenders fully, are high—sometimes as high as 20 percent a day. Although Yunus's motivation is not primarily commercial, the high interest rates and a relatively low default rate (in part because groups of women related to or friends with the borrower often agree to guaranty repayment of the loan), said to be only 1 percent, enable the Grameen Bank and its imitators (collectively referred to as "MFIs"—microfinance institutions) to cover their costs. The MFIs provide other services to poor entrepreneurs as well, but the loans ("microcredit") are the most interesting feature of this experiment in helping poor countries throw off their poverty.

Microfinance began with the Grameen Bank in the 1980s, and to date the bank has disbursed almost $6 billion in loans to some 6 million people. The total number of borrowers from all microfinance institutions is expected to reach 100 million by next year. The aggregate value of these loans is a drop in the bucket so far as alleviating Third World poverty is concerned, but the award of the Nobel Prize is a vote of confidence that may encourage continued growth of the program.

What exactly microfinance has to do with "peace" is obscure. The causes of war are complex, and it is by no means clear that poverty is a major one. In any event the actual contribution of microfinance to peace must be slight and speculative.

So the award of a Nobel Peace Prize to Yunus was questionable, but that is not to criticize Yunus's project. The experiment is a worthy one, though its success has yet to be demonstrated despite glowing appraisals by Kofi Annan and others. It may simply be the latest development fad.

It does however seem superior to philanthropy in the sense of handouts, which in this case would mean giving grants (or heavily subsidized loans) to small entrepreneurs on the basis of competitive applications. For that is a competition in rhetoric. Middlemen would spring up to assist the applicant in writing a persuasive application, and the fees charged by the middlemen would be a good example of how the prospect of obtaining economic rents (crudely, something for nothing) channels the expected rents into costs. And the grants would frequently be misallocated. The high interest rates that the microfinanciers charge induce self-selection by the borrowers: a borrower has to have confidence in the project for which he is seeking microcredit in order to be willing to assume the burden of servicing his debt. Of course such confidence is sometimes, and perhaps among the poor often, misplaced.

An obvious question is why, if microfinance is remunerative, commercial banks and other commercial lenders did not enter the market long ago; for as I said, microfinance began in the 1980s. One possibility is that regulations designed to protect the solvency of banks limits their ability to make risky loans. Usury laws may be an obstacle too, if they are differentially applied to ordinary lenders as distinct from microfinanciers—yet the Grameen Bank seems to be an ordinary stock corporation, not a nonprofit. More important may be the existence of a close substitute for microfinance in the form of informal loans by relatives and clan members, a method of financing that is feasible (and extremely common) in societies in which the clan and the extended family can discipline members by threat of ostracism and other informal sanctions. The total capital possessed by the family or clan might be slight by usual commercial standards, yet if only one or a few members have any real entrepreneurial prospects, the limited capital may be sufficient to finance their tiny projects. So microfinance is perhaps best understood as a device for easing the transition from an economy based on trust to a normal commercial society.

As a substitute for trust, microfinance has obvious drawbacks. Extremely high interest rates, though justified not only by the risk of default (and the opportunity cost of money, that is, the riskless interest rate) but also by the very high transaction costs of a tiny loan (since those costs are largely fixed, rather than varying with the size of the loan), burdens the borrower with very heavy fixed costs, since he must repay the loan regardless of the success of his enterprise. The higher a producer's fixed costs relative to his total costs, the riskier his enterprise, since if demand for his product falls or his marginal costs rise he will find it extremely difficult to adjust by cutting output; the cut will reduce the revenue out of which he has to pay principal and interest on the loan. Borrowing at astronomical interest rates seems an unlikely formula for commercial success—and the more unlikely the poorer the borrower.

In the family or clan alternative, trust may provide an extremely low-cost substitute for the transaction costs involved in microfinance. Perhaps then microfinance will occupy a narrow niche in capital markets between family and clan resource pooling at one end and commercial lending at the other. Indeed, the fact that the overwhelming majority of microfinance borrowers are women suggests that the particular market failure that microfinance corrects is discrimination against women in the family and clan capital markets.

An alternative form of microfinancing would be equity rather than debt financing, on the model of private-equity firms like Blackstone and the Carlyle Group. Of course these multibillion dollar firms have no interest in making $100 loans in Bangladesh. But the Grameen Bank could presumably furnish equity in lieu of loans to its customers, thus sharing the risk with them and so reducing the risk to them; and it is a superior risk sharer because of size and diversification. But maybe the bank would find it too difficult to evaluate projects, or would fear being inundated by applications from the impecunious.

I end on a skeptical note. The evidence for the efficacy of microfinance in stimulating production and alleviating poverty is so far anecdotal rather than systematic. The idea of borrowing one's way out of poverty is passing strange. And I am unaware of any historical examples of nations that climbed out of poverty on the backs of small entrepreneurs financed by credit. Also, recall that Grameen Bank has lent almost $6 billion to some 6 million persons. This implies an average loan of almost $1,000, which in a country like Bangladesh is not chicken feed and makes one wonder how much of the Grameen Bank's loan portfolio is actually microfinance. (Yet the bank's financial statement indicates that the average loan balance in 2005 was only $85—I don't understand how this squares with the aggregate figures that I gave above, which are also published by the bank!) Then too, the bank has been in operation since 1983, which is more than twenty years and indicates that the average number of borrowers is only three hundred thousand a year, with presumably many repeat borrowers. Bangladesh has a population of almost 150 million people. It is true that the microfinance movement is growing—and as it grows we may see default rates rising and the microfinanciers adjusting, as the Grameen Bank may already have done, by greatly increasing the minimum size of loans. Think back to that low default rate for the Grameen Bank. The bank does not have written loan agreements and does not sue defaulters or invoke other legal remedies against them. The natural inference to draw is that the bank is extremely selective in its choice of persons to whom it is willing to lend, and such selectivity, if imitated by other microfinanciers, must greatly limit the scope and impact of microfinance.

I suggest, albeit tentatively, that there may be a good less to microfinance than its boosters claim.

48

WORLD INEQUALITY

December 10, 2006

WORLD INEQUALITY—BECKER

A recent UN report on world inequality of wealth (UN Department of Economic and Social Affairs, *World Economic and Social Survey: Diverging Growth and Development* [2006]) attracted widespread media coverage. The report finds that the richest 2 percent of adults own half the world's assets, which clearly indicates a very skewed world distribution of assets. When put into context, however, the inequality in wealth appropriately defined is not nearly as large as the report might suggest, and wealth inequality in the world has almost surely become smaller over time, not larger as some in the media reported.

The UN report was prepared by very good economists, and does a commendable job in what it tries to do. That is to measure the value in 2000 of the world distribution of physical and financial assets, net of any debt—this is usually called net worth. The authors had direct wealth data for countries that have more than half the world's population, and an even larger share of its wealth, and they infer wealth in countries missing from their data. Their results do show both considerable inequality in assets, and a long tail at the upper end of asset holdings—called skewness in statistical language. The report does not even attempt to show what happened to world inequality over time, even though some of the media reports that it demonstrates that inequality greatly increased in recent decades.

World inequality in wealth is to a large extent determined by inequality across nations. Comprehensive data on what happened to the distribution of assets in the world over time are not available, but the income data show a sizeable decline, not increase, in world income inequality since 1980. This is mainly but by no means entirely due to the remarkable rate of growth in incomes in two quite poor nations, China and India, which contain about 37 percent of the world's population. Studies also show that both the number of and the fraction of the world's population who live on either $1 or $2 of income per day has fallen quite sharply during the past twenty-five years, again partly due to China's and India's growth.

Earnings, not incomes from physical or financial capital, are the predominant determinant of incomes for the vast majority of persons in the world in rich as well as poor nations. Put differently, human capital, not assets, is the most important form in which people hold their wealth. Human capital is itself determined by education, training, nutrition, and other forms of health investment. Human capital wealth that determines earnings is about three times as large as wealth in the form of physical assets of all types. Such wealth from human capital is much more equally distributed and is much less skewed in its distribution than are assets.

Even earnings and money incomes exclude the contribution of better health to people's "real" income, defined as the incomes that produce well-being. World inequality in health among countries has declined greatly since 1960 when measured by life expectancy at various ages, even though the AIDS epidemic in Africa has largely eliminated the gains in life expectancy in that continent after 1970. Inequality in "full" income among countries has declined much more rapidly than inequality in per capita GDP since 1960, where the growth in full income is defined as the sum of the growth in GDP plus the value placed by individuals in different countries on the improvements in their life expectancy—for definitions and various results on world inequality, see the article by Becker, Philipson, and Soares in the *American Economic Review,* March 2005.

Income inequality within the United States and many other countries has indeed grown a lot since 1980, in part due to much greater returns on education and other human capital, and in part due the somewhat related growth in incomes at the upper end that Posner discusses. This widening inequality appears to be largely due to technological and other changes, such as globalization, that have increased returns to persons with more education and other human capital, including high-end abilities. However, inequality in life expectancy has fallen within most of the developed countries as a result of more equal access to health care—in the United States due mainly to the growth since 1970 of Medicare and Medicaid. So while inequality in full income probably also grew, and perhaps substantially, it grew more slowly than did inequality in earnings and incomes on assets.

My discussion should not be construed as complacency about the inequality found within countries like the United States, or among countries. For example, America should do a much better job of providing a way for able young persons from more disadvantaged backgrounds to finish high school and go to college—the past twenty-five years have been devastating for persons with little education. This is not an easy problem, but Head Start and related early childhood programs seem to be effective, legalization of drugs would reduce the temptation for inner city youth to drop out of school to sell drugs, and I also support greater competition among schools. Unlike Posner, I do not support the estate tax because it brings in little tax revenue relative to the large costs involved in legally avoiding this tax—through trusts and the like—and also in illegally evading this tax (see my more extended discussion of the estate tax in my post on May 15, 2005).

Many other poor countries should be following China and India's example and open up their economies to competition and world trade, so that they too can grow faster. Similarly, the rich countries have to reduce their restrictions on imports of goods produced by developing countries, and by countries that want to be developing.

To conclude, it is worth remembering that world inequality in "real" incomes has declined, not increased, a lot during the past twenty-five years. Much more can be done to equalize opportunities both within and between nations, yet it is unwise to concentrate attention primarily on inequality in assets. This is one component of inequality, but it is by no means the major determinant of inequality in well-being.

SHOULD WE WORRY ABOUT THE RISING INEQUALITY IN INCOME AND WEALTH?—POSNER

Economic inequality is growing in the United States and other developed countries, and also in rapidly developing countries, notably China and India. Becker and I blogged about economic inequality on April 23, almost eight months ago, but indications that inequality is surging at the very top of the income distribution merits a further look, as does the recent study of world income inequality that is the focus of Becker's comment. Recent reports in the media document phenomenal returns to hedge-fund operators, private-equity investors, and other finance specialists, astronomical CEO salaries, enormous returns to software entrepreneurs, a stampede of lawyers and doctors to Wall Street, $200,000 law firm signing bonuses for twenty-seven-year-olds who have clerked for the Supreme Court, enormous philanthropic gifts ($100 million gifts to colleges and universities by alumni are no longer unusual), and soaring demand for products bought only by superwealthy people, such as full-sized passenger airliners converted at great expense to private airplanes, $40 million homes, paintings costing tens of millions of dollars, and automobiles costing several hundred thousand dollars. There are now almost eight hundred billionaires in the United States and countless millionaires, and one out of every five hundred U.S. households have an annual income of at least $1 million.

Now this is to look only at the top of the income distribution. It is not to consider the income distribution as a whole, let alone poverty. In the more conventional focus on earnings by quintiles, one sees little change in recent years. But since 1980 the percentage of total personal income going to the top 1 percent of earners has risen from 8 percent to 16 percent. It is the top of the distribution on which I'll be focusing.

What are the causes, and what are the effects, of this trend in the income (and of course wealth) of the highest-earning segment of the distribution? Part of it is reduced marginal tax rates, because high marginal tax rates discourage risk taking. Consider two individuals: one is a salaried worker with an annual income of $100,000 and good job security, and the other is an entrepreneur with a 10 percent chance of earning $1 million in a given year and a 90 percent chance of earning nothing that year. Their average annual incomes are the same, but a highly progressive tax will make the entrepreneur's expected after-tax income much lower than the salaried worker's. Many of the people at the top of the income distribution are risk takers who turned out to be lucky; the unlucky risk takers fell into a lower part of the distribution. It is rich people as a class who are growing relatively richer, not necessarily individual rich persons.

Marginal income tax rates on the wealthy have not declined much in recent years, however; but the income tax rate cuts since 2001 have favored the wealthy. Another and more important factor in the recent wealth surge is a growing return to high IQs; outstanding success in highly complex fields such as finance and software is highly correlated with high levels of intelligence. And increased size of markets as a consequence of increased international trade provides greater returns to successful innovations.

I am more interested in the effects of the increasing incomes of the rich—though one might ask: *are* there any effects, other than those that are perfectly benign? Even though the federal income tax is increasingly a proportional rather than a progressive tax (though it is still somewhat progressive—the average tax rate for the top 1 percent of earners—24 percent—is roughly twice that for all federal taxpayers), the more skewed the distribution of income, the higher the proportion of taxes that is paid by the rich. And in fact the top 1 percent of earners pay more than one-third of all federal income taxes today, which is a boon to the rest of the population. Very wealthy people also provide patronage for the arts, funds for high-risk ventures (actually, art is one of those ventures), and money for philanthropic enterprises. And there is very little envy of the rich on the part of other Americans, in part perhaps because of the much-derided but very real "trickle down" effect. This is due partly to philanthropy but more to the enormous consumer surplus generated by products such as Microsoft Windows, the brainchild of persons who are now billionaires. It is also due in part to the fact that, given diminishing marginal utility of income, income increases at lower levels in the income hierarchy increase personal welfare more than increases at higher levels do. Moreover, real wealth is a function of improvements in the quality and variety of products and services, and these improvements benefit all classes of the population.

All this is not to say that the existence of a stratum of exceedingly wealthy people is altogether to the good. There are three potentially bad consequences for our society:

1. The existence of enormous financial returns to IQ deflects high-IQ people from entering careers in which the social returns may greatly exceed the

private returns: government service, basic science, and teaching. The quality of both the civil service and the public schools appears to be falling.

2. Massive philanthropy directed abroad can interfere with a coherent foreign policy. Major philanthropies such as the Gates Foundation do not coordinate their spending decisions with U.S. national goals.
3. Huge personal wealth may play a disproportionate role in political competition. Personal wealth confers an enormous advantage on a candidate, but also permits a person who does not want to be a candidate to exert an influence on candidates and policies, as in the case of Richard Mellon Scaife and George Soros. The fact that a person is a highly intelligent speculator, such as Soros, is no guarantor of political insight or wisdom; and the fact that a person has inherited a vast fortune, such as Scaife, is no guarantor of ability of any sort. More important, however, heavy campaign spending by the wealthy force nonwealthy candidates to spend increased time and effort on fundraising, which makes a political career less attractive to nonwealthy persons and makes nonwealthy politicians less well informed about policy and more dependent on interest groups than if campaign spending were lower.

Are these consequences serious enough to warrant remedial action? I think not, except that they may provide some grounds for wanting to retain, perhaps even to strengthen, the estate tax. The disincentive effects of taxing estates are much less than those of income taxation.

49

FOREIGN AID

January 21, 2007

SHOULD THE UNITED STATES PROVIDE FOREIGN AID?—POSNER

The United States is frequently criticized for the meagerness, relative to the nation's aggregate wealth, of its contribution to what is called "overseas development assistance," which is to say government financial aid (other than for military purposes) to poor countries. Although U.S. ODA spending has increased substantially since 9/11, as a percentage of gross national income it is, at .22 percent, at the very bottom of the twenty-two wealthiest countries in the world. (Norway is at the top, with .93 percent.) Aggregate private giving by U.S. foundations, businesses, nongovernmental organizations, colleges (for scholarships), and religious organizations almost equals the government's expenditure; yet even ignoring private contributions by other countries, which though lower in percentage terms than American private giving are not negligible, total U.S. public/private ODA would as a percentage of gross national income fall short of many of the other wealthy nations. (For a useful compendium of statistics and commentary, see "Sustainable Development: The US and Foreign Aid Assistance," www.globalissues.org/TradeRelated/Debt/USAid.asp, visited January 20, 2007.)

These figures are meaningless from an ethical standpoint. To begin with, there is a big difference between the amount given and the amount received, administrative costs to one side. Most U.S. foreign aid requires the recipient to spend the money for U.S. goods and services, which are often much more expensive than those available elsewhere. Suppose the U.S. gives a foreign country $1 million for the purchase of goods in the United States that could be purchased elsewhere for $750,000. Then the net transfer is not $1 million but only $750,000.

Nor should administrative costs, often inflated, be ignored, or the waste that is endemic in government programs. The largest recipient of U.S. foreign aid today is Iraq, and it seems that much of that aid has been squandered.

On the other side of the ethical balance, however, the statistics ignore the benefits that the United States confers on foreign countries by virtue of its enormous defense expenditures (including financial assistance to foreign militaries, but that is only a small percentage of the total defense budget). The United States spends more than 4 percent of its gross domestic product on defense, compared to a world average of 2 percent—and only 1.9 percent for Norway. We really are the world's policeman, holding a security umbrella over a large number of nations, which would have to spend much more on defense were it not for that umbrella. Of course we do not do this from the goodness of our heart, but to protect our national security—but then very little that government does is motivated by altruism toward foreigners.

My own, unfashionable view is that charitable giving, both governmental and private, is more likely to increase than to alleviate the poverty, ill health, and other miseries of the recipient populations. That is a familiar proposition with regard to antipoverty policy on the national rather than international scene. We generally and I think rightly applaud the substitution of workfare for welfare, because welfare promotes dependency by taxing work heavily—if welfare is cut off when the recipient's income reaches, say, $20,000 a year, so that if he was receiving welfare payments in cash or kind worth $2,000 an increase in his income to $23,000 will net him only $1,000 ($23,000 – $2,000=$1,000), this means that his marginal income tax rate is .67—a potent discouragement to working.

Something like this occurs, I believe, on the international scale. Receipt of money enables a government to avoid grappling with the political, social, and economic conditions (cultures, institutions) that are impeding economic development. It has been argued that countries that have enormous natural resources (mainly oil) relative to population seem not to benefit from that gift, as wealth without effort does not create good attitudes toward work, enterprise, and savings, at the same time that it enables the government to defer consideration of its social and other problems. Foreign aid has similar effects. Moreover, the more "generous" the foreign aid, the worse these effects. When foreign aid becomes a significant part of a nation's income, the result is likely to be inflation, waste, corruption, rent seeking, and indefinite postponement of needed economic and political reforms. Insignificant foreign aid does not have these bad effects, but, by the same token, has few good effects.

Of course the donors, both public and private, can and often do attach conditions designed to assure that the money they give is used for constructive purposes. But, first, they do not know what these countries need (the major theme of William Easterly's 2002 book *The Elusive Quest for Growth),* and, second, unless foreign assistance is a large fraction of the total income of the recipient country, the effect of the assistance, however many strings are tied to it, will tend to be that of an unrestricted grant. If a country spends $100 million on health care, and receives foreign assistance for health care of $20 million, it may decide to reallocate $20 million of the health care expenditures that it makes out of its own resources to some other purpose, in which event the restriction on the grant will have no effect. This is a general problem of charitable giving and public welfare, but it is particularly difficult to solve when the donor is dealing with a foreign country.

This point is pertinent to foreign aid for such projects as eliminating (realistically, greatly reducing) such Third World plagues as HIV/AIDS and malaria. The former can be effectively combated with a combination of public health education and free condoms, and the latter with DDT spraying in people's bedrooms. These are projects within the financial capacity of most Third World countries.

The substitution effect will disappear if the foreign money is given for a purpose on which the recipient nation spends nothing (or less than the grant). But if the nation does not value the project, often this will be because the project has little value to the nation.

The chalice is poisoned in still another way. The "generous" gifts from wealthy countries—plumming themselves on their greater (apparent) generosity than the United States—enable those countries to hide, perhaps even from themselves, the extent to which their tariff policies immiserate poor countries. Most of them are agricultural producers with costs much lower than in wealthy countries, which use tariffs to shield their farmers from Third World competition even though their farmers are much wealthier that those in the Third World, and would be even without tariff protection. The nonfarmer taxpayer in a wealthy country in effect pays his country's farmer twice: in higher food costs or in taxes that finance farm subsidies, and in the taxes that support the government's foreign aid program.

No doubt some foreign aid, including nonmilitary aid, advances the foreign policy objectives of the donor nation (though quite possibly at the expense of the populations of the recipient nations), rather that just lining the pockets of domestic producers and enabling publics to feel better about (or simply ignore) their nations' tariff policies. The focus of my discussion has been on the question whether the recipient nations benefit at all. My guess is that they do not. It is just a guess, but it has support in empirical research. I mentioned Easterly's book, and there is much more. And sometimes gross data can be highly suggestive. Africa has received some $600 billion in foreign aid since 1960, yet most African nations are poorer today than they were then. I am mindful that recent economic research has tended to find a positive relation between foreign aid on the one hand and economic growth and improved health in recipient nations on the other; for a recent summary, see Steven Radelet, "A Primer on Foreign Aid" (Center for Global Development, Working Paper No. 92, July 2006). Considering that aggregate overseas development assistance amounts to $92 billion a year (2004), some positive effect can be expected. Yet I remain skeptical. The studies necessarily ignore the tradeoff between foreign aid and tariff reductions; if the former reduces pressure for the latter, the net effect of the aid on the recipient nations could be negative.

IS THERE A CASE FOR FOREIGN AID?—BECKER

My answer is essentially "no," with a few small qualifications. Posner gives the main arguments against aid, so I will not go over them.

William Easterly among others has written several articles that examine the empirical evidence on the relation between foreign aid and economic growth—see, for example, chapter 2 of his book *The Elusive Quest for Economic Growth.* He and others have discussed foreign government aid to countries in Africa, Pakistan, and other Asian countries, and typically have not been able to find any noticeable positive effects of aid on a country's economic growth

In this book Easterly discusses in detail aid to Ghana in the early 1960s that helped it build a huge dam and the largest man-made lake in the world. This project was at the time supported by some economists with extravagant claims about what it would accomplish: create a new fishing industry, generate electricity, encourage a new aluminum smelting plant, and other benefits. At a huge cost, it accomplished few of these goals—there is a smelting plant run by a private multinational that has had slow growth in its output—but little else that is positive. Indeed, the lake had some serious negative consequences, such as destruction of considerable agricultural land because of the wide area flooded, and the importing to those living near the lake of waterborne diseases, such as malaria, river blindness, and hookworm.

India is my favorite example to illustrate the failure of government foreign aid. From the 1950s until the end of the 1980s more private and government aid went to India than to any other country. Yet during that same time period, India had a very modest growth in per capita income of about 1 percent per year—sometimes resignedly called in those days the "Hindu rate of growth." I am not claiming that foreign aid was the main source of India's mediocre performance, but it clearly did not overcome the bad economic policies of its government. In fact, aid may well have encouraged these policies as the India government could always count on foreign aid to help it out of the worst aspects of any mess caused by its restrictions on foreign trade, severe controls over private investment even by Indian companies, and neglect of basic education, roads, and agriculture.

Fortunately, in the early 1990s, the Indian government recognized that the real cause of its economic problems was not insufficient aid, but its own policies. Reforms at that time include opening up more investments to the private sector, greatly lowering tariffs, quotas, and other barriers to foreign trade, and changes in its thinking about relying on rich countries to help its development. Indeed, India can legitimately claim that now one important obstacle to its growth comes from the very same rich countries that had been important donors because of their import restrictions that hinder the access of Indian farmers and manufacturers to their markets.

Foreign aid programs other than of a humanitarian nature are destined to fail because they involve transfers of resources from one government to another. No economist who has closely examined the evidence concludes that the reason why some poor countries fail to have significant economic growth is because their governments have insufficient resources. The complaint is typically that governments do the wrong things with the resources they have, including their regulatory powers. They discourage entrepreneurship, give cronies special advantages in investments or in rights to import and export, overregulate labor markets, spend too much on public prestige projects, such as domestic airlines and large dams that of little use and yet drain valuable resources, neglect basic education in order to create expensive universities, and so on. Foreign aid only makes it easier to continue to promote projects and policies that are not merely neutral with respect to growth, but hinder any take off into rapid growth.

Donor nations are also subject to political pressures that influence the form their aid takes. They attach various strings to the aid that help powerful interest groups in their own countries at the expense sometimes of the aid having any chance of helping recipient countries grow faster. Given the distortions away from effectiveness on both sides of the donor-recipient equation, it is no surprise then most foreign aid has been at best ineffective, and at worst negatively affects the growth prospects of recipients.

Does my discussion mean that I oppose all foreign aid except sometimes for military assistance, and for humanitarian purposes? My answer, to repeat, is yes. However, I include in humanitarian assistance aid to combat some of the major diseases in poor countries, although I prefer such aid to be from private foundations and other groups since they tend to be more effective than governments—see my January 1, 2007, post on private charities. However, if governments of rich countries do give resources to help fight diseases in poor countries, they should give to private groups in these countries. If they have to give to government agencies, they should stipulate in the grants that recipient governments have to match their own tax revenues in specified proportions to the amounts received in aid.

AFTERTHOUGHTS TO PART VIII

POSNER AFTERTHOUGHTS

My major rethinking with respect to my posts in this part of the book concerns the "democratic peace" notion—that democracies are unlikely to go to war with each other. Mature, wealthy democratic countries are indeed unlikely to go to war with each other, because these are countries dominated by commercial values. But many countries are democratic without being mature or wealthy; examples that come to mind are India, Pakistan, Iran, Iraq, the Gaza Strip (under the rule of Hamas), and Venezuela. Not that these are as democratic as the United States, Japan, and other wealthy countries; they have (India perhaps least) strongly authoritarian elements; what is unclear is whether their democratic elements make them more peaceful than they would be if they were out-and-out dictatorships. I am increasingly skeptical. The example of Hamas is revealing: power founded on democratic preference has not brought responsibility.

The wealthy democracies are nations in which a commercial class emerged that successfully challenged the power of kings, nobles, and clergy and brought about a cultural revolution inimical to militarism.

When democracy, better termed populism, precedes such a revolution, there is no reason to suppose that it will be unaggressive. The experience with Hamas suggests (and there is other evidence) that populist regimes in the Middle East and Central Asia are likely to be extremist and violent.

BECKER AFTERTHOUGHTS

I claimed that economic progress tends to lead to political freedom, but recent work has challenged this conclusion. See Daron Acemoglou and James Robinson, *Economic Origins of Dictatorship and Democracy* (2005). The more traditional view had been based mainly, although not entirely, on comparisons of changes in different countries, which may be biased because of unobserved persistent differences among countries. Acemoglu and Robinson rely more on changes within countries. I still believe that the view I expressed is generally right, but more research is necessary before one can be as confident of this as the opinions expressed in my discussion.

Small nations continue to thrive at least as well as large ones, and in some dimensions perhaps better. For example, the current financial crisis started in the United States, and has spread to Great Britain, Japan, Germany, and Russia, to name a few large nations. Small nations like Iceland and Ireland have also been seriously affected, but probably on the whole small nations have done better since they participated less in some of the exotic financial instruments that helped expand this crisis.

Inequality in life expectancy within as well as between countries has generally decreased during the past several decades. However, the advantages of a college education in the United States in reducing the risk of dying apparently has increased rather than decreased during the past several decades. See Yun Sanchez, "The Longevity Gains of Education" (Ph.D. diss. in progress, Department of Economics, University of Chicago, 2008). If so, this would mirror the increasing earnings advantage of college education during this time period.

I claimed that in order to stimulate the Palestinian economy, Hamas would modify its opposition to Israel. I still believe that is likely to happen, but Hamas's opposition has not changed much since I wrote that. Of course, it often takes many years for such changes to occur, and by that standard not much time has passed since my optimistic assessment. Still, I am a bit surprised that there was not a little thawing in the relations between Hamas and Israel.

FRONT COVER FLAP

In the five years since nobel prize- winning economist Gary S. Becker and renowned jurist and legal scholar Richard A. Posner began writing a blog together, the Becker-Posner Blog has established a reputation as a reliable source of lively, thought-provoking commentary on current events. Readers around the world look forward to its pithy and profound weekly essays that highlight the valuable insights offered by economic reasoning when applied to unexpected topics.

Uncommon Sense gathers the most important and innovative entries from the blog, arranged by topic, along with updates and even reconsiderations when subsequent events have shed new light on a question. Whether it's Posner making the economic case for the legalization of gay marriage, Becker arguing in favor of the sale of human organs for transplant, or even the pair of scholars vigorously disagreeing about the utility of collective punishment, with reference to Israel's battles with Hezbollah and Hamas, the writing is always clear, the interplay energetic, and the resulting discussion deeply informed and intellectually substantial.

To have a single thinker of the stature of a Becker or Posner addressing questions of this nature would make for fascinating reading; to have both, writing and responding to each other, is an exceptionally rare treat. With *Uncommon Sense,* they invite the adventurous reader to join them on a whirlwind intellectual journey. All they ask is that you leave your preconceptions behind.

BACK COVER FLAP

GARY S. BECKER is University Professor at the University of Chicago and the author of many books, including *Human Capital: A Theoretical and Empirical Analysis.* He was awarded the Nobel Prize in Economics in 1992 and the Presidential Medal of Freedom in 2007.

RICHARD A. POSNER is a judge of the U.S. Court of Appeals for the Seventh Circuit, senior lecturer in law at the University of Chicago Law School, and the author of numerous books, including *How Judges Think.*

BACK COVER MATERIAL

"In the vast wasteland that most assume the blogosphere to be, Becker and Posner's work is a gem. Authentic, responsive, and enormously fun, it should be read both in real time, and in the reflection of a published work."

LAWRENCE LESSIG

"If Becker has a single guiding principle, it is that the economic way of looking at behaviour applies more broadly than originally thought, and people make rational choices about crime, marriage, parenthood, education, even drug addiction.... After initial fierce resistance within the profession, and equally fierce support from Chicago school greats such as Milton Friedman, Becker is now regarded as one of the most influential economists of the 20th century—arguably, the most influential of all."

TIM HARFORD, FINANCIAL TIMES

"For sheer intimidating cerebral megahertz, Posner has few rivals on the bench—or anywhere else, for that matter.... His books and writings make him, by a wide margin, the most frequently cited legal scholar of the past half-century."

FORTUNE

D

F

L

M

N

O

P

Books For ALL Kinds of Readers

At ReadHowYouWant we understand that one size does not fit all types of readers. Our innovative, patent pending technology allows us to design new formats to make reading easier and more enjoyable for you. This helps improve your speed of reading and your comprehension. Our EasyRead printed books have been optimized to improve word recognition, ease eye tracking by adjusting word and line spacing as well as minimizing hyphenation. Our EasyRead SuperLarge editions have been developed to make reading easier and more accessible for vision-impaired readers. We offer Braille and DAISY formats of our books and all popular E-Book formats.

Made in United States
North Haven, CT
05 November 2026

21767033R00330